CONSERVATIVE WOMEN

ST ANTONY'S SERIES
General Editor: *Alex Pravda, Fellow of St Antony's College, Oxford*
Recent titles include:

Craig Brandist
CARNIVAL CULTURE AND THE SOVIET MODERNIST NOVEL

Jane Ellis
THE RUSSIAN ORTHODOX CHURCH
Triumphalism and Defensiveness

Y Hakan Erdem
SLAVERY IN THE OTTOMAN EMPIRE AND ITS DEMISE, 1800–1909

Dae Hwan Kim and Tat Yan Kong (*editors*)
THE KOREAN PENINSULA IN TRANSITION

Jaroslav Krejčí and Pavel Machonin
CZECHOSLOVAKIA 1918–92
A Laboratory for Social Change

Jill Krause and Neil Renwick (*editors*)
IDENTITIES IN INTERNATIONAL RELATIONS

Joseph Nevo
KING ABDALLAH AND PALESTINE
A Territorial Ambition

William J. Tompson
KHRUSHCHEV
A Political Life

Iftikhar H. Malik
STATE AND SOCIETY IN PAKISTAN
Politics of Authority, Ideology and Ethnicity

Barbara Marshall
WILLY BRANDT
A Political Biography

Javier Martínez-Lara
BUILDING DEMOCRACY IN BRAZIL
The Politics of Constitutional Change, 1985–95

Conservative Women

A History of Women and the Conservative Party, 1874–1997

G. E. Maguire
Lecturer in British Studies
University of Paris XII–Val de Marne
Paris

Published by PALGRAVE MACMILLAN
Houndmills, Basingstoke, Hampshire RG21 6XS and
175 Fifth Avenue, New York, N. Y. 10010
Companies and representatives throughout the world

PALGRAVE MACMILLAN is the global academic imprint of the Palgrave
Macmillan division of St. Martin's Press, LLC and of Palgrave Macmillan Ltd.
Macmillan® is a registered trademark in the United States, United Kingdom
and other countries. Palgrave is a registered trademark in the European
Union and other countries.

ISBN 0–333–68695–0

This book is printed on paper suitable for recycling and
made from fully managed and sustained forest sources.

A catalogue record for this book is available from the British Library.

Transferred to digital printing 2002

Printed and bound in Great Britain by
Antony Rowe Ltd, Chippenham and Eastbourne

*This book is affectionately dedicated to my family:
to Henri, Tommy and Kevin
It would not have been possible without their love
and support*

Contents

Acknowledgements

Many persons have helped me with this research, and to all of them I owe heartfelt thanks. First and foremost, I would like to thank the Conservative Party and in particular its archivist, Dr Martin Maw, for his immense assistance. I am also extremely grateful to Alistair Cooke, OBE, for giving me special permission to consult Conservative Party archives up to 1975. I must also express my boundless gratitude to Colin Harris and the staff of the archival centre at the Bodleian Library in Oxford who were all very kind and helpful.

Thanks must also be given to the House of Lords Record Office for allowing me to consult the Davidson and Bonar Law Papers, to the British Library, where I did a great deal of research, to the Public Record Office and to Reading University Library. On a personal note, I owe an immense debt to Dr Michael Hawcroft of Keble College Oxford for all his help – the book literally would not have been written without him. Dr Beatrice Heuser and Dr Cyril Buffet were kindness itself and provided me with much help. Finally, I must also thank Fr Philip Whitmore and everyone at Clergy House at Westminster Cathedral who are always indulgent and always kind about receiving me and helping me in any way possible.

Thanks are also owed to many people at the University of Paris XII. First and foremost, I must express my gratitude to Evelyne Hanquart-Turner and her research group for funding part of my research. I must also thank Ulrika Dubos and the Department of English for giving me a grant towards research and for being so understanding about my absences.

I certainly cannot forget the help given to me by my in-laws, Roger and Line Zuber, who proofread and criticized the manuscript. Nor can I fail to acknowledge all the assistance of my mother Gloria Smith and my niece, Marie Ford. Last but not least, I must thank my family, to whom this book is dedicated. They have put up with so much from me that I really do not even know how to start. Special thanks must go to Tommy and Kevin for being so understanding about a mother who always seemed to be glued to a book or the computer. Finally, I must give my heartfelt thanks to my husband, Henri, for encouragement, understanding, and, on a more practical level, proofreading and always intelligent criticism. This book would not have been possible without them.

List of Abbreviations

CWAC	Central Women's Advisory Committee of the Conservative Party, later called WNAC
EPCC	Equal Pay Campaign Committee
ILP	Independent Labour Party
LGC	Ladies Grand Council of the Primrose League
NSOWS	National Society for Opposing Women's Suffrage
NUSEC	National Union of Societies for Equal Citizenship, the Fawcett Group after 1918
NUWSS	National Union of Women's Suffrage Societies, Millicent Fawcett's non-militant suffrage organization
PORD	Public Opinion Research Department of the Conservative Party
WAUTRA	Women's Amalgamated Unionist and Tariff Reform Association
WNAC	Women's National Advisory Committee of the Conservative Party, earlier called CWAC
WSPU	Women's Social and Political Union, the Pankhursts' militant suffrage group
WTUL	Women's Trade Union League
WUTRA	Another abbreviation for WAUTRA, this time without the 'Amalgamated'

Introduction

In an influential work published in 1981, Olive Banks identified three intellectual traditions, dating from the eighteenth century, that exist within the feminist movement: that of evangelical Christianity, that of the Enlightenment, and that of socialism.[1] She sees evangelical Christianity as giving birth to the zeal of nineteenth-century female reformers, notably in the anti-slavery movement. From their religious beliefs sprang a desire for social reform, and this, in turn thrust women, for the first time, into the public spotlight. The Enlightenment was the basis of a second branch of feminism which emphasized the importance of reason over age-old tradition, and she places John Stuart Mill and Mary Wollstonecraft squarely within this tradition. Women are seen as having natural rights which have been denied to them. The third tradition she identifies is that of 'socialist feminism' with its emphasis on communal and child care and open sexual relationships. Now there is undoubtedly much truth in this analysis, but there is also one major error. For Banks and for many other historians, feminism is essentially a movement of the left. There has been, until recently, a tendency to neglect the right.[2]

It is tempting to see right-wing political movements as reactionary and to deny their progressive tendencies. And yet, in the history of Great Britain, the right has also made important contributions to women's rights. The Primrose League, a Conservative organization, was the first political group to admit women. Conservatives like Lord Robert Cecil, the Earl of Lytton, Lady Selborne and Lady Betty Balfour worked tirelessly for women's suffrage – sometimes even uniting their efforts with those of the Pankhursts or Millicent Fawcett.[3] It was a Conservative-dominated coalition government that gave women over thirty the vote in 1918 and an entirely Conservative one that gave women the right to vote on the same terms as men in 1928. The first woman member of Parliament, Lady Astor, was a Conservative. It was Harold Macmillan's government that introduced equal pay for teachers and non-industrial civil servants. Later, Edward Heath ordered the formation of the Cripps Committee, whose job was to examine the legal disabilities against women and recommend legislation to remove them. Finally, and most obviously, the Conservatives were the first and, to this day, the only, party to choose a woman leader. Women have mobilized in mass numbers since the days of the

1

Primrose League for the Conservative Party. It has been estimated that, if women had not been given the vote, the Labour Party would have been in power almost continuously since 1945.[4] It would not be going too far to say that women have provided the basis for Conservative Party dominance in the twentieth century.

Of course, the Conservative Party can hardly be viewed as a radical feminist organization. It has many reactionary elements within it, as the women's suffrage campaign clearly shows. However, on the whole, the Conservatives' record has been no worse than that of the Labour Party. After all, trade unions have not generally been renowned in history for their feminism. The danger has existed, at least until recently, that the history of feminism would simply be viewed as the history of left-wing feminism. This study is an attempt to redress the balance by analysing the relationship between women and the Conservative Party. It seeks to examine not only the attitude of women to the party and the official attitude of the party towards women, but also men's attitude towards having women in the party. It will consider the role of women at all levels, from that of the voter and the grassroots organization to the national party structure and Parliament. The primary objective of this study is to examine the evolution of women's role within the party and try to assess whether it has always been one of progress. Essentially the relationship between women and the Conservative Party can be classified into three periods, which correspond to the three sections of this book. First, there is the period before women got the vote. During this time, women moved from exercising political influence in the background through family ties to exercising it in the open through the Primrose League and (it must be admitted to a much lesser extent) through the Conservative and Unionist Women's Suffrage Association. The second part considers the beginning of overt political power from 1918, when they first voted, to 1945. This period saw the party organize in order to incorporate women both within the party structure and in Westminster. Finally, the third part will examine the relationship between the postwar Conservative Party and women as voters, party activists and representatives in local or national government. In particular, it will discuss the phenomenon of Margaret Thatcher and her association with the party. Finally, we shall look at the post-Thatcher period until the devastating Tory defeat of 1997.

Part I
Before the Vote

Part 1
Before the Vote...

1 Women in the Political Background

There is a cliché that says that behind every great man there is a woman. Like all clichés, there is an element of truth and of exaggeration in it. In any case, few people would deny that women – or rather certain women – have exercised political influence through their relationships with men. As wives, mistresses, mothers, daughters or simply friends, women have listened to men's problems and offered their advice. This is true in politics as much as in any other field. Until this century, only a few women in Britain could vote in certain local government elections, but in spite of this many people have argued that women still possessed political power. In 1864, one anti-suffragist argued that: 'There can be no more baseless assumption than that the polling-booth is the main source of influence in politics. Women already enjoy greater influence in other ways, both public and private, than the franchise would give them.'[1] In the light of events since then, this interpretation is controversial – to say the least. It is also clear that even if women did exercise some background political power, there were very few who did so. Furthermore, most of these were, by definition, from the upper class. This should not come as a surprise because, with few exceptions, Britain before the twentieth century was governed by an oligarchy based on the aristocracy. Much of the history of Britain before the First World War is that of a country coming to grips with the idea of democracy – and, as part of this, with the acceptance of a political role for women.

This chapter aims to examine the background part that women played before they gained the right to vote and to try to evaluate exactly how effective it was. The Conservative Party is a particularly good place to study this phenomenon because until recently the party was dominated by great aristocratic families who often intermarried. In this family-based governing class, a woman's role was likely to be greater, although perhaps more retiring, than in the trade union-based Labour Party. For this reason, the Conservative Party gave an excellent opportunity for gifted women in these families to exert power behind the scenes. The greatest of these could be important political players in their own right – although ultimately frustrated ones as we shall see when we examine the case of Lady Derby. More commonly, women in these families had a limited role as political hostesses and confidantes to their husbands. Strangely enough – or perhaps not so strangely – many of them were against giving the vote to women. They certainly had never felt particularly deprived or disadvantaged, and living as they did in wealth and having access to the most powerful men in the country, they could hardly feel that they suffered from serious disabilities. This reinforces the class-based nature of female political power before the vote, but this point should not be exaggerated. The late nineteenth and early twentieth centuries were also a period of increasing female participation in left-wing movements: notably the Women's Co-operative Guild and socialist societies like the Fabians and the Independent Labour Party (ILP). Women were entering the political arena at all levels of society. Here, however, we are concerned with the part played by women in the Conservative Party and that inevitably means upper- and middle-class women. In this chapter we shall analyse the traditional and the not so traditional roles played by women aristocrats in the Conservative Party and examine to what extent these changed in the period leading up to women being granted the vote.

In many ways Mary Anne Disraeli represents the traditional role accorded to women in the Conservative Party. She was not intelligent enough to be threatening, and she was sublimely devoted to her husband. Her main duties were limited to entertaining (at which she was generally quite good in spite of her personal peculiarities) and taking care of her husband. Disraeli himself dedicated his novel *Sybil* to her, calling her 'a perfect Wife', and the stories of Mary Anne's adoration of Disraeli and her extreme solicitude are legendary. There is the story of how, having severely cut her face before a dinner party, she persuaded the hostess to sit her at the opposite end of the table from Disraeli – whom she knew would arrive late and without his eyeglass – so that he would not be upset by her injuries. In another, even better known case, she remained silent while her hand was crushed in a carriage door so as not to upset Disraeli before a major speech in Parliament. More important, she helped pay Disraeli's debts, used her influence with friends as much as possible to assist his career, and provided a happy home life for him. She never went to bed before he returned from Parliament – even if it was at three in the morning – and she always had a hot meal waiting for him. She invested a great deal of time and money in organizing political parties for him, although her own behaviour at them could be eccentric.[2] She is a clear example of the wife in the background, although she did meet with Disraeli's constituents during elections. She is in many ways emblematic of women's political role before the development of organizations like the Primrose League.[3]

Lady Salisbury, although she did not take her devotion to her husband to the extremes of Mary Anne Disraeli played a similar part. Georgina Salisbury hosted innumerable parties in London and at the family estate at Hatfield and was forced to take the leading role at these gatherings because of Salisbury's shyness and dislike of social occasions. She was far from being a great political hostess, for she could be quite rude to people she disliked – even when they could be of use to her husband. On the whole, though, her parties probably helped Salisbury's career. She was also Salisbury's confidante and adviser on political matters. Their correspondence shows that he sought for and listened to her counsel. She was a shrewd and intelligent woman, famous for her wit, and Salisbury was not the only one who sought her advice. She corresponded with many famous men, notably Disraeli, and offered them her observations on the political situation.[4] Like Mary Anne Disraeli, she used her own personal friendships, with Gladstone for example, to help Salisbury whenever possible. We can, however, see two major differences between Georgina Salisbury and Mary Anne Disraeli. First, Georgina married into the aristocracy while Disraeli was always on the fringes of noble society. Georgina belonged to the extraordinary Hotel Cecil, which – if families were rated for over-achievement – would deserve the highest award. Along with Salisbury the family counted Lord Cranborne, Lord Hugh and Lord Robert Cecil, her sons, all talented men active in Parliament. There were also her daughter, Lady Maud, a leader in the Conservative suffragist movement and Maud's husband, Lord Selborne, a leading politician. Furthermore, two nephews, Arthur and Gerald Balfour, would become active in politics, and Arthur would replace Salisbury as prime minister after the latter's resignation. This, of course, does not completely do justice to the family for we do not have the space here to mention all their cousins and relations by marriage. In one way or another, the Cecils were related to a large part of the aristocracy. Since the personal dimension intruded so much into the public dimension of politicians' lives, women were bound to be present – and perhaps even to be consulted – when important political decisions were made.

Georgina differed from Mary Anne in a second way – in that of being active in political organizations herself. The period of Salisbury's dominance of the Conservative Party saw the foundation of the Primrose League – the first political organization in Britain to give women a major role. There is no doubt that she was at first rather repelled by the Primrose League. She detested one of its founders, Lord Randolph Churchill, and harboured dark suspicions about any of his actions. Like many other aristocrats too, she found the whole thing rather laughable with its medieval sounding titles and often absurd ceremonies. Furthermore, like many others, she did not think it was right for women to give speeches and assume a public role in politics. However, she quickly realized that it could be extremely useful to Salisbury and got involved in it.[5] As Salisbury's wife she immediately became a leading figure in the League and served as a member of the Ladies Grand Council. Thus we can see how even before women got the right to vote their role in politics was changing. In Mary Anne Disraeli's generation a political organization that incorporated women was unheard of. In Lady Salisbury's day not only was such an organization created but it became a major force in the country. To a large extent this new participation by women was due to changes in the election laws. The 1870s and 1880s saw a vast attack on electoral corruption and, with the Third Reform Act, a massive expansion in the franchise. The larger electorate and the new rules against corruption meant that vast numbers of unpaid volunteers were necessary for canvassing and other party work. Women were now not only welcome but indispensable for these new tasks, and politics became fashionable for them.

These new laws obviously weakened the power of the aristocracy, but they did not destroy it. The Hotel Cecil was perhaps simply the most spectacular example of what was common throughout Britain: extensive intermarriage between aristocratic and gentry families. The case of Lancashire well illustrates this phenomenon for the Stanleys, the Earls of Derby, were related either directly or indirectly to almost every other major family in the region. The future seventeenth earl of Derby, for example, married the daughter of the Duke of Manchester. After the latter's death, the dowager Duchess of Manchester married the eighth Duke of Devonshire, who was a major power in national politics. And this does not even begin to consider links with the lesser aristocracy and the greater gentry.[6] Given the ties between these families, it is not surprising to see that women were often used as intermediaries to pass information on to their husbands. Devonshire, for example, was in contact with his stepdaughter about the political career of her husband.[7] Disraeli, at the beginning of his career, had certainly been made to feel more welcome by the women than by the men. It was women who first promoted him and introduced him to the great figures of the time. Years later, when J. C. C. Davidson, then a minor figure in the Conservative Party, wanted to warn Bonar Law against trusting Lloyd George too much in 1916, he did so by writing to Law's sister. He knew of her influence over the Conservative Party leader and hoped that by convincing her, he might be able to get her to use her influence with Law.[8] More frequently, women themselves were active in writing to friends to try to help the career of a husband, son or protégé.

Essentially, political wives were expected to support and advise their husbands, use their influence on his behalf, and be the organisers and hostesses at often lavish affairs involving hundreds of guests. Having a wife was not, of course, absolutely necessary to a man's political success – both Arthur Balfour, a bachelor, and Bonar Law, a widower, made it to 10 Downing Street without a wife – but it certainly did not hurt. Balfour, of course, had his Cecil connections to assist him on the social side, and Bonar Law, who even more than Salisbury detested social occasions, had the last and the greatest of all Conservative political hostesses, Edith, Lady Londonderry, to help him. The role of political hostess was undoubtedly a very important one during this early period when the parliamentary Conservative Party lacked the necessary structures to consult with each other on political questions. Nowadays a number of groups exist in which backbenchers can express their point of view to the party leaders, the most important one probably being the 1922 Committee, but this did not, of course, exist until after the First World War. In this early period the leaders kept in touch with their backbenchers to a large extent through social gatherings. Social occasions provided a necessary forum for communication within the party. For this reason, a major political hostess could be extremely powerful – if only because she determined the guest list and, therefore, could be of immense assistance to young and ambitious MPs. It would, however, be a mistake to assign too much power to the political hostess. Obviously there were many other more important factors that contributed to an MP's career – notably, how well he spoke in Parliament, his reputation for hard work and diligence, his personal popularity, and his intelligence – but a hostess could always help smooth the way. Cultivating a political hostess and getting invited to her parties was an obvious starting point for a young and ambitious MP, particularly if his family connections were not especially brilliant.

Perhaps the most remarkable case of a woman who tried to exercise political power behind the scenes (and sometimes not very far behind the scenes) was that of Mary, Lady Derby.[9] Her father had been a great friend of the Duke of Wellington, who had become very fond of the bright and admiring young girl. Wellington seems to have taught Mary much of what she knew about politics. In 1847 at the age of 22 she married the second Marquess of Salisbury. He was over thirty years her senior and a widower with several grown children – one of whom was the future prime minister. The second marquess was a minor politician in his own right, and Mary quickly became enamoured of political activity. Highly intelligent, there is no doubt that she was ambitious and wanted to be important in some way. To this effect she became a great political hostess and cultivated friendships with major and minor political figures. Being a woman, however, she could never hope to hold political office herself, and most of her activity was devoted to seeking office for young protégés. She became the confidante of several younger Cecil men as well as the close friend of the Queen of Holland and Lord Clarendon, the diplomat. Among the promising young politicians whose careers she helped were Robert Lowe (the future Lord Sherbrooke) and Lord Stanley, later the fifteenth earl of Derby. The extent of her influence can be seen from the fact that Lord Clarendon told her of ministerial appointments in Gladstone's 1868 government before most of the appointees knew it themselves. She was even allowed to inform her friend Robert Lowe of his appointment. She described what happened:

> He [Robert Lowe] came and I told him he was to be Chancellor of the Exchequer. He had no idea of it. He promised to write the next day and fulfilled it when he accepted office. I had known all his troubles during the last two years and a half – had encouraged him in his honest truth speaking, had told him his day would come; he had never believed it and I thought it curious I should have been the person to give him this news.[10]

The fact that she was given such a task shows the extraordinary respect and admiration that many politicians felt for her. Her political role, however, remained extremely limited: she was informing others of their appointment to the cabinet – a decision in which she had played no role – and was not herself becoming a member. She was being granted a courtesy not real power.

The person whose career she worked hardest to advance, however, was undoubtedly Lord Stanley. He was a serious and ambitious young politician, whose career was undoubtedly already greatly helped by his father's prominent position. His father, with Benjamin Disraeli, had been one of the few important figures in the Tory Party to break with Robert Peel over the latter's decision to repeal the Corn Law in 1846. The result of this split was the formation of the modern Conservative Party with the elder Derby as its leader and Disraeli as its major figure in the House of Commons. The fourteenth earl became prime minister of minority governments from 1858–9 and from 1866–8. It was under his premiership that the Second Reform Act of 1867 was passed. Given his own gifts and his family background, Stanley obviously was someone with a great future. Stanley had been a school friend of Lord Robert Cecil, the future Marquess of Salisbury and Mary's stepson, and it was through him that they met. She very quickly became his close friend and political confidante. It is perhaps not surprising to discover that, two years after Lord Salisbury died in 1868, Stanley, now the Earl of Derby, and Mary were married. Derby was often criticized for indecisiveness and for not infrequently voting with the Liberals – and the latter fact could hardly endear him to Disraeli. Still, he was undeniably an important political player and there is no doubt that he was absolutely devoted to his wife. Through her marriage Mary would finally get a chance to exercise real influence in politics, although, at the same time, it limited her since from this point on she focused primarily on advancing his career.

Mary's importance was shown in 1874 when Disraeli won the election and formed his government. Her stepson, now Lord Salisbury, had been one of the greatest critics of the Second Reform Act, viewing anything that smelled of democracy with deep disgust. He also distrusted Disraeli whose unorthodox background and political opportunism seemed to him to be entirely disreputable, and he refused to have anything to do with the new prime minister. Disraeli, however, very much wanted Salisbury in his government. As a member of the government Salisbury could hardly indulge in much criticism of it – at least not without first resigning. He had already begun courting Salisbury even before the election. He had done so by paying a visit to Beresford Hope, MP for Cambridge University. Hope hated Disraeli, but his wife, Lady Mildred, was less hostile and was also Salisbury's sister. Disraeli's aim was to begin overtures through her.[11] No one knows what happened during the encounter, but Disraeli continued his advances through Lady Derby. Disraeli felt that Mary Derby was the ideal person to act as intermediary between the two men: on the one hand, she was the wife of a leading cabinet member and Disraeli's own friend, while, on the other hand, she was Salisbury's stepmother and had kept a warm relationship with him.

She, naturally enough, was more than ready to undertake such a task. Lord Salisbury described his first meeting with Lady Derby:

> I went to my Lady's. Her mission, of course, was very simple. Her question was whether I would refuse sans phrases, or whether I would entertain the matter. I said it must depend in the first instance upon their proposed policy. She told me they had a scheme for offering (as a compliment) a place in the Cabinet to Lord Russell – and trying through him to get the Duke of Somerset to join. That is all moonshine, but D[israeli] evidently wants to strengthen his government as much as possible. I told her further that I would not take any other office but India. We then went and interrogated Derby. I went through all the possible questions I could think of.[12]

Her mediation turned out to be a success. The result of this meeting was a letter from Disraeli who informed Salisbury that: 'Lady Derby tells me that she thinks it very desirable, and that you do not altogether disagree with her, that you and myself should have some conversation on the state of public affairs.'[13] Lady Derby succeeded in her objective, and Salisbury agreed to join Disraeli's cabinet.

There is no doubt that Mary had scored a political success, although one that was obviously based on the complicated family relationships of the Conservative Party and thus fundamentally did not break with the traditional role given to women. Mary, however, wanted to go further. Her political power was based not only on her husband's influence but also on her wide knowledge of political affairs – a knowledge that she was only too willing to show. Perhaps she felt that as a woman – and thus obviously disqualified from any important public role in politics – she had constantly to prove to men that she was a political figure and that she could make a valuable contribution. Whatever the reason, she cultivated the friendship of men in all parties and tried to use the knowledge she gained to help her protégés and her party. At first at least she regularly informed Disraeli of what she had learned, and their correspondence is in many ways remarkable. In 1865, for example, she used information she had received from friends to inform Disraeli of developments in the cabinet. In one case she wrote: 'I think I know from good authority that a Committee of the Cabinet sat for the first time upon Reform on Saturday and went over the returns, but no one of them had any fixed ideas upon the subject. I'm told that it will be impossible for an announcement to be made in the Queen's Speech that a Bill will be submitted to

Parliament.'[14] After Disraeli's wife died and before the rise of Lord Salisbury, Mary Derby seems to have become the Conservative Party's most important hostess, and needless to say she often wrote to Disraeli on matters relating to social occasions. But this is only part of her correspondence with him. Any rumour she heard, she frequently reported to the party leader, even when her husband was opposed to doing so. It was not unusual for her letters to include phrases like 'Stanley does not know that I am doing it or he would reproach me for taking up your time' or 'I am doing all this unknown to S[tanley] so pray take no notice of my share in it and forgive me if I am wrong.'[15] Her goal was not only to advance the careers of her friends but also to inject herself into political affairs as much as possible.

Under Disraeli's government, Derby was given the Foreign Office, and Lady Derby became almost as active in foreign affairs as Derby himself. Since her remarriage she had formed a new and rather dangerous friendship with Count Shuvaloff, the Russian ambassador. Since the Franco-Prussian War it was obvious that France was in decline and that the balance of power had shifted towards Germany and more precisely towards the Dreikaiserbund, the League of the Three Emperors, which included Germany, Austria and Russia. It was of course an old British practice to try to prevent any country from becoming too dominant in continental Europe, and Disraeli was quite convinced of the necessity of curbing the Dreikaiserbund. Disraeli felt that Britain needed a strong and active foreign policy, while his foreign secretary Derby was devoted to inaction and isolationism – and through his wife he remained on friendly terms with the Russian Embassy.[16] The potential for conflict was thus obvious. To complicate the matter further, there was the question of the Ottoman Empire which was already the sick man of Europe. It had long been Britain's policy to give support to this dying empire. Disraeli instinctively clung to this old policy in spite of the fact that the Turks were undeniably corrupt and violently oppressive, particularly against their Christian subjects. His views can be summed up quite easily: he wanted to strike a blow against the Dreikaiserbund, maintain British independence and shore up the Turks.

The matter came to a head in the summer of 1876 when the *Daily News* began publishing horrifying accounts of Turkish massacres of Bulgarian Christians. Disraeli tried to ignore the matter at first, but events forced him to take them into account. Public opinion in Britain was profoundly shocked by these massacres, and Disraeli was completely out of touch with feeling in the country. Gladstone, however, was not. The great Liberal had retired from politics, but the amorality of Disraeli's stand in the Eastern Question made him decide to return. In September 1876 Gladstone published his own analysis of the situation, *The Bulgarian Horrors and the Question of the East*. The pamphlet caused a sensation throughout the country and caused Disraeli's support for the Turks to become even more unpopular than it already was. To further complicate the matter, there was a deep disaccord between Disraeli and his foreign minister. Derby was deeply distressed about the massacres. Lady Derby was of course kept informed of developments throughout the crisis by her husband, but deeply interested as she was in foreign affairs, she sought information from other sources. She wrote frequently to the Home Secretary, R. A. Cross, asking for any information he could give and also discussed the matter with her stepson, Lord Salisbury. She also cultivated another source of information, Count Shuvaloff. Shuvaloff was obviously eager to confide in Lady Derby, knowing that she would pass all the information he gave her on to her husband, the foreign secretary. However, Lady Derby went much further than this: she had always enjoyed confiding political secrets to her friends, and now she did the same thing with Shuvaloff. Considering the strained nature of Anglo-Russian relations at this time, Lady Derby's actions can hardly be considered as ethical and may perhaps be criticized with worse names. There seems to be no doubt, though, that this decision was a joint one and that Derby was fully aware of the fact that his wife was revealing secrets to the Russian ambassador. We may indeed wonder why Derby and his wife took such a drastic step, but their motives appear to have been mainly noble: they hoped their actions would preserve the peace.

With Derby's permission then, Lady Derby revealed details of cabinet meetings and government decisions. Shuvaloff not only reported this news to his government but also to Sir William Harcourt, an important Liberal politician. Thus, not only the Russians but also the Liberals were aware of the workings of Disraeli's cabinet.[17] Of course, this leakage could not be kept secret for long, and Disraeli and the Queen soon learned of it. The Queen was furious at the discovery and felt that both Derbys should be punished for their confidences. Disraeli, realizing that the issue was political dynamite, behaved in a calmer manner. He responded by establishing his own direct links with British representatives abroad and thus going around Derby. Obviously, the whole situation created terrible tensions in Disraeli's cabinet. It may seem strange to us that he did not react more strongly. Perhaps he still felt a lingering gratitude to the house of Stanley – after all, he had worked closely with Derby's father for years – or perhaps the Stanleys were simply too powerful in Lancashire for Disraeli to dare an open break. Then again, perhaps he simply found it useful to have a way of feeding information to the Russians or maybe he simply wanted to avoid increasing public attention on the issue. In any case Derby, although remaining foreign secretary, retained little power or control over policy. In November 1877, for example, Disraeli sent a message warning the Tsar that if Russia persisted in assaulting Turkey, Britain would be forced to ally herself with the latter. Lord Derby was not even informed of this message for fear he would reveal it to his wife and she in turn would tell Count Shuvaloff.[18] By December, Victoria, feeling that the Derbys had got off too easily, was insisting to Disraeli that something had to be done and soon after decided to take matters into her own hands. She charged Dean Wellesley with expressing to Lady Derby the Queen's disapproval of her actions. This the dean did, but Lady Derby remained unrepentant.

The situation could only end with Derby's dismissal or resignation, and this was exactly what happened. In March 1878 Derby finally resigned. This result was a blow to Lady Derby who clearly loved power, but she immediately went to work to mend fences with those former colleagues of her husband who had been less hostile and to open communication with the Liberals. She even continued to give (unasked for) advice to Disraeli. In October 1878 she wrote to him about recent information she had received from Shuvaloff and suggested that he should immediately send a special envoy to the Turks. She even went so far as to tell Disraeli: 'It strikes me as so evident that Lord Salisbury or Lord Lyons ought to go at once tomorrow.'[19] At the same time, she was acting as a go-between for Gladstone and Derby. Gladstone was actively courting Derby, but, strangely enough, it was always Lady Derby who replied to his letters. Soon Gladstone began to write directly to Lady Derby.[20] Derby's natural indecisiveness caused him to hesitate for a long time: he did not finally break with the Conservatives until 1880, and he refused to accept office under Gladstone until 1882. At this point, Derby agreed to take over the Colonial Office, but he never recovered the earlier prominent position he had had under Disraeli. He did, however, retain his tendency towards independent voting, and in 1886 he broke with Gladstone over home rule. Derby would never hold political office again.

The life of Lady Derby is, in many ways, one of the most remarkable of any Victorian woman, and yet it clearly shows the limitations women faced at this time. Obviously an intelligent and ambitious woman, she dared to try to play a role, although undeniably a background one, in politics. To some extent she succeeded: several times she intervened effectively, but she never really managed to be taken seriously by men. Ultimately her success was based entirely on the extent to which men were willing to confide in her and use her as a go-between. Her family connections placed her in a position where she could meet important men, and she impressed them with her intelligence and understanding of politics and particularly of foreign policy. She dreamed of power and to some extent she got it, although she sometimes made serious errors of judgement in using it. She was unable to resist showing off the power she had and used her knowledge often indiscreetly and, in the case of Shuvaloff, unpatriotically. In marrying Derby she got what she wanted, a rising political star, and, unfortunately for both of them, if she helped make him, she also helped bring him down. To some extent Lady Derby's life is a tragedy, for in spite of all her talent, the fact of being of woman kept her from exercising real political power. One cannot but imagine that she would have been in many ways a far more powerful foreign secretary than the indecisive Derby, although she would have undoubtedly entered into far more conflict with Disraeli.

By far the most important nineteenth-century example we must consider is that of Queen Victoria. Although young Victoria had, under the influence of Melbourne, been an ardent Whig, she had later moved towards the Conservatives. By the time Disraeli became prime minister, Victoria was undeniably a Conservative woman, although one who, for constitutional reasons, had to maintain some discretion about revealing her political preferences. Victoria's reign also coincided with a major change in the nature of the monarchy. As queen, Victoria obviously exercised power, but the extent of her power declined as her reign went on. At the beginning of her reign, during the Bedchamber crisis of 1839, Victoria was able to prevent Peel from taking office and keep her beloved Lord Melbourne in power. Even so, it seems clear that Peel did not really want to take office at this time. If he had forced the issue, he almost certainly would have won. The constitutional balance that had existed at the time of George III had already disappeared. By the late Victorian period, she had lost even more power. In 1880, after the Conservative election defeat and Disraeli's resignation, Victoria, in a desperate attempt to avoid the return of Gladstone, asked Lord Hartington (the future duke of Devonshire) to take power. Hartington, however, very sensibly refused, for he recognized the need for Gladstone and his popularity in the country. She was thus not even given the illusion of power in this case.

In opposition to Gladstone who ignored the Queen as much as he thought constitutionally proper – when he was not lecturing her – Disraeli paid court to her with almost ridiculous obsequiousness. His first meeting with her upon becoming prime minister in 1874 set the tone of their relationship. Victoria describes it saying: 'He knelt down and kissed hands, saying: "I plight my troth to the kindest of *Mistresses*"!'[21] In many ways their correspondence is almost as remarkable as it is silly. The effusive flattery of Disraeli's letters may seem ridiculous to us now, but they did keep a lonely old widow amused. On one occasion, Disraeli went so far as to say that his world would be as joyless as when Proserpine was in the underworld but for Victoria's gift of primroses which 'remind him that there might yet be spring & tho' Proserpine be absent there is happily for him a Queen to whom he is devoted at Windsor'.[22] On another occasion he insisted on how much value he placed on her advice: 'It may be unconstitutional for a Minister to seek advice from his Sovereign, instead of proffering it; but your Majesty has, sometimes, deigned to assist Mr Disraeli with your counsel, and he believes he may presume to say, with respectful candour, that your Majesty cannot but be aware how highly Mr Disraeli appreciates your Majesty's judgment and almost unrivalled experience of public life.'[23] Although his written adoration of her reached the level of absurdity, in reality he rarely paid much attention to Victoria's views. Sir Henry Ponsonby, the Queen's Liberal-leaning private secretary, observed that: '...it seems to me that he communicates nothing except boundless professions of love and loyalty and if called on to write more says he is ill'.[24] Although Ponsonby suffered from a certain political prejudice, there is much truth in this statement. It seems likely that both Victoria and Disraeli were playing a game, but it was a game that pleased both of them and hurt no one.

Victoria was sensible enough to reserve much of her influence for the questions that were most important to her, and there is no doubt that the Church was one such question. Much of her correspondence with Disraeli concerned Church appointments and here they could have ardent disagreements. They were not as intense as Victoria's conflicts with Gladstone on the question because, unlike Gladstone, Disraeli usually did not feel strongly about the Church. He did, however, have a tendency to promote men who were either friends of his or friends of friends of his. On several occasions Victoria voiced her disapproval of this:

> For the *future* she would wish Mr Disraeli to try and select, for Canons or high positions in the Church, people whose literary or other merits point them out for promotion, rather than merely from their birth. If *both* can be combined right and well, but if not it is very *important* that merit and true *liberal* broad views should be the recommendation.

Victoria went on to insist that: 'It is by such appointments alone that we can hope to strengthen the very tottering fabric of the Established Church.'[25]

On several occasions she went so far as to submit her own suggestions to Disraeli, and she was ready and willing to campaign vehemently in favour of the former tutor of her son Prince Leopold for the position of Canon of Westminster in spite of his relative youth. In doing so, she was not above trying to pull Disraeli's heartstrings with her own form of melancholy writing. She insisted that 'the appointment would greatly gratify her poor sick boy, and cheer him much'. She concluded by adding: 'The Queen feels sure, that Mr. Disraeli would find this appointment popular, and would be glad to gratify poor Leopold. There is no change in his condition.'[26] Disraeli was occasionally forced to admonish her for her intrusions into clerical appointments. After her aforementioned letter, he felt obliged to tell her:

> It is his [Disraeli's] duty to impress upon your Majesty, that the utmost discretion is requisite in advising your Majesty to confer patronage upon the Broad Church party. He feels sure he is speaking with perfect warrent when he says that the great mass of the Conservative party, in and out of Parliament, view the Broad Church school with more suspicion and aversion than they do the Ritualists; and he could not have carried the Public Worship Bill last Session, had not he given assurances to several influential persons, that the Ministry would, in no way, identify itself with the Broad Church movement. He hesitates not to say, that any marked sympathy of that kind would lose not only votes in the House of Commons, but at public elections.[27]

Disraeli's message was clear: Victoria's power was severely limited by the demands of politics and by the need to secure re-election.

However much he was willing to please her in little things, he, no more than Gladstone, was going to disregard political realities.

On the other hand, Victoria was a firm supporter of Disraeli's position on the eastern question and, as we have seen, was scandalized by the conduct of Lord and Lady Derby. Like Disraeli, she incorrectly believed the Russians to be ultimately responsible for the Bulgarian atrocities. She argued that: 'Hearing as we do all the undercurrent, and knowing as we do that Russia instigated this insurrection, which caused the cruelty of the Turks, it ought to be brought home to Russia, and the world ought to know that on their shoulders and not on ours rests the blood of the murdered Bulgarians!'[28] She was more than happy to confirm Disraeli in all his prejudices and to encourage him in his eastern policy in spite of public disapproval. Thus, Disraeli listened to Victoria in this case because she happened to be saying what he wanted to hear. This does not mean that Victoria had a great deal of influence on him. He certainly made her life as easy as possible and was more than ready to do things to please her, such as have her proclaimed Empress of India. Even here, though, he had strong political motives: he wished to identify the Conservative Party with the monarchy and with the empire in order to associate it with patriotism in people's minds. But, as we have seen, he did not hesitate to gently rebuke her at times – although always in his inimitable style. In one such case in 1875, for example, he wrote: 'Were he your Majesty's Grand Vizier, instead of your Majesty's Prime Minister, he should be content to pass his remaining years in accomplishing everything your Majesty wished; but, alas! it is not so.'[29] Politics was his ultimate guideline, and when political needs differed fundamentally from Victoria's wishes, Disraeli did not hesitate to choose the former.

Victoria's relationship with Salisbury was considerably less colourful although there is no doubt that her political sympathies were with him. She clearly found Salisbury considerably more agreeable than Gladstone and the Liberals, although she did consent to intervene with Salisbury over the Third Reform Act. Conservative opposition to the Third Reform Act of 1884 was threatening to cause a constitutional showdown between the House of Commons and the House of Lords. At all costs, Victoria wanted to prevent such a conflict. While the Queen was, if anything, even more afraid of democracy than was Salisbury, the situation in the country was tense. Both she and Gladstone feared riots if the bill was rejected. The Queen did her best to mediate between the two sides, and she certainly helped provide an atmosphere of conciliation. The extent of her role in this crisis is quite controversial, but it seems clear that her intervention was important but not decisive.[30] She wrote directly to Salisbury and asked him to consent to 'a personal conference between the two Parties in both Houses'.[31] The situation was resolved without a major crisis, and she undoubtedly had a part in that. The following year, however, what little sympathy she might have possessed for Gladstone disappeared after General Gordon's death at Khartoum. She sent an uncoded telegram to him and other leading Liberals, rebuking them for what had happened. Since it was not in cipher, the contents were immediately leaked and published in the press.[32]

In any case, her sympathies were obviously with the Conservatives, and she was clearly pleased when they returned to power in 1885. Apart from all personal considerations, her own devotion to the empire and Palmerstonian views in foreign policy clearly pushed her in that direction. She did not hesitate to voice her sadness when the election at the end of that year did not go well for them:

> The Queen has been much distressed, she must say, at the unsatisfactory turn the Elections have taken. But it must be observed that the extreme Radicals have *not* succeeded, that many of the minorities are very large and greatly larger than *last* Election, and that Conservatives have gained many seats since '80. The feeling of the country is therefore very healthy in *that* respect. The Queen thinks, however, *most* of the country and of our *foreign relations*, and of the *absolute* NECESSITY of having strong and able and safe men to conduct the government of the Empire, such as is the case in Lord Salisbury's hands. She therefore looks to *him* to help and advise her in this critical juncture.[33]

Here, she does not even make a token effort towards impartiality. She is quite clear about her support for Salisbury and the Conservatives.

Victoria certainly saw herself as having a role in policy-making. Equally clearly, neither Gladstone, Disraeli nor Salisbury were willing to give her such a role. Gladstone was in many ways the most respectful of the Crown's constitutional position among the three men. He took care to write her regularly and at length about government decisions, but he made it evident that he was not consulting her but informing her. Furthermore, there is no doubt that Victoria disagreed with him politically, disliked him personally and was particularly irritated because he did not even try to give her the illusion of possessing power. In response, Victoria had no hesitation about corresponding with Conservative leaders about Liberal government policy.[34] She opposed the Liberal cabinet on many questions of policy and often criticized them privately. After Gordon's death, the issue that probably upset her the most was Irish home rule. Victoria was violently hostile to this policy and made no attempt to keep quiet about it. She showed Salisbury her correspondence from the government and even sometimes her replies. She even went so far as to contact Salisbury about the best time for a dissolution after the home rule bill had been defeated, which was an obvious constitutional violation.

Victoria clearly had a major role in politics, but there is no doubt that part was still extremely limited. This was the case, not so much because Victoria was a woman, but because the Crown's power was continually declining. The growth of democracy and the rise of political parties inevitably caused the monarchy to lose most of whatever power still remained to it. By the end of Victoria's reign the Crown had become little more than a figurehead which Edward VII could not and did not even try to restore. However much Victoria might try to influence policy decisions, in most cases – unless her views reflected popular opinion in the country – she could do little. Still, there is no doubt that Victoria enjoyed political influence and power, even when Gladstone was in office. Her active hostility could make the life of any prime minister difficult. She was also a major public figure in the nation and, especially in her later years, held in real reverence. There is no doubt that Disraeli was trying to make political capital from this reverence by associating himself and his party with her. She may have been little more than a symbol, but as such she possessed real power. In spite of her own hostility to women's suffrage, Victoria would be used by the suffragists as the classic example of a woman who could exercise effective and responsible political power. If Victoria could do this, they argued, other women could as well. The very fact that Victoria was so admired and unthreatening made her a strong argument in favour of granting women more political rights.

Occupying a very different position from Victoria were the Londonderry women who undoubtedly were the queens of the Conservative Party social scene in the late nineteenth and early twentieth centuries. First there was Theresa, the wife of the sixth Marquess, and then her daughter-in-law, Edith. Nor is it possible to forget the role of Frances, duchess of Marlborough, who was a Londonderry by birth.[35] The Londonderry women had a well-deserved reputation for being particularly formidable. It was said that, during the sixth

Marquess's period at the Board of Education, Theresa had been so interested in anything pertaining to County Durham that she actually chaired at least one departmental meeting in spite of her husband's presence and the fact that she had absolutely no official position. One observer described the occasion:

> A curious scene was to be witnessed in the bow-window of the Lord President's room this morning. For more than two hours Lady Londonderry presided over a departmental consultation as to the steps to be taken in dealing with the Durham County Council in its treatment of the voluntary schools of the county. It is true the Lord President was nominally a party to the conference, but he remained at the end of the table in isolated dignity, while Lady Londonderry held the Permanent Secretary and the subordinate official immediately concerned in close communion.

Another commentator remarked that: 'It is certainly a new departure...when a Minister's wife undertakes to look into matters of departmental administration in the very seat of her husband's authority, and leaves to him the simple functions of an interested listener.'[36] There is little doubt that Theresa was a far more dominant personality than her husband and that she was passionately interested in at least some political questions. At the same time Theresa was hostile to women's suffrage and, along with other politically active female aristocrats like the Duchess of Marlborough, signed an anti-suffrage petition in 1889.[37] Given the obvious influence she already possessed she saw small need for the vote.

Her daughter-in-law, Edith, was in many ways an even more powerful figure and reigned over, first, the Conservative Party, and then Ramsay MacDonald's National Government until the mid-1930s. Austen Chamberlain asserted that he could tell how his own career was going by the number of fingers (from two to ten) she used when she shook hands with him.[38] Her habit was to give a spectacular reception at Londonderry House before every parliamentary session for the leaders of society and Tory politics (who were, of course, often the same people), and she would stand next to the current party leader to welcome the guests as they arrived. The very fact of greeting the guests with the party leader is in itself suggestive of the extent of her power. There is no doubt that Edith was an inveterate snob, but her snobbery was based on power and not on class. Bonar Law, an unlikely background figure in the party, may not have interested her before he became party leader, but he certainly did afterwards.

Perhaps her most amazing relationship was with the Irish nationalist leader, Michael Collins. She arranged a meeting between Collins and her husband, who owned large estates in the north of Ireland, in April 1922, while the new Irish Free State was preparing its constitution. There was a brief correspondence between the two on matters relating to that meeting which was not particularly successful. It is clear, however, that she and not her husband had worked for the meeting and that she, and not her husband, was disappointed by its lack of results.[39]

Lady Londonderry is notorious in Labour Party legend because of her relationship with Ramsay MacDonald, the first Labour prime minister. They met in 1924, just after the formation of the first Labour government, at a party given by the king and queen. They hit it off at once, and MacDonald invited her and her husband to Chequers. There is certainly an element of political opportunism in the alacrity with which they accepted MacDonald's offer. In fact, their names are the first to appear in the visitors' book at Chequers under MacDonald's premiership.[40] To her critics, she certainly deserved her nickname of Circe the Sorceress because of the spell she cast over MacDonald – a spell that led him to break with the rest of his party in 1931 and form a coalition with the Conservatives. Of course, many other factors pushed MacDonald towards this momentous decision, and Lady Londonderry perhaps played only a small role. It seems more likely that his attraction for Lady Londonderry was a symptom of his rightward movement rather than the cause. In any case, a more unlikely couple can hardly be imagined: the illegitimate Scots Labour Party leader and the grande dame of Conservative party politics. The ageing, lonely (and perhaps social-climbing) widower, MacDonald, was clearly smitten with her, however, and she did not hesitate to take advantage of this infatuation. It is certain that Stanley Baldwin, leader of the Conservative Party at this time, and his party chairman, J. C. C. Davidson, were intent on modernizing the Conservative Party and breaking the aristocratic grip on it. They thus were not terribly fond of the Londonderrys. Partly for this reason and partly because of his own minimal talents, the career of Lord Londonderry, a background figure at best, had not been as brilliant as Lady Londonderry had hoped.[41] No wonder that neither spouse hesitated a second about rushing off to Chequers at MacDonald's invitation, and MacDonald, in turn, gave both Londonderrys a new lease on life. It is noteworthy that after MacDonald's retirement, one of Baldwin's first actions was to remove Lord Londonderry from his ministerial position. Lord

Londonderry further discredited himself in 1938 by writing a book in which he praised Hitler.[42] Both he and his wife seem to have been quite captivated by the German dictator, at least until war began. But, of course, by that time, the days of the great hostesses were fading, and they did not survive the Second World War.

Lady Londonderry, however, was more than just a seductress and hostess. In many ways she was a very modern woman and a feminist. She had been a strong supporter of the suffragists before the war: not, of course, of the radical Pankhursts, but of the much more moderate Millicent Fawcett. She had actually gone so far as to write a letter to *The Times* on the subject – a fact which had quite horrified her mother-in-law, the in many ways even more formidable Theresa. Edith was also very active in the First World War. She did quite a lot of work with hospitals, even founding one herself. However, her major achievement was undeniably her role in the foundation of the Women's Legion in 1915 of which she became president. The Women's Legion was started to free men in the army from non-combat positions for fighting. Women replaced men as cooks, drivers, dispatch-riders, and worked in agriculture. Gradually these women were given uniforms and, in 1917, organized into regular Women's Armies. In her memoirs, she describes the elation she and other women felt at the sudden freedom the war gave them and presents the prejudice that they frequently encountered:

> I always wore uniform, and never before was life, from the feminine standpoint of dress, so delightful. You wore it at functions, you wore it for every day, at funerals or weddings. It led indeed to some strange experiences. Some people were always rude to a woman in uniform, and in their Departments, in connection with the work, a uniformed woman was always kept waiting to the last, and usually squeezed out of the lifts by the porters, and when I had to give my name they were incredulous or laughed outright. I was lunching one day at Lady ____'s house, and on ringing the bell the parlour maid looked at me with suspicion. I thought I must have come to the wrong door, and said, 'Is Lady So-and-so not in?' 'Yes,' replied the maid. 'If you will go down by the area and give me a message I will see if Lady ____ will see you! She is very busy and has company to lunch.' I then gave my name. I could see she was shocked and horrified.[43]

After women got the right to vote in 1918, Lady Londonderry became one of the first women justices of the peace. She was thus much more than a social butterfly. She was undoubtedly a feminist and one who made, in her own way, a not unimportant contribution to the liberation of women. Her role in the Women's Legion shows her to have been independent-minded enough to go against the prejudices of her class. To some extent she seems to have even taken a certain pleasure from shocking them – which may perhaps explain something about her relationship with Ramsay MacDonald. They both enjoyed the shock their friendship gave to those around them.

The life of Edith Londonderry also shows how much the position of women – even without the vote – had evolved since the days of Mary Anne Disraeli. The Primrose League and similar organizations in other parties had brought women out of the background and into the visible business of politics. Already in Theresa Londonderry's generation we can see the result as she became actively, although unofficially, involved in politics. These early pioneers and the desperate need for labour during the First World War allowed Edith to go much further. There is, however, something rather pathetic about each of these women. Even Edith Londonderry, the most uninhibited and liberated of them, found herself ultimately dependent on a man for her political power, whether it be her husband or Ramsay Mac-Donald. However powerful a woman may appear to be, she can have no real political base but her personal influence over men. She does not have a political career herself (although Edith Londonderry was active after women got the right to vote but for whatever reason did not try to enter Parliament herself). There is undeniably a major evolution in women's position during this period – one which made possible their achievement of the vote in 1918 – but they faced a great deal of prejudice and their role remained ultimately severely limited and dependent on the acceptance of men.

Having looked at these examples of women in political life, we must try to see what conclusions we can draw about this period. First, women, even if they stayed in the background, clearly exercised an important influence simply because the Conservative Party during this period was, to a large extent, based on family alliances. Furthermore, these family links were strengthened through social contact which was far more important at this time than it is today when politics has become professional. During this period the Conservative Party was based on a small, inter-married political elite, and this very fact increased the influence of women who were related to men in this elite. Through their role in arranging marriages, settling family differences and offering advice to their men in private, these aristocratic women exercised real political influence. However, the effect of the power behind the throne can and often is exaggerated. Ultimately whatever power these women had was based on their relationships with men. They could offer advice, and they could introduce rising young men to the party leaders, but they could rarely do more. One clear sign of this is that, while young men intent on advancement frequently confided in these hostesses, they tended to grow more distant as they rose in politics. This happened even to Lady Derby, and it can hardly be doubted that she was a political force primarily because of her husband. Without the vote and other political rights the power of women was quite simply extremely limited.

On the other hand, this period clearly shows a growing role for women in the political life of the country. Each generation possessed more political power than the one before and exercised it in a more public manner. While these aristocratic women continued to be influential behind the scenes, they also became more and more visible, and their role in politics became more and more accepted. The late Victorian period saw women at all levels of society acquire a number of rights and a great deal of political experience which paved the way for their receiving the vote after the First World war. One of the main reasons for this was the growth of political or semi-political organizations that included women among their members. Through these groups, women began to exercise overt political power, albeit in a severely limited fashion. They also began to be taken seriously by men for their political views. One of the first and most important of these groups was the staunchly Conservative Primrose League, and we should now turn to a more detailed consideration of that organization.

2 The Primrose League

The foundation of the Primrose League can only be understood against the background of politics in the 1880s. The 1880 election defeat had severely demoralized the Conservatives and as a result they began to fight among themselves. As long as Disraeli remained as uncontested leader, the situation could be kept under control but in 1881 Disraeli died, leaving no obvious heir as party leader. The stopgap solution found was to make Sir Stafford Northcote leader in the House of Commons and Lord Salisbury in the House of Lords. Of course, this could only work as long as the Conservatives remained in opposition for once they returned to power only one of the two could be prime minister. The House of Commons was already the more powerful of the two houses, which should have given Northcote an advantage, but his personality worked against him. Northcote was one of the least aggressive Conservative Party leaders in history. To make matters worse, he had once been Gladstone's secretary and retained a great deal of respect for and deference towards the Liberal leader. Many Conservatives quickly became disenchanted with Northcote's performance in the House. The most important of these, at least for our purposes, was undoubtedly Lord Randolph Churchill. Churchill, the rather dissipated third son of the Duke of Marlborough, was determined to have a meteoric political career. He and three friends: Henry Gorst, Henry Drummond Wolff, and, more tepidly, Arthur Balfour, Salisbury's nephew, formed a group known at the time and since as the 'Fourth Party'. The Fourth Party attacked Gladstone and his government in vitriolic terms, although their real target was their own leaders. The basic aim of the Fourth Party was the crucifixion of Northcote, a task which they accomplished with much skill and, it must be added, with considerable inadvertent assistance from Northcote himself. The Fourth Party could certainly sting, as Gorst's famous remark that he wanted 'to point out that the right hon. Gentleman at the head of the Government had forgotten to answer the Question which the Leader of the Opposition forgot to put'.[1] His point was clear: Northcote was simply not critical enough of Gladstone's government.

All of this, of course, inevitably helped Salisbury to emerge as uncontested party leader. Questions of competence aside, it was clearly in the Fourth Party's interest, and particularly Churchill's, to have Salisbury as party leader and eventually as prime minister. Churchill wanted to rise quickly in politics, and, if Northcote could be pushed aside, Churchill would then become the leading Conservative figure in the House of Commons. Churchill may have presented himself as the great spokesman of 'Tory democracy', but in reality most of his actions were motivated by personal advancement.[2] At the same time as his personal assault on Northcote, Churchill launched an attack on the National Union, which was the central organization for all Conservative clubs and societies and thus, in many ways, the heart of the Conservative Party itself. There was therefore a power struggle not only for control of the House of Commons but also for control of the Conservative Party structure. Churchill insisted that the party did not give a voice to rank-and-file party members and called for a democratic and self-governing Tory Party.[3] In 1883 Churchill was elected to the Council of the National Union and became shrilly vocal in presenting its complaints. At the same time, Churchill's innate restlessness and his unscrupulous desire to rise as quickly as possible, made him think that a new Conservative organization, outside the party structure, might be a good idea. The Primrose League began as one element in the power struggle between Northcote and Churchill.

As near as anyone can tell, the origin of the Primrose League lies in Lady Dorothy Nevill's lunch parties.[4] Churchill, Wolff and Gorst had noticed the popularity of Disraeli's memory both in the country and in the party. They therefore determined to harness Disraeli for their own purposes. It was generally believed that Disraeli's favourite flower had been the primrose. The main evidence for this was that Queen Victoria had sent him primroses during his last illness and had had a wreath of them made for his funeral. In any case, the question of whether Disraeli really liked primroses is completely beside the point. What was important was that the flower summoned up the image of an increasingly revered leader and, perhaps more importantly, of the Queen's close relationship to the Conservative Party. The Primrose League then was to be an organization outside the Conservative Party but devoted to the memory of Disraeli and to certain of his presumed ideals: the monarchy, the empire and the Church of England. It was also supposed to be a vehicle for Randolph Churchill's ambitions. Churchill and his friends quickly interested Sir Algernon Borthwick in their project. Borthwick was the owner of the strongly Conservative *Morning Post*. Disaffected by, as he saw it, the lack of recognition given to him by the Conservative Party leadership, Borthwick decided to support Churchill. He and his wife would both play an important role in the Primrose League. The League, which would open the way to women in politics, thus can hardly be said to have a very noble origin. As the historian Martin Pugh has demonstrated, the Primrose League began as 'yet another Fourth party machination', but it grew into much more than that.[5]

On 17 November 1883 the Primrose League officially began, and Churchill and his friends formed the Grand Council. Membership was open to 'all classes and all creeds except the atheists and enemies of the British Empire'.[6] Churchill seems to have had no clear idea as to what he intended the Primrose League to be; most likely it was simply another vehicle to use in his quest for power. Beyond that, he seems to have thought little about the League. It was Wolff who had the strongest influence on it. He wanted a popular organization but one like the Ulster Orange Order or the Freemasons that was cloaked in ceremony and even a little mysticism. In imitation of these bodies, the League created a hierarchical structure complete with medieval sounding titles, honours, and rituals. Perhaps the most extraordinary thing about the Primrose League was its decision – once again largely at the instigation of Wolff – to admit women to membership. The League would thus become the first major political organization to allow women a major role. As we saw in the first chapter,[7] Gladstone's Electoral Corrupt Practices Act of 1883 had severely restricted the number of paid political helpers that a candidate could use during an election. The basic result of this act was to make the establishment of a system of unpaid volunteers absolutely vital. Furthermore, the Third Reform Act had increased by over two million the number of voters and the Redistribution Act that followed had completely redrawn the constituencies of Britain. The result was certain to be chaos, from the point of view of the political parties, unless large numbers of unpaid canvassers could be found. The National Union and its constituency organizations were in too poor a condition to provide these workers, so either the National Union had to be completely reorganized and rejuvenated or an alternative organization had to be created. The Primrose League, and more particularly its women members, turned out to be the ideal source for this unpaid labour. It is no wonder then that Churchill was soon able to negotiate Salisbury's acceptance of the organization and win himself a cabinet seat.

But even beyond this, the Primrose League turned out to be a tremendous asset to the Conservative Party. First, it was a meeting place for members of different classes. Disraeli had said: 'I have never been myself at all favourable to a system which would induce Conservatives who are working men to form societies confined merely to their class.'[8] The League allowed dukes and workmen to meet while at the same time reflecting the hierarchical structure of society which was so beloved of Conservatives. There were two classes of membership: one for the workmen and one for the upper and middle classes and special titles given to each group. Conservatism has always stressed the idea of a hierarchical society while at the same time proclaiming an ideal of social unity. The League quite obviously illustrated these beliefs. Herbert Gladstone, the son of the great prime minister, had sneered at the League as 'only fit for duchesses and scullery-maids', which was completely missing the point. As a grand councillor responded: any group that 'enabled duchesses and scullery maids to meet on equal terms was of the greatest value'.[9] This was the obvious truth in a country that was becoming more and more democratic. Since the League also presented social functions, this attracted many people, particularly in rural areas where there was little competition. However, this was clearly not the only reason for the League's success, for it very often flourished in urban, working-class areas too. By 1900 the League claimed to have 1.5 million members, most of them working-class.[10] The working class joined the Primrose League for a number of reasons of which deference to their social superiors formed only a small part. Obviously many working-class members found it thrilling to go to a tea party at a stately house given by a duke and duchess. But there was much more than this in the success of the League. In the cotton towns near Manchester the League enjoyed a remarkable success without having any great aristocratic patrons.[11] The League provided a respectable form of entertainment for them and their families without rowdiness or excessive use of alcohol. But there is no doubt too that they felt a certain sympathy for Conservative aims. Imperialism was popular, and both the Primrose League and the Conservative Party had strongly associated themselves with it. Certainly, the reason the working class joined often varied according to the area. In regions with a heavily Catholic population, Catholic workers often became members of the League because it had no Protestant overtones. What is clear in every case is that the League provided an essentially recreational function and one that was in harmony with the new insistence on respectability to be found in the upper levels of the working class.

The second, and perhaps greatest cause of the Primrose League's success, was that it decided, almost from the beginning, to admit women. The decision to admit women had been made very early, in December 1883. An addition to the rules was made which stated that: 'Ladies may, on the recommendation of a Ruling Councillor or a Habitation and a payment of the entrance fee and subscription, become honorary Members and shall be entitled Dames of the Primrose League.'[12] Notice the use of the word 'honorary', which tells us a great deal about what role the organization's founders envisioned for women. There is no doubt that the women were to be subsidiary to the men's group. Churchill's mother, the Duchess of Marlborough, and his wife, the American Jennie Jerome, were among its first members. Other aristocratic ladies soon joined up. The participation of the nobility was certainly an important element in the League's success. As we have seen, many members of both the working class and the middle class found it extremely tempting, and even gratifying, to go to League functions in aristocratic homes and to talk on more or less equal terms with duchesses. In its mixing of classes, the League was one of the greatest forces for democracy in the country. For rural families, in particular, it also provided entertainment and an escape from everyday boredom. Of course, there was always some attempt at political propaganda at League functions, but it was often very brief. All of this leads us to conclude that it seems likely that most people joined the League more for its social element than for its political conservatism. This, of course, does not mean that the League did not provide valuable services for the Conservative Party. As we have seen, the League gave numerous and generally remarkably efficient volunteer workers during and between campaigns. The League certainly played a significant role in the Conservative dominance of the late-Victorian period, although ultimately the home rule controversy was more important.

In political and social terms, the success of the Primrose League depended on its female membership. With women and even children present, the League could claim to be a wholesome family organization, and the presence of the aristocracy made it even more prestigious socially. But the women were also the basic reason for its formidable political success. To some extent, women's involvement in the Primrose League was a natural outgrowth of their already important involvement in philanthropic work. Through their socially accepted charitable endeavours, upper-class women were already usually in closer contact with their community than were their men folk. They already moved between different classes, and they already knew a great deal about families in their area. Obviously, this knowledge could be extremely useful in a political context, while the fact that these ladies were often already known figures for their charitable work made them receive a warmer welcome in working-class areas then men might have had. Women thus were ideally situated for canvassing work and for maintaining the voter register in an up-to-date condition. The philanthropic tradition for women thus gave them a solid basis within the community which they later exploited to great advantage when they moved into political work. Furthermore, the fact that they had more free time than men also made women obvious political volunteers. From the very beginning, the Primrose League stressed the importance of female help, although they did so in terms of women's traditional role. In 1885, Jennie Churchill insisted that women made the best canvassers because of 'the persuasive gentleness characteristic of their sex'.[13] To a large extent, the Primrose League revolutionized the role of women in politics while, at the same time, protesting that what they were doing was in no way revolutionary. It was simply an extension of women's customary role and was presented in such terms.

Already Randolph Churchill's re-election campaign in Woodstock in 1885 had shown the importance of women workers. At that time all ministers, when they entered the cabinet, were required to resign their seats and seek re-election. As part of the agreement between Churchill and Salisbury, Churchill had been given the India Office. The demands of his work were great, and Churchill felt unable to leave London to conduct an election campaign, so he therefore sent his wife. The Primrose League barely existed at that time in Woodstock and so Jennie was forced to rely on her own efforts and any assistance her friends could give her. Most of the campaign work was actually done by herself and her sister-in-law, Lady Georgiana Curzon, although the assistance of the Churchill family and their imposing presence at Blenheim Palace certainly helped too. In her memoirs, Jennie describes the elation that campaign gave her:

We were most important, and felt that the eyes of the world were upon us. Revelling in the hustle and bustle of the committee rooms, marshalling our forces, and hearing the hourly reports of how the campaign was progressing, I felt like a general holding a council-of-war with his staff in the heat of a battle. A. was doubtful, B. obdurate, while C.'s wife, a wicked abominable Radical, was trying to influence her husband, whom we thought secure, to vote the wrong way. At once they must be visited, and our arsenal of arguments brought to bear on them. Sometimes with these simple country-folk a pleading look, and an imploring, 'Oh please vote for my husband; I shall be so unhappy if he does not get in'; or, 'If you want to be on the winning side, vote for us as, of course, we are going to win,' would be as effective as the election agent's longest speeches on the iniquity of Mr Chamberlain's unauthorized programme or Mr Gladstone's 'disgraceful' attitude at the death of Gordon. In some ways the work was arduous enough.[14]

Lady Randolph worked so hard and made such an impression in the constituency that rhymes or songs were soon being written by the locals about her campaign tactics:

> Bless my soul! that Yankee lady,
> Whether day was bright or shady,
> Dashed about the district like an oriflamme of war.
> When the voters saw her bonnet,
> With the bright pink roses on it,
> They followed as the soldiers did the Helmet of Navarre.[15]

Randolph Churchill won the election and to a large extent because of his wife's efforts. The Primrose League would soon repeat what had happened in Woodstock throughout the country and show that women did indeed have a role in politics.

The upper level of women members of the Primrose League, in keeping with its custom of using high sounding titles, were known as 'dames'. The first women to belong were aristocratic friends of Henry Drummond Wolff and included Lady Dorothy Nevill and her daughters, the Churchill family and others. These cultivated aristocratic ladies found the League rather ridiculous and often laughed heartily at its undeniably kitsch accoutrements. Lady Knightley, for example, said: 'It all sounds rubbish.' However, this did not mean that she dismissed it. She went on to comment acutely that 'I can quite believe that the paraphernalia helps to keep Conservatives together – means in short, an army of unpaid canvassers.'[16] This was in effect what happened, for membership did not remain limited to aristocratic ladies. There were two levels of membership in the Primrose League. The upper level was that of knight or dame, for which the person paid one guinea, but there also existed a lower and much cheaper level of membership, that of associate member. At the first general meeting (officially known as the Grand Habitation) in July 1884, membership was announced as being 3500 knights and 370 dames.[17] Over the following years the ratio between knights and dames decreased steeply: in September 1885 it was at three to one; in November 1885 at two to one; in January 1886 at three to two; and in March 1887 at five to four. An examination of associate members shows the same phenomenon, giving, as Martin Pugh has estimated, a nearly fifty-fifty ratio between men and women in most habitations.[18] His calculations led him to conclude that hundreds of thousands of women must have belonged to the Primrose League during the Victorian period, and most of these were obviously not upper-class.

Not only were there nearly as many women members as men members, but, in general, the women were more active. Most of the habitations were mixed, that is, included both men and women. Of these mixed habitations, the figures for 1887–9 show that one in four of them were led by women. Furthermore, in many cases where the leader (or Ruling Councillor to give the official title) was a man, he had a female deputy. There seems to be little doubt that in some cases the man was simply a figurehead while the deputy, called a Dame President, actually did most of the work.[19] Other offices were also frequently held by women, although at the national level women were less important. The Primrose League was governed by a Grand Council which remained limited to men until after the First World War. However, a Ladies Grand Council (LGC) was formed practically as soon as women were allowed to become members, and Frances, Duchess of Marlborough was made its president.[20] The Ladies Grand Council was officially subordinate to the Grand Council, but it possessed a great deal of power because of its better fund-raising abilities. All members of the LGC had to pay a guinea a year for membership, which was quite separate from any other fees they had to pay to the League. The LGC thus never had to ask for money from the Grand Council, rather they were in a position of being able to give it. The inaugural meeting of the LGC took place on 9 April 1885 and was addressed by, among others, Arthur Balfour the nephew of Salisbury. The ladies' attitude towards the press, however, reveals a great deal about the ambivalence of their attitude to the Primrose League and to their role in it. They decided to invite reporters both from the fashion and the political sections of the *Morning Post*.[21] The ladies were clearly unsure as to whether their organization was simply a fashionable society one or whether it was a serious political group. Then again, perhaps they wanted it to be both: in any case, this is what they achieved.

The LGC was also far more dynamic than its male counterpart, and much of the Primrose League's spectacular expansion, particularly from 1885–7, must be credited to the dames' enthusiasm. The LGC itself grew at a remarkable rate. Three months after its formation it counted 362 members, and by February 1886 the figure had reached 796.[22] By 1892 the figure had reached 1370.[23] Ladies coming to London during the season would be co-opted and then when they returned to their own areas would form new habitations.[24] It was estimated in February 1886, that approximately 400 habitations had already come about through the efforts of the members of the LGC. The same report asserted that:

> Turning to the operations of the League undertaken in connection with the late general election, your committee have pleasure in announcing that of the many thousands of canvassers furnished by the PLM, more than one-half were obtained by means of the organization at the disposal of the LGC. It should also be mentioned that not less than 10,000 non-resident voters – the canvassing of whom forms so important a feature in the operations of the League – were induced to vote by Ladies. In addition to canvassing, your committee have to report that 326,000 leaflets were issued from the offices of the Ladies' Council, and the sum of £360 was expended in holding meetings for the promotion of constitutional principles.[25]

No one could deny that, from the very beginning, the LGC had been a success of the first order.

Given all this, it is not surprising to see that male members often felt threatened by the women's branch. The Primrose League challenged the accepted orthodoxy of the time in that it was a political organization in which men and women mixed on more or less equal terms. The paradox was that, being a Conservative organization, its members felt it necessary to deny that this challenge was taking place at all. Women being deeply involved in campaign elections was a novelty, and of course many men (and not only men) began to protest that such behaviour was unbecoming for women. As we have seen, Jennie Churchill was one of the first to break this taboo, and other women soon followed. The general election of 1885 saw large numbers of women getting involved in a political campaign for the first time – and most of these women were Conservatives. Even so august and old-fashioned a figure as the Duchess of Marlborough joined her daughter-in-law, Jennie Churchill, in canvassing Randolph's new district in Birmingham. Once again, Jennie describes what happened:

The Duchess of Marlborough, my mother-in-law, came down to help me. It was the first time that women had ever indulged in any personal canvassing in Birmingham, and we did it thoroughly. Every house in the constituency was visited. The Duchess would go in one direction, and I in another; the constituency was a large one, and the work arduous. The voters were much more enlightened than the agricultural labourers of Oxfordshire; the men particularly were very argumentative, and were well up on the questions of the day. The wives of the Radicals were also admirably informed, and on more than one occasion routed me completely.[26]

These first female canvassers were almost always aristocratic, but what became acceptable for the aristocracy was quickly imitated by the middle class. Soon, instead of a few noblewomen, groups comprising dozens of dames were methodically canvassing constituencies. The dames of the Primrose League certainly played a role in the Conservative election victory of 1885 and thus proved their worth to the men in their party.

Jennie's quote, however, leads us to the next consequence of women's participation in the Primrose League. For if women were quickly becoming a major force as canvassers during elections, they also very often lacked the necessary political knowledge to make them truly effective in their task. Notice how Jennie talks about the arguments she had with men who opposed Conservative policies, and notice too that she often found herself unable to answer them. It was obvious that if women were to do good work in an election campaign, they had to receive a certain degree of education on political topics. Now, as we have seen, women had long been involved in philanthropic work, and this was an accepted part of women's sphere. Canvassing, to some extent, could be viewed as a simple extension of women's accepted role in charitable organizations. Meresia Nevill, for example, insisted that: 'As a rule I consider women the best canvassers, in as much as they are used to district visiting. They have the habit of going among the poor.'[27] Thus many a worried male (or female for that matter) could argue that canvassing was simply an extension of women's natural function in society. It was more difficult to say the same thing about political education, but it was clear that if women were to become more effective canvassers, then greater knowledge of the issues was absolutely vital. So the Primrose League found that an important part of its work was simply educating its own members.

This education could take many different forms. As we have seen, many Primrose habitations had been originally founded by women, and these women had needed some training before doing so. The LGC had, almost from the beginning, been forced to provide this training: 'Upon all these ladies the duty of forming Habitations wherever they did not already exist was specially urged, and by means of meetings, pamphlets, and circulars, they were fully instructed as to the methods of carrying out this work, while through the Ladies' Office, and by means of the Ladies' Secretary, every assistance was given them with the same object.'[28] But this, of course, was only the beginning of the ladies' work. Once the habitation had been founded, it had to be kept going and even expanded. Obviously also there was a great deal of work to be done during an election, but the report emphasized that work was also necessary between elections. The ladies' job during such a period was 'spreading sound political opinions' through activities like debates and lending libraries. All of this, of course, required the ladies to keep abreast of political events and of major issues in the country. The *Primrose League Gazette* advised members that:

'Ladies will find it desirable,' she [Lady Lechmere] said, 'to keep well posted up as to the chief speeches of the last Session, and at Public meetings.' This is a so obviously important precaution that it ought not to need emphasis, but by reason of its importance it is worth while to impress it strongly upon those to whom the recommendation appeals. Women's success in political discussion depends principally upon their ability to shatter the delusions and sophistries which form so conspicuous a portion of the Radical's argumentative stock-in-trade, and unless they take care to 'keep well posted up', and to arm themselves with hard facts, they will not be so well able to further the cause which they wish to promote.[29]

Women were thus expected to know and be able to discourse intelligently about the major issues of the day.

If women were forming habitations, canvassing, fund-raising and organizing political debates, the next obvious step was for women to participate in those debates themselves and to even make speeches on their own. Here we are coming to a radical departure. Speaking on political questions before large groups could hardly be considered as a traditional role for women, and the first dames to do so seem to have been rather shocked at this fact. The Countess of Jersey began one speech she gave to the LGC by saying: 'I feel that I should owe you an apology for addressing you were I not acting strictly under orders.

Our Presidents and the Ladies of the Grand Council have thought it well that one of their number should very briefly explain the motives which have actuated them...'[30] Lady Jersey was not alone in finding herself forced to justify (not least of all to herself) this new public role for women. The Primrose League was, after all, a conservative organization, and a clear tension existed between the women's (not to mention the men's) fundamentally conservative view of the world and the new, unorthodox role they found for themselves. This could go to absurd lengths, such as in Mrs Courtney Lord's justification:

> 'Public speaking,' said Mrs Lord, 'is manifestly out of our province, so far, at least, as the addressing of very large audiences is concerned. Neither by constitution, nor by taste and feeling are we adapted for the part of sharing in the gladiatorial combats of the platform. But while our independent work belongs to a less ambitious, and less turbulent sphere, there is every reason why we should develop the faculty of "thinking aloud", and of putting our thoughts into clear and persuasive speech. It is not alone at occasional mass meetings and political demonstrations that converts are to be gathered. Smaller and more systematic gatherings may be made even more fruitful, and it is at these that the "Silvery Eloquence" of the ladies may be heard at once to more advantage and to more effect.'[31]

The distinction she makes may seem to us to be a question of hair-splitting, but her message to the men was clear: we do not intend to try to rival you for leadership; we are content to stay in the background. It was widely believed that in everyday life, women and men had their own separate spheres: women's sphere was at home, that of men in the world. These first lady members of the Primrose League believed that the same was true in politics. A small gathering was acceptable because it could take place in someone's home. A large gathering obviously could not be explained away in the same fashion. Of course, the difference between the two is tiny, but it served to reassure that first generation.

In this way, the women tried to establish a difference between themselves and the feminists: after all, they were ladies and knew how to behave in society. They accepted its basic tenets and certainly were not going to try to revolutionize it. Women of the Primrose League protested endlessly that they were not at all like those horrible and vulgar (and mostly middle-class) women who were agitating for women's rights. Lady Montagu, presenting a paper to the LGC on

'Why Should Women Care for Politics?' argued that the dames were quite a different kettle of fish: 'Until the establishment of the Primrose League, the few women whose names were at all prominently brought forward in connection with political movements belonged to a school of thought which repelled rather than attracted the great mass of their sex, and the subjects they took up, as well as the manner in which they dealt with them, aroused alarm and disgust among all those who valued beyond any political success the preservation of the refinement and dignity of womanhood.'[32] Lady Montagu argued that the Primrose League was 'a just and fitting outlet' for women: it allowed them to participate in politics while at the same time remaining feminine. It is this phenomenon that particularly characterizes conservative feminism: the women behave in a feminist way while all the time protesting that they are not feminist at all. A woman may spend her waking hours on politics but at heart her first love is her family.[33] Some may view this as pure hypocrisy, but it does fulfil a certain psychological need for the woman. She can think of herself as old-fashioned when she is not at all.

There is thus very frequently a tension over the role of women. This certainly was the case in the League. Many men were obviously asking the same question as Lady Montagu, and at least some of them were answering that women should not care for politics. Much time then was spent by women leaders trying to reconcile their own fundamentally conservative view of society and the place of women within it with the radical new role they had carved for themselves in politics. Their attempts were generally not very convincing, and to us today may even seem to be absurd. Since the most obvious role for a woman is that of mother, many ladies tried to justify their political involvement in such terms. The Countess of Jersey, for example, gave the following, extremely typical justification: 'Is it nothing to women which path the nation takes? Have we not cast the greatest stake into the wheel of destiny? Our stake is the welfare of our children.'[34] Lady Montagu went considerably farther. She argued that:

> Why should women care for politics? The simplest and shortest answer to this question – the answer which would have been given if Alice had asked it in Wonderland – is, Why not? And indeed, if retort, not persuasion were our object, we might go no further, and leave the burden of a proof – a heavy one, I think – on the side of the questioner. But we, the Dames and Women Associates of the Primrose League wish to go much further: we assert not merely that

there is no reason why women should not care for politics, but that there are most convincing reasons why they should care. We say that whether they will or no, the circumstances of women's lives must be affected, directly or indirectly, by political events, and therefore, that if it is said, by or for women, that they need not care for politics, this cannot mean that they have the option of escaping the effect of political events upon their lives, but only that they need not take interest in the principles and causes of which those events are the outcome, need not forecast their consequences, and may decline to promote or avert, by such means as lie within their reach, the good or evil which may result from them.[35]

However much Lady Montagu might protest that the dames were well-mannered ladies and not wild-eyed feminists, there was little difference between their positions in the end. Women, Lady Montagu argues, should be interested in politics because their lives are affected by it. If you accept this position, you can hardly deny the vote to women. There was, of course, a difference in presentation: after all, middle-class women had to be louder and more forceful in their demands to be heard. Aristocratic women started from a more privileged position and so could afford to be more ladylike while still achieving their aims. The feminists had to bang down the doors; the Primrose dames could afford to politely knock before entering.

It follows logically from this fact that the women of the Primrose League were usually not strongly involved in the suffragist movement. The League itself was officially neutral on this question, but by the very fact of being a body that involved women in politics, it was almost certain to be drawn into the controversy, at least to some extent. This very fact would make it suspect to more reactionary outlooks. In 1897, for example, when faced with widespread rumours that the League supported women's suffrage, the LGC responded by saying:

The statement that the Primrose League favours and promotes the granting of the franchise to women is incorrect. The Primrose League has always abstained from promoting any matter of these opinions and confines itself to the furtherance of its three principles; i.e. respect for religion, the support of the constitution, and the Imperial ascendancy of the Empire.[36]

This was the paradox of the League: a political organization that was driven by women and yet which refused to take a stand on whether women should vote or not. It was a paradox and yet a logical one, for to have taken a position on the question would certainly have divided the League and caused sharp in-fighting. Its value in campaigns would probably have been destroyed. One need only look at the Liberal women's organization to see what would have happened. The Liberals split over the question and it effectively paralysed them. By refusing to take a stand on the issue the Primrose League avoided that.

The fact is that the Primrose League achieved a certain recognition for women in politics simply because it was a success. The dames showed that they could get Conservative voters to the polls and help ensure Conservative victories. Conservative members of the House of Commons frequently acknowledged that they had entered Parliament, to a large extent, through the work of the dames.[37] The women were believed to have made a substantial contribution to the Conservative victory in the general election of 1885. The men in the League readily acknowledged the contribution of the women. Lord Salisbury, himself, paid tribute to the League and the role that it had given to women:

> The old Conservative Associations have done, and do still, an infinite amount of service, but in some respects and for some purposes they were better fitted for the old suffrage, the old arrangements of party, than they were for those which now exist. The Primrose League is freer. It is more elastic. It brings classes more together, and I think its greatest achievement of all is that it has brought the influence of women to bear on politics in a way that has never before been the case.

Lord Salisbury, however, was notably sympathetic towards women in politics and was known to be in favour of giving at least some women the right to vote.

Other men, however, were not always as open-minded as Salisbury. There was frequently something rather condescending about the way the men congratulated the women. One knight told the dames that:

> They relied greatly on the help of the ladies in the Primrose League. A woman had an instinct in her far better than the grosser nature of man, who required argument and proof before he would put his hand to anything. In woman's breast was implanted an instinct to protect what she loved. What they held most beloved was gravely threatened at this moment. Therefore, the ladies of England, members of the Primrose League, came forward in thousands at the last election. In many constituencies they were the best

canvassers. He had seen them in dozens in the committee-rooms, directing envelopes, sending circulars, writing letters, and omitting nothing that could be done to secure the return of the candidate, and where they had put their shoulders to the wheel the Unionists had won.[38]

The speaker undeniably acknowledges the excellent work that the women had done, but he cannot resist being patronizing towards them still. Men decide where they stand on an issue through their reason, women through their emotions. This was a common belief at the time, and one that was frequently used to justify women not being given the vote.

The other main argument against female suffrage was that women were much too apathetic to vote. They simply left political decisions up to the men in their families, and most of them really had no real desire for the vote. Obviously the work of the dames proved at least this argument to be wrong. The League showed that women were interested in politics and able to master the issues. Without even endorsing women's suffrage, the League showed that women were quite capable of exercising it and therefore deserved it. Primrose League women were expected to be as well informed on political questions as men: when they went out canvassing they had to be better than men in debates. It presented women in leadership roles as instructors and public speakers. It showed women's intelligence and capacity for hard work. After having known the Primrose women, it was difficult for a man to maintain his old stereotype of women, although, as the previous quote shows, some men, in spite of the evidence, refused to acknowledge this. They remained trapped in their limited view of women. Perhaps they simply depended too much on their emotions and not enough on their reason. In any case, as time went on, men had to accept that the women of the Primrose League played an important role within the Conservative Party.

Of course, the Primrose League was not an isolated phenomenon, but part of a general movement of women into the political arena at this time. Most analyses of this phenomenon have focused on the left which has given a rather slanted picture. The most important of these left-wing groups, from our standpoint, was probably the Women's Co-operative Guild. Originally called the Women's League for the Spread of Co-operation, it had been founded in 1883 and by the Edwardian period had a membership of around 30 000 women. It was thus much smaller than the Primrose League. Furthermore, like the Primrose League, the Guild, at least at first, strongly stressed the traditional role of women. Co-operation was seen as being simply an extension of women's natural role as homemaker. Most of the early members were middle class, and they usually accepted the middle-class perception of women's role. The Guild's founder and first General Secretary was Mrs Alice Acland, and the motto she created for the Guild emphasized its fundamentally conservative view of women's role: 'study to be quiet and do your own business'. Like the dames of the Primrose League, she carefully tried to show that her organization was not like radical feminist groups.[39] Furthermore, she emphasized that women did not really have a head for business, and so should not try to thrust themselves forward in that domain. She also disapproved of public speaking by women, although within a year this became generally accepted within the organization. In spite of its relative conservatism, male co-operators were frequently hostile to the Guild – often simply because they did not want their wives to leave the house.

As the Guild developed, its working-class membership expanded, and like the Primrose League, its leaders found it necessary to provide for the education of its members. Courses had to be developed to improve women's efficacy in organizing and administering co-operatives and in presenting its advantages to outside groups. The not unnatural result of education was that women became more interested in things outside the Guild and thus became more politicized. Logically enough, given the nature of this organization, the politicization tended to be leftward, and the Guild slowly became more and more concerned with questions of social reform. In 1889 the leadership changed, and this transformation speeded up. The Guild began to take an interest in questions like divorce and women's suffrage.[40] There is no doubt that the Guild, although starting from a similar view of women, became far more radical than the Primrose League in its assertion of women's rights. After its first days, it strongly endorsed anything that made women more independent of their husbands and advised that women should be ready to assert themselves against their husbands. This was something the League never would have officially at least, dared to do. Note the use of the word 'officially', for, as we have seen, the League also encouraged women to act in an independent fashion – although protesting that it respected traditional roles. On the other hand, the more vocal radicalism of the Guild contributed to a certain hostility towards it within the labour movement. This, of course, was also linked to the fact that the Guild was a segregated organization for women while the Primrose League was far more integrated.

The story of women in the trade union movement is considerably less cheerful. Women workers certainly qualified as among the most oppressed and exploited, but, in spite – or perhaps because – of this women were slow to organize into trade unions. Furthermore, even when they succeeded in forming trade unions, these unions usually did not survive for a very long period of time. On the other hand, the Women's Trade Union League was in many ways a success. By 1904 it had around 126 000 members, but most of these women came from professions traditionally dominated by low-paid female labour.[41] The WTUL was not, however, a major part of the trade union movement, and its leaders, notably Margaret Bondfield and Mary MacArthur, were generally tolerated at trade union conferences because they did not insist too strongly on feminist demands. They can in no way be viewed as having an influential role in the TUC. The trade union movement, with few exceptions, was centred around male interests. Since the trade unions were the most important group in the foundation of the Labour Party and since the party at first had no individual members, it is safe to say that women were only a peripheral element in the new party.

Thus, although the role of women within the labour movement has attracted a great deal of scholarly attention, it seems that, in spite of some important individuals, their role was probably far less important than it was in the Conservative Party. Although some women belonged to the Independent Labour Party (ILP) from the very beginning, their numbers and importance were never great. The early history of the Labour Party shows the same phenomenon. There was no woman present at the conference that founded the Labour Representation Committee – as the Labour Party was called until 1906 – and only a small number were present in subsequent conferences. However, in 1906 the Labour Party recognized the need for a women's branch and the Women's Labour League was founded. The WLL can hardly be described as an immediate success and by 1913 it possessed only 4000 members.[42] Its first chairman was Margaret MacDonald (wife of Ramsay), and she managed to present at the same time both a radical and a fundamentally conservative view of women's role. She argued that: ' In the old crusades, men did the fighting and women watched and waited but now they wished to fight side by side.' At the same time she emphasized that women had special contributions to make in areas that touched on home life like child care and the elderly.[43] There was, in fact very little difference in her rhetoric – at least with regard to women – and that of the Primrose League. As time went on, the Women's Labour League became increasingly involved in the struggle for women's suffrage – a fact which did not endear them always to the men in the movement. The men tended to be focused on the achievement of universal male suffrage, and the women, dependent on them for money, refused to support any measure to give some women the right to vote if it did not include the enfranchisement of all men. For this reason, the Women's Labour League rejected the Conciliation Bills, which proposed the enfranchisement of a limited number of (mostly upper- and middle-class) women, that periodically appeared in Parliament after 1910. The Women's Co-operative Guild did not have such scruples – it supported the Conciliation Bills – which may partly explain why it attracted more hostility from men than did the Women's Labour League. It must be stated though that the Women's Labour League did receive support from many men in their struggle. In 1912 Arthur Henderson moved a resolution at the Labour Party Conference which stated that the Labour movement could not accept a franchise bill that did not include women.[44] The Labour Party thus had the most progressive official policy in relation to female suffrage, but women remained a peripheral part of the organization.

The story of women's organizations in the Liberal Party is considerably less inspiring. At first there was a notable hostility towards the participation of women in politics from the Liberals – perhaps because most of these women were Tory and they were also undeniably effective. Sir Henry James had been able to send light-hearted congratulations to Jennie Churchill after her husband's victory at Woodstock in 1885, in which he stated that: 'You must let me very sincerely and heartily congratulate you on the result of the election, especially as that result proceeded so very much from your personal exertions. Everybody is praising you very much.'[45] After witnessing a few years of Primrose League work, James was considerably less magnanimous. In 1887 he gave a speech in which he strongly insinuated that Parliament would soon be forced to legislate against the participation of women in elections.[46] The Liberal leadership, however, seem to have felt that such legislation was impracticable, but they did repeatedly try to show that the League was violating the Corrupt Practices Act. In this they continually failed. In the end, they simply decided to copy the Primrose League, but their attempts, perhaps because of their own comments against such organizations, were usually pale imitations of their model. The Ladies' Liberal Federation was never as great a success as the Primrose League and very quickly fractured over the question of women's suffrage. In 1892 a majority of members voted in favour of female suffrage, and Mrs Gladstone resigned as its president. The Federation split into two groups over the question. Until the First World War the effectiveness of the organization would be severely hindered by its feud between rival women's groups and with the party leadership over women's suffrage. In 1888 the Federation had only 10000 members, which was tiny in comparison with the League. The WLF grew considerably during the Edwardian renaissance of the party, reaching 66000 in 1904 and even 133000 in 1912.[47] However, Liberal women frequently felt frustrated by a party whose leaders were so opposed to women's suffrage. It was probably fortunate for the Conservatives that they were not in power during this period or the Primrose dames might have felt equally frustrated with their leadership. As it was, the more suffragist ones could always imagine that their party leaders would have done better if they had been in power. In any case, it was certainly lucky for the Conservative Party that its dames were far less concerned with women's rights than with the political victory of their preferred party.

The important thing to remember about these Liberal and Labour groups was, first, that they were considerably smaller than the Primrose League. The second major observation is that women's role in them did not differ significantly from their role in the League. Martin Pugh has summed up the situation very well:

> All remained either segregated or outside the official party organization in some sense. All felt the same pressure to play down women's suffrage for fear of dividing the party. On the other hand the Conservative experience is distinctive in certain respects. Through the Primrose League it was vastly more successful in mobilizing women than its rivals; and it provided for more opportunity for men and women to work together throughout the country over a period of several decades. But the corollary of this co-operation was that the league's ladies would never be assertively feminist.[48]

As Pugh asserts, the Primrose League, although less interested in feminist questions than the other groups, probably still played a more important role in the emancipation of women. More than any of the other organizations for women it showed that women could be successful at political work – to such a point that the men of the League were, to some extent, dependent on the women in financial terms.

However, it must be admitted that for all its success, the Primrose League was also a potential source of weakness for the Conservative Party because it provided a duplicate party organization. There is no doubt that the National Union was jealous of the success of the League and could not help viewing contributions made to the League as so much money lost to the real party organization. A rivalry between the two groups undeniably existed. However, as long as the Conservative Party did not include women, this rivalry could be contained. The League could simply be viewed as a body for organizing volunteer female workers. In any case, there was no arguing with success, and as long as the League provided necessary workers and did vital work that the National Union was itself less able to do, there was very little the party hierarchy could do against it. However, as we shall see, when the Conservative Party would finally be forced to admit women in 1918, the Primrose League would be effectively absorbed and go into a long decline.

The Primrose League was thus a major phenomenon of Victorian Britain. It was in many ways an intermediary organization between the largely oligarchic structure of politics before the Third Reform Act and the mass structure that would emerge after the 1918 Reform Act. Strongly hierarchical, it comforted those Conservatives who feared that anarchy would be the result of working men getting the vote. The success of the League showed that most workers retained a clear respect and fascination for the aristocracy. As the greatest mass political organization of the Victorian period the League provided the basis for the modern Conservative Party, and – most important from our point of view – women were there from the very beginning. Far more effectively than the other parties, the Conservatives managed to organize women at an early date and give them a place within the party. Women proved to be valuable workers, and, although many men still maintained a patronizing attitude, the women were too successful to be pushed aside completely. They clearly had earned their place in the party structure. An analysis of the Primrose League also certainly explains a great deal about the immense success of the Conservative Party in twentieth-century Britain for the party's obvious electoral dominance has been based on its support from the very groups who made up the Primrose League. In particular, the Conservative Party has triumphed in the twentieth century to a large extent because of its success among women. Millicent Fawcett, the Liberal Unionist suffragist leader, gave perhaps the greatest tribute to what the Primrose League had achieved for women:

It is an undeniable fact that the Primrose League has done more to give women the position which has been so long and so rigidly withheld than any other organization in this or in any period of the world's history. The originators of this movement showed their judgement and their discrimination when they included women in their ranks...It is admitted by friend and foe, that the Primrose League...has rendered the organizational help of women in such a way as no help has ever been given before at Parliamentary or municipal elections. It has been the frank and universal admission of successful Conservative candidates that they have been lifted into Parliament by the Primrose League.[49]

To some extent, Fawcett's praise is too great, for the League was an essentially patriarchal institution, and one which, as we have seen, remained neutral on the question of women's suffrage. On the other hand, by showing that large numbers of women from all classes could master political issues and play a valuable role in the political landscape, the League did undoubtedly advance the cause of women's rights. After the success of the League it became more and more difficult for men to say that women were incapable of exercising the vote intelligently.

3 The Conservative Party and the Campaign for Women's Suffrage

The history of the suffrage movement in Great Britain is more than just that of the Pankhursts and the Women's Social and Political Union (WSPU), although they have, by far, monopolized scholarly attention. Any woman interested in politics – even socially conservative ones – could desire the right to vote and to gain overt political power. As we saw in the previous chapter, the Conservative Party, through the Primrose League, mobilized the largest number of politically aware females. Although the League played down the suffrage question it should not be surprising still to discover that a large number of people in the Conservative Party – both men and women – desired at least some women to get the right to vote. Upper-class and upper-middle-class women tended to be better educated and more politically knowledgeable than many men. There is no doubt that as women became more and more politically involved, they also became more and more aware of the injustice of their exclusion from the franchise. Lady Knightley is a classic example. Absolutely fascinated by politics, she was heavily involved in her husband's political campaigns. Like most upper-class and upper-middle-class ladies, she had never particularly felt herself to be disadvantaged or in need of the vote – that is until in 1885 she accompanied her husband when he went to vote. As she said: 'I felt – for the first time personally – the utter anomaly of my not having the vote.'[1] As time went on, others began to feel like her. This, of course, by no means meant that they were democrats. They did not necessarily, or even usually, desire all women to get the right to vote but rather preferred richer women to have it. Maud Selborne, Salisbury's daughter, wrote to Austen Chamberlain in 1910 to insist that a limited form of women's suffrage might actually prevent, for a short time at least, the arrival of universal male suffrage. She believed that he should try 'to enlist the naturally Conservative force of property owning women on the Unionist side'.[2] Many others felt like her that it could obviously only work to the Conservative Party's advantage.

It is important to understand that opinion on the franchise was linked to the question of class. Those Conservatives who opposed women's suffrage very often did so not because they were against it in principle but because they feared that it would lead to universal suffrage. They reasoned that, if the register were so weighted in favour of their party, the Liberals, when they returned to office, would introduce universal manhood suffrage. This, they believed, would almost certainly lead to revolution or worse. Lady Salisbury was convinced that even limited women's suffrage '*must* lead to manhood suffrage the moment the other side come in again'.[3] Such people considered the vote to be a privilege based on personal fitness and not a right. They were terrified at the idea of tinkers or homeless persons getting the right to vote.[4] Lord Salisbury himself, when he had been Lord Robert Cecil, had broken with Derby and Disraeli because of his opposition to the Second Reform Act. For a long time, he had hoped to be able to return Britain to its pre-reform paradise, but then he discovered that, surprisingly enough, Britain after the Second and Third Reform Acts voted more often Conservative than it had before. Even so, the very success that the Conservatives had enjoyed since 1874 was argument enough against any further reform. Most people could see no reason to tamper with a winning system. The question of votes for women, then, was inexorably linked to the question of universal manhood suffrage.[5]

However, it must still be noted that the end of the nineteenth century saw important gains for women's rights. In 1857 a divorce court was established which made it easier for women to get a divorce on the grounds of adultery in combination with cruelty or desertion. A man, of course, could get a divorce on the grounds of adultery alone. Married Women's Property Acts in 1870, 1882 and 1893 finally gave married women the right to own property themselves. Until then when a woman married all her personal property automatically was transferred to her husband, which had, of course, led to many abuses. In the same year the Criminal Amendment Law was passed which was designed to protect young girls from moral crimes. From 1876 women were allowed to register as doctors, and they made other professional breakthroughs during the period, although they were banned from practising law. It was also at this time that the first women's colleges were founded at Oxford and Cambridge, although women remained ineligible to take university degrees there until well into the twentieth century. Finally, women gradually acquired voting rights in local government during this period. Widowed or unmarried women ratepayers gained the right to vote in municipal elections in 1869. The following year unmarried women householders were given the school board franchise, and soon after a woman joined the London School Board. As time went on, more women, although still a tiny number, sat on school boards and, eventually, became poor law guardians. It would not be until 1894 that married women would gain the right to vote in local elections and even then only if they had a different qualification from their husband – which obviously excluded most women. Women's participation in these bodies did have an effect and, in some cases, led to major innovations like school meals. In 1888 Salisbury's government passed the Local Government Act which, among other things, created county councils. Unmarried women householders were given the right to vote, and, in fact, three women were actually elected in London. The House of Lords, however, ruled that they could not take their seats on the grounds that the right to vote for members of a body did not give the right to sit in that body.[6] It would not be until 1907 that women received the right to sit on county councils. Still, there was no doubt that during the late Victorian and Edwardian period women were slowly gaining new rights, and it became increasingly evident that it was only a matter of time until some women, at least, got the right to vote in parliamentary elections.

The women's suffrage movement was essentially, at least at first, a middle-class movement. The upper-class woman, as we have seen, possessed influence through her social position and through her closeness to male policy-makers. Women factory workers, however exploited, possessed some degree of financial independence, and even those working-class women who did not work were probably too preoccupied with other things to agitate for the vote. The Pankhursts and the Fawcetts, for example, were both solidly middle-class families, and most of their supporters shared their social origin. One sign of this was that the Liberal Party, with its predominantly middle-class membership, was the most divided of all political movements over the suffrage question. Of course, it had been a Liberal, John Stuart Mill, who had first placed the question of women's suffrage on the national agenda in his *The Subjection of Women*, written in 1869. In this work he had detailed the injustices from which women suffered, notably in the realms of the law and education. He argued that the only way to end these disabilities was to give women the right to vote. Mill was, of course, well in advance of his time, and most of his ideas were laughed at. His work, however, did show that women's rights, at this stage, were fundamentally linked with the middle class and, to a lesser extent, with the Liberal Party. Women's suffrage divided the Liberals far more than it did the Conservatives or Labour. We saw in the previous chapter how the Women's Liberal Federation split over the question, and to some extent, women's usefulness as campaign workers in the party was destroyed by their in-fighting over this issue.

The first suffrage society for women, the Manchester Woman Suffrage Committee had been formed in 1866, and other cities soon followed. In the same year, a group of women started a petition in favour of female suffrage and gathered over 1400 signatures, including many prominent Victorian intellectuals. Mill himself presented this petition to Parliament when a second reform act was being considered, but it made no appreciable impact at the time. Later, in 1867, when Derby and Disraeli were proposing their own successful act, Mill offered an amendment to include women. A vote was taken, and the bill was defeated by 194 to 73. In any case, the question did not disappear, for in 1868 the National Society for Woman Suffrage was formed to unite the local committees. This organization, however, had a very difficult existence. An effective national body did not come until 1897 when the National Union of Women's Suffrage Societies (NUWSS) was formed. The NUWSS was decidedly non-militant and quite unlike the later WSPU. It was by far the largest organization working to gain votes for women. By 1909 it was estimated to have 70 affiliated societies with 13 161 members. This grew to 480 affiliated societies and 53 000 members in 1914.[7] Not only was it far larger than the WSPU, but it also had a fundamentally democratic structure. Its president, Millicent Garrett Fawcett, although no stranger to controversy, was elected, and the membership possessed the right to decide policy questions at annual or semi-annual conferences. From the very beginning the organization included members from both the Conservative and Liberal parties, although Liberals probably dominated. As time went on it attracted more and more working-class women and Labour supporters, which – given the Labour Party's somewhat more progressive viewpoint on women's suffrage – was certain to have an effect.

This, of course, did not mean that upper-class women or Conservative Party sympathisers were not supporters of women's suffrage or active in the movement. Lady Dorothy Nevill, Lady Frances Balfour, Lady Betty Balfour, Lady Selborne, Lady Londonderry and many others were active in the campaign for women's suffrage. These women had all been involved in politics practically from their birth and were important members of the Primrose League. Like Lady

Knightley, they felt the profound injustice of taking men, most of whom knew far less about politics than they did, to the polls to vote, while they waited outside. As in so many other areas, Conservative women tended, at first at least, to work in the background. Rather than forming their own suffrage association or even getting involved in already established organizations, they generally preferred to talk to their men folk and try to convince them of the need to give the franchise to women. They nagged, and they pestered. Some of them, like Lady Constance Lytton, a militant, and Lady Betty Balfour, a non-militant, even managed to get themselves arrested. It was not until 1908, when the suffrage campaign was reaching its frenzied zenith, that Lady Selborne formed the Conservative and Unionist Women's Suffrage Association. She was soon joined by Eleanor Cecil, Betty Balfour and Lady Londonderry, among others. The organization started its own journal to promote their ideas, *The Conservative and Unionist Women's Franchise Review*. The arguments presented in this journal were typically Conservative and already familiar to us: that giving the vote to certain 'qualified' women would help avoid the catastrophe of universal male suffrage. At one point the journal went so far as to hypothesize that the arrival of adult male suffrage would very possibly 'bring civil war in its train'.[8]

It is interesting to note the dominance of the Cecil clan here once again. The Cecils were, as a whole, unusually devoted to the question of women's suffrage. Lord Salisbury himself in a speech in Edinburgh in 1886 had stated that:

I am now speaking for myself only, but I do earnestly hope that the day is not far distant when women also will bear their share in voting for Members of Parliament... and in determining the policy of the country. I can conceive of no argument by which they are excluded. It is obvious that they are abundantly as well fitted as many who now possess the suffrage, by knowledge, by training, and by character, and that influence is likely to weigh in a direction which, in an age so material as ours, is exceedingly valuable – namely in the direction of morality and religion.[9]

In other words, Salisbury thought that women would be likely to vote Conservative. The younger generation was even more strongly in favour of women's suffrage. Not only Maud Selborne but her two brothers, Lord Hugh and Lord Robert supported the cause. Lord Robert's wife, Lady Eleanor, was also an important figure, as were their cousins by marriage, Lady Frances and Lady Betty Balfour.

Strangely enough, the Conservative women's suffrage movement reflected the Cecil dominance of the Conservative Party during this period.

Soon after its foundation the Conservative and Unionist Women's Suffrage Association joined the NUWSS and here an obvious conflict developed. The NUWSS was, in principle strictly non-party, but its policy was clear: 'To disregard party and support the friends and oppose the enemies of Women's Suffrage, to whatever party they may belong.'[10] The problem was that the Labour Party – unlike the two other ones – was officially committed to giving the right to vote to women, and so, by definition, the NUWSS supported more Labour candidates than those from other parties. Furthermore, in 1913, they drew even closer to Labour. Millicent Fawcett described how this happened:

> It remains to add a few words about the recent development in the National Union policy at Parliamentary elections. That policy always has been and continues to be, to support at a contested election that man among the candidates whom we believe to be the best friend of Women's Suffrage. Up to last May we arrived at a decision on this point solely on the strength of the replies given by the candidates to a series of questions. The breaking of pledges by supposed friends of Women's Suffrage was a painful feature of the defeat of the Conciliation Bill at the end of March. In consequence of this, at a special Council meeting, held in May, the National Union resolved henceforth to judge which among candidates at a contested election was the best friend of Women's Suffrage, not only by the replies given by individual candidates, but by the attitude on the suffrage question of the Party to which the candidate belongs.[11]

This quite obviously referred to the Labour Party, although Fawcett was at pains to insist that this rule did not apply to proven friends of women's suffrage like Lord Robert Cecil. Fawcett certainly did not feel comfortable with this course, and she took advantage of the First World War to end it.

Obviously, this policy of supporting Labour candidates caused a certain anguish both to Liberals and Conservatives involved in the organization. Many people warned Balfour and Bonar Law, who followed Balfour as party leader, about the dangers of allowing the Labour Party to take over the women's suffrage question for they feared that women would become embittered against the Conservatives.

Since most of them believed that women would one day get the right to vote, there seemed to be no reason to create a large group of electors hostile to the party. Lord Selborne asked Bonar Law in 1911 to speak out in favour of women's suffrage since: 'as the women will get the vote sooner or later, I think it is of great importance to our party in the future that the Radicals should not be able to say that the Unionists did nothing to keep the cause on.'[12] Other people echoed his warnings, while some suffragists became increasingly frustrated with the party's lack of response on the question. No less a person than Lady Betty Balfour, sister-in-law of the party leader, Arthur Balfour, resigned her office as Dame President of the Woking Habitation of the Primrose League to protest an anti-suffrage statement by her MP. She felt that: 'To continue to work for a Member holding such views seems to me an absurdity.'[13] More and more frequently, other women were beginning to feel like her. Lady Eleanor Cecil was anguished by this dilemma. As she wrote to Maud Selborne:

> It seems to me we shall soon have to make up our minds between our Conservative followers (if they exist!) and our radical allies. We can't hope to make a really effective appeal to Conservative women who are at all keen about our party (and it's just these women we ought to get) if we are never to say anything which may offend Common Cause. This policy would also and does in fact – leave us at the mercy of Antis who say we are all Socialists. In that is there much point in a Conservative Suffrage Society which is afraid to avow its Conservatism?[14]

Here then was the dilemma faced by all Conservative suffragists: whether to be first a Conservative and second a suffragist or vice versa. Suffragism forced them toward the Labour Party, which was hardly a prospect that attracted women like Cecil and Selborne. On the other hand, they were getting very little positive response from their own party. Note Cecil's anguished 'if they exist!' They wanted to attract Conservative women to their organization but, at the same time, realized that the NUWSS's alliance with the Labour Party was forcing them away. Furthermore, this was giving ammunition to the anti-suffrage groups – most of whom were right-wing – and who were using this alliance to paint the entire feminist movement as left-wing. Until the war came this dilemma remained insoluble. Cecil and Selborne were unable to find a balance between their feminism and their conservatism.

Cecil and Selborne were also aware of another argument being used against the franchise for women by extreme right-wing anti-suffragists.

Lord Cromer, for example, argued that women should not have the vote because of their strong involvement in philanthropic work. He feared that: 'woman's sympathy and emotion might lead her to move forward from philanthropy into a sentimental socialism which would offend against all the laws of political economy and greatly extend state influence'.[15] This reasoning, of course, was all part of the conflict going on at the same time between the Liberals and the Conservatives over old age pensions and other social reforms. This argument was reinforced by the close links between the NUWSS and the Labour Party. This, in turn, increased Cecil and Selborne's desire to show that feminism could be Conservative, but, as we have seen, they found this difficult. Strong suffragists did, of course, exist both in the Conservative Party and in the Primrose League. Battles did occur over the question, but on the whole most Conservative suffragists subordinated their suffragism to their Conservatism. Obviously the suffrage issue did not divide the Conservative Party as much as it did the Liberal Party. As we saw in the previous chapter, the Primrose League remained officially neutral on the question while the Women's Liberal Federation tore itself to pieces over it. The Conservatives were further helped by being out of power during the worst part of the suffragette agitation.[16] It was the Liberals who bore the full brunt of the fury.

Obviously, the Conservative and Unionist Women's Suffrage Association was devoted to constitutional action and did not believe in using the same methods as the WSPU. Given the fact that many anti-suffrage MPs were friends or relatives, this can hardly be surprising. Members of the groups found it extremely easy to lobby Conservative, and sometimes even Liberal, leaders through letters and social contacts. They did not need to use militancy to draw attention to themselves and usually felt that the violence and authoritarianism of the Pankhursts was a betrayal of feminism. At the height of the suffragette disturbances many Conservative suffragists actually wanted to protest publicly against the activities of the WSPU but discovered that many women in their organization were reluctant to do so. Lady Eleanor Cecil observed to Maud Selborne that:

> Many [in the Conservative Suffragist Society] don't approve of the militants but they are afraid of offending them, hope to profit by their deeds, and have a sentimental sympathy for certain individuals, consequently they won't commit themselves to a definite public protest – extraordinarily silly and short-sighted I think.

Sarah Bailey and I have been pounding at them for the last month and shall only succeed – if at all – because some of the militants have been throwing corrosive acid about and have narrowly escaped blinding an innocent man. Rather a shock to sentiment – and so far to be welcomed.[17]

Certainly, as this quote shows, there were Conservative women who sympathized with the militants. Lady Constance Lytton was one such. She risked her life on hunger strike and suffered forced feeding for her cause. But she was the exception. Most Conservatives felt little sympathy for the WSPU and its activities. The hostility of the Conservative suffragists towards the militants was shown quite clearly when Eleanor's husband, Lord Robert Cecil one of the staunchest parliamentary advocates of women's suffrage, introduced the Public Meetings Bill. This bill was specifically designed to control the activities of the WSPU and was passed after a remarkably short debate in both houses of only ninety minutes.

Such feelings, however, did not prevent the Conservative suffragists from being in touch with the Pankhursts or even from, if the occasion arose, co-ordinating policy with them. Lord Robert Cecil was in close contact with Christabel Pankhurst after 1910. When Christabel renounced militancy in June 1911, after Asquith promised a reform bill, Cecil advised his sister, Maud Selborne, to work with her so as to avoid an overlapping of efforts. He was even rather surprised by Christabel's willingness to compromise on the suffrage question:

Heard from Christabel yesterday down the telephone and we have now arranged for a meeting of the Conservative suffragists in the House of Commons to be held on July 10th . . . That is very satisfactory as far as it goes. Christabel is evidently anxious that the Bill should not be extended. Whether this is due to hostility to Lloyd George or to a desire to keep the Bill as it is I do not know. But she wishes us to strengthen her hands in her negotiations with the Radical Suffragists by saying that we are strongly opposed to any extension of the Bill. I feel a little difficulty myself in saying that I would not support an extended Bill, but I think that is what she would really rather like us to say.[18]

It is certainly a peculiar circumstance to find the militant suffragette Christabel Pankhurst trying to convince the son of Lord Salisbury to be more conservative on a measure for women's suffrage than he was inclined to be.

As this episode illustrates, there is no doubt that not only Christabel but also her mother Emmeline tended towards conservatism. Emmeline Pankhurst, after all, finished her life as a Conservative candidate for Parliament, and, after her death, no less a person than Stanley Baldwin unveiled her statue at Westminster. As early as 1907, it was Christabel Pankhurst who warned the then Conservative leader Arthur Balfour that people within both the NUWSS and the WSPU were seeking to ally their movement with Labour. She insisted that she was not in favour of such a course: 'I am very anxious that the whole women's suffrage movement (and not our own society alone) shall remain independent of the Labour party, because I am far from being persuaded that the Labour party can or will take effective action upon this pledge.'[19] Of course, to some extent this can be explained by rivalries between Christabel and her sister Sylvia who was a socialist and close to Keir Hardie, the Labour Party leader. It also represents a not unnatural suspicion of Labour, and more particularly trade union, attitudes towards women. In 1905 Emmeline Pankhurst had hoped that the Labour Party annual conference would endorse a bill for limited women's suffrage that had been introduced into Parliament during the previous session. Instead the conference had resolutely voted against it, saying: 'That this Conference, believing that any Women's Enfranchisement Bill which seeks merely to abolish sex disqualifications would increase the political power of the propertied classes by enfranchising upper and middle class women and leaving the great majority of working women still voteless, hereby expresses its conviction that Adult Suffrage – male and female – is the only Franchise Reform which merits any support from the Labour Members of Parliament.'[20] However comprehensible this policy might seem, it was one of the reasons that tilted the Pankhursts towards militancy. They felt that all the political parties had pushed women's suffrage to the side and so if they wanted them to take it seriously they would have to do something to dramatize the cause.

Christabel, as we have seen, particularly distrusted the labour movement. She felt that there was a fundamental hostility between the trade unions and the feminist cause, as she explained to Balfour:

The working-class vote is now largely controlled and organised by Labour politicians and T[rade].U[nion]. officials. These men are very ready to propose restrictions on working women's labour. There are some who advocate the entire exclusion of women, whether married or single, from certain industries. There are those who also desire to close wage earning occupations to married women.[21]

Christabel was quite correct in her observations. As we saw in the previous chapter, the trade unions can hardly be viewed as particularly favourable to women's rights, and, to some extent, this is comprehensible. Since women were paid less than men, employers were always tempted to hire a woman. The predominantly male trade union movement viewed this as unfair competition and wanted to end it. Their solution, however, was not to try to secure equal pay for women but rather to attempt to have them banned from working at certain times or in certain professions. Christabel, unlike her sister Sylvia, was first and foremost a feminist. The Labour movement was primarily interested in universal male suffrage and only coincidentally in female suffrage. Since the Liberals were in power and showed no inclination to grant women the right to vote, logically there was only one other possibility and so Christabel turned her attention to Balfour and the Conservatives. She began an at times flirtatious correspondence with Balfour in 1907 that lasted until 1911.

It would be wrong to portray the Conservative Party as being particularly reactionary on the question of female suffrage, although there is no denying that its attitude was ambivalent at best. Obviously some Conservatives like Lord Robert Cecil and Lord Selborne were wholeheartedly committed to at least a limited form of female suffrage. Others, notably the party leadership, had a more nuanced attitude. Disraeli had expressed support for a limited form of it at a very early period. We have already seen that Salisbury spoke in favour of women's suffrage as early as 1886, but subsequently during his years in office he did nothing about it. This was pretty much the position taken by the two following leaders, Arthur Balfour and Bonar Law: both stated their support for women's suffrage and then explained that they were speaking for themselves alone. Many rich Tory ladies also supported the WSPU which was, to some extent, reliant on them for funding. Furthermore, the Conservative Party, more than any other, depended on women to function. The work of the Primrose dames was widely recognized and respected. It was not illogical for Emmeline and Christabel to reason that a party whose leaders had repeatedly spoken in favour of female suffrage and who depended on women volunteers offered the best chance of giving them at least some form of suffrage. Previously, the WSPU had demanded 'the Parliamentary vote for women on the same terms as it may be granted to men', but now this was changed to 'Tax paying women are entitled to the Parliamentary Vote'.[22] The WSPU then broke with the Labour Party and began a kind of courtship of Conservative Party leaders. Since the Conservatives were out of power such a move could have no immediate benefit for them, and, in fact, in the short term at least it probably worked against them. The Liberals were only too ready to believe that the WSPU was yet another Tory attempt to embarrass them, while the Pankhursts' policy change did nothing to move Labour towards a less stiff position on the question.

While Christabel's reasoning may sound logical on the surface, she knew very little about the inner workings of the Conservative Party. While the Tory Party may have been perfectly happy to envision the use of illegal resistance of their own over home rule, they distinctly did not approve, as we have seen, of the Pankhursts' form of militancy. Furthermore, neither Balfour nor Bonar Law were willing to take the risk of committing the Party to such a policy. Of course, they obviously had important reasons for doing so. Balfour explained to Christabel Pankhurst that if the electoral system of the country was 'to be interfered with on the ground of abstract right, (as for instance "one man, one vote") then unquestionably it is impossible for any reasonable man who appeals to such political logic not to carry his argument to its legitimate conclusion; and its legitimate conclusion undoubtedly is that what are the "rights" of one sex are the "rights" also of the other.' Lest she should consider this declaration as grounds for optimism, he repeated several times in his letter that he saw no immediate need to reform the constitution.[23] He was even more candid with another female correspondent, explaining that: 'Of course, one of the great difficulties in dealing with the question is that, while opinion is deeply divided on the subject, the division does not follow Party lines – a Party Leader, therefore, could hardly take it up seriously, in the present state of public feeling, without risking the destruction of his party.'[24] Here then was the crux of the problem: women's suffrage would divide the Conservative Party. That is why no leader dared take up the question until after the First World War, when hostility towards women's suffrage – and, more importantly, universal manhood suffrage – had declined.

There is no doubt that Balfour had very good reasons for fearing the division of the Conservative Party. In fact, during the period of his leadership, the party was convulsed and nearly split in two over the issue of tariff reform. In 1903 Joseph Chamberlain, who had broken with the Liberals over home rule and had subsequently accepted office under the Conservatives, announced his conversion to a policy of 'imperial preference' or 'tariff reform'. He toured the country presenting his vision of a glorious future for the empire. The core of his policy was the need to break with free trade and to reintroduce protection. Tariffs, however, would not be introduced against goods from within the empire, thus, he hoped, linking the dominions, the colonies and the mother country together in a close bond. This, in turn, would guarantee that Britain would remain a major world power in a period when she was being surpassed economically by larger countries like the United States and Germany. Not only this, but Chamberlain claimed that tariff reform would improve the living conditions of the working class and provide the finances necessary for social reform. The whole thing did sound rather wonderful – perhaps too wonderful – but it meant the end of free trade, which had been the dominant economic orthodoxy in Great Britain since the repeal of the Corn Law in 1846. Nothing could be better calculated to reunite the Liberals – who had been feuding over home rule – and to divide the Conservatives and that was exactly what happened. The Conservative Party tore itself to pieces over the issue.

Conservative women as well as Conservative men fought over it. The Primrose League, in spite of its devotion to empire, was dominated by the free traders. In response to this, Chamberlain formed a new group, the Tariff Reform League, which had a sister organization, the Women's Amalgamated Unionist and Tariff Reform Association (WAUTRA). Chamberlain's group fought a kind of civil war with the League, much to the disadvantage of the latter which lost many members. The Primrose League never really recovered from this, and after refusing some years later to be incorporated into the regular party structure, faded away into a shadow of its earlier self. The result of the tariff reform crisis was that the Liberals won the 1906 general election and stayed in power until the First World War forced them to form a coalition government. Balfour's concern, like Bonar Law's after him, was to reunite the party and keep it united until they could win another election. In this Balfour was tragically helped by the collapse of Chamberlain's health in 1906, who became a paralytic and remained that way until his death in 1914. The enforced absence of Chamberlain gave Balfour a chance to reunite his party, and he was certainly not going to risk a conflict over a new issue like women's suffrage. He was so worried about this problem that, when Christabel Pankhurst asked him to pronounce publicly on his support for her cause, he replied: 'Though I rather think I have given expression to them [his views on the question] in public before now, I should not like to utter them as leader of the Party, and in answer to a formal deputation, without some consultation with my colleagues.'[25]

It is obvious that, if the party leadership feared the question could be a divisive one, it was because many members – in spite of the brilliant work done by the Primrose dames – were hostile to the cause. An examination of voting records on all the women's suffrage bills presented to Parliament shows that Conservatives passed through three distinct phases on the question.[26] From 1867 to 1883 Conservatives consistently voted against suffrage bills by a margin of three or four to one. However, the following period, from 1884 to 1908 showed a reversal of this trend for, with one exception, suffragists were consistently in the majority. Clearly, in true conservative fashion, the party MPs had first instinctively reacted against anything new. However, as time went on they adjusted to the idea and gradually came to accept it. Undoubtedly, this surprisingly progressive spirit owed a great deal to the efforts of the Primrose dames, who, during this period, were showing candidates exactly how valuable women could be in politics. Significantly, the National Union also approved suffrage resolutions at this time: in 1887, 1889, 1891, 1894, 1907, 1908 and 1910. This is not really remarkable, for who better than party agents in the constituencies could know the excellent work that women were doing for their cause. After 1909, however, the results become less clear. A majority voted against suffrage bills in five out of seven cases.[27] This, of course, was because the whole question of women's suffrage had become mixed up with the question of male suffrage. As we have seen, many Conservatives who were in favour of a limited form of women's suffrage (which would undoubtedly have benefited their party) were strongly against universal male suffrage. Thus their vote on these bills tells us more about their attitude to democracy than to women.

Women's suffrage, then, was frequently intermingled with other questions as an analysis of votes on the subject clearly shows. It could certainly be used as a cover for blatant political manoeuvring by even confirmed supporters. In 1906, for example, the Liberals introduced a bill to end the system of plural voting which had always worked strongly in favour of the Conservatives. Robert Cecil proposed an amendment which would have made the new act come into force only after the next election unless women's suffrage had first been introduced. This was an obvious attempt to seduce the Liberal and Labour suffragists to oppose the government, and, of course, it did not succeed. To some extent, however, it did work against the Liberals for it helped to convince the Pankhursts and other extremists that the Liberal government would never be sympathetic to their demands. It was one more element in their move towards the militancy which would so embarrass the government. At the same time, the Liberals did not see their bill become law. The Conservatives controlled the House of Lords and the latter still retained its veto power. Any particularly controversial piece of Liberal legislation could easily be demolished there. The attitude of both the Liberals and the Conservatives then was part of a complicated struggle for political power in Edwardian Britain. It was so tied in with other questions that it cannot be analysed in isolation.

The pre-war period thus was a time of fierce hostility between the Liberal and Conservative Parties. Women's suffrage played only a small part in that drama. Far more important were the issues of the power of the House of Lords and home rule for Ireland. The Conservatives, as we have seen, were using the House of Lords to block major legislation by the Liberal government, particularly when it concerned social reform. This caused a great deal of bitterness and until this major constitutional question was solved there could be no real progress on the question. There is no doubt that the House of Lords was so reactionary that, even if Balfour had ordered them to vote for a women's suffrage bill they would not have done it. Home rule also preoccupied both parties after 1910. The results of the two elections of that year had made the Liberals depend on the support of the Irish Nationalists to remain in power. This support, of course, was only forthcoming if the Liberals agreed to introduce home rule. The Conservatives were equally determined to do everything in their power – including support for armed rebellion – if home rule was applied to Ulster. The debate on universal manhood suffrage further embittered the situation. In such an atmosphere, members on both sides of the House of Commons considered women's suffrage to be a relatively unimportant sideline. As we have already seen, it was often used as an arm against one side or the other. Robert Sandars of the Conservative Party urged other members to employ it in 1913:

I have been rather busy over the Franchise Bill. The general idea is that it will have a most disastrous effect on our party if it goes through. I am trying hard to get our people to support the women's vote in some form; it seems to me if we get the two questions mixed up together there must be an appeal to the country before the Bill becomes law.[28]

His purpose for supporting women's suffrage was clear: if they could force a general election over the question, there was a strong chance the Tories would win. Both the Conservatives and the Liberals used the franchise reform in this rather cynical fashion to try to secure an advantage for their party.

A further problem was that, if the Conservative leadership was tepidly in favour of women's suffrage, much of the rank and file were not. There were always more Liberals than Conservatives in favour of giving the vote to women in spite of Christabel Pankhurst's wishful thinking. While backbench Conservative hostility to women's suffrage has probably been exaggerated in the past, there is no doubt that many Conservatives figured in the lists of the anti-suffrage movement. The Women's National Anti-Suffrage League had been formed in 1909 as a response to the suffragette agitation. Its chairman was Lady Jersey of Primrose League fame. In 1910 they amalgamated with the Men's Committee for Opposing Women's Suffrage and formed the National Society for Opposing Women's Suffrage (NSOWS). The leading male figures in the group were Lord Curzon and Lord Cromer. Curzon, at least, was an important figure in the Conservative Party and would later hold cabinet office. Many other members of the NSOWS also belonged to the Conservative Party, while still other Conservative politicians sympathized with their aims. Austen Chamberlain, a future party leader, felt quite strongly hostile to the demand for votes for women, exclaiming at one point: 'Lord! how I do dislike the suffragists en masse'.[29] Now Austen Chamberlain was, of course, the son of Joseph Chamberlain who, as we have seen, had caused a split in the Conservative Party just a few years before. It is therefore impossible to imagine that Balfour would have dared provoke a new split over the party about such a – from his point of view – unimportant question. The anti-suffrage group were just too strong.

In fact, in spite of much talk and a number of bills, nothing would be done on the question until after the First World War. It has traditionally been asserted that women's work during the war changed men's attitude and made possible the introduction of a limited amount of female suffrage in 1918. There is certainly some truth in this for numerous commentators at the time insisted that they had changed their minds on the question precisely because of what they had seen during the war. Asquith, notably, announced in 1917 that the work women were doing to support the war effort had caused his hostility to women's suffrage to completely vanish. Stanley Baldwin gave an even more memorable speech in 1928 during the debate on giving the franchise to women on the same terms as men:

> I used to vote against women's suffrage. I was taught by the war, which taught me many things. I learned during that time – when the young manhood of the nation was passing through the Valley of the Shadow of Death – I learned, I hope and believe, to see such things as wealth and prosperity, and worldly success in their proper proportion, and I realized, as I never did before, that to build up that broken world half the human race was not enough; it must be the men and women together.[30]

Asquith and Baldwin were not the only ones. Over and over again, politicians repeated that they were now convinced that women should have the vote. The question to consider though is whether they really meant it or whether they were simply using the war as an excuse to give some dignity to a reversal made for other reasons. Then again, perhaps a little of both was involved. Lord Balfour of Burleigh, who was personally opposed to women's suffrage, summed up the situation well: 'I think really what happened was that the War gave a very good excuse to a large number of excellent people, who had up to that time been on the wrong side, to change their minds.'[31]

A major change had obviously occurred during the war, but, given the complexity of the suffrage question and the number of other factors involved, it seems unlikely that it was voted simply because men were impressed by women's war work.[32] There is no doubt that, if some men admired women's contribution to the war effort, others felt threatened by it. The war actually aggravated tensions between men and women. Since women were paid less than men and were usually ready to accept poorer conditions, men feared that they might lose their jobs. We have already observed the tensions that existed between feminists and the trade union movement. Furthermore, since women's suffrage was part of a party battle over franchise reform, the formation of a coalition government in 1915 created a spirit of inter-party co-operation and made possible a resolution of the problem. The coalition also brought into the cabinet sympathizers like Robert Cecil and Arthur Henderson of the Labour Party. The Speaker of the House of Commons was appointed to lead an all-party conference on electoral reform. This conference eventually reached a compromise solution over the question. They proposed to base women's suffrage on the local government franchise: all women who voted in local government elections or wives of such voters, if they were over thirty years of age, would be eligible to vote in parliamentary elections. This, of course, ensured that women could not possibly be a majority of electors, although, at the same time, it made another reform act in the near future inevitable. This proposal was accepted by the government and voted by Parliament. It became law in 1918.

Some historians have asserted that the vote was granted in 1918 because of the earlier work done by the suffragettes. Certainly there were few people at the time who took this point of view. Stanley Baldwin, in the speech quoted earlier, does not once mention the suffragettes. Other commentators considered them to have actually hurt the cause through their militancy. In any case, the term militant can hardly be applied to Emmeline and Christabel Pankhurst during the war. They rallied round the flag in an almost excruciatingly patriotic way. The WSPU basically ceased to function during the war. The fact is, though, that the WSPU had already started to decline before 1914, and the Pankhursts probably found the war a convenient and dignified way to extract themselves from an embarrassing situation. What is likely too is that the government, fearing a return of suffragette violence after the war, moved to prevent such a thing. In any case, at the crucial moment Christabel was touring the United States and Emmeline was on her way to Russia. On the other hand, it must be stated that, in countries where there had been no history of suffrage agitation, like France or Belgium, women's suffrage was usually not voted after the war – in spite of the fact that women might have participated even more in the war effort than they had done in Britain. Furthermore, it must be said that the constitutional branch of the movement, the NUWSS, was a bit more active. After first signing an appeal for peace from the International Woman Suffrage Association in a last-minute hope of averting war, Millicent Fawcett, once the irrevocable had occurred, called on all her members to support the government. She accepted that it was unlikely that a suffrage measure would be voted during the war (in this she was, of course, wrong) but she still paid close attention to the political scene. She was in close contact with politicians and received regular reports from sympathizers in the government like Henderson and Cecil.

One thing does seem clear from an examination of the debates over the Representation of the People Act – that women's suffrage was a minor element in it. Far more than the war work done by women, Parliament was concerned by the massive sacrifices made by men during the war. It was the death and maiming of hundreds of thousands of young men that swept aside the old hostility to universal male suffrage and made possible an agreement on women's suffrage. The first concern of politicians was to see that servicemen got the vote. It seemed the only fair thing after what they had been through. Even Mrs Pankhurst had it announced that she would accept the enfranchisement of servicemen even if women were not included.[33] As late as 1924 the Duchess of Atholl, a Conservative woman MP, moved the rejection of an equal franchise bill because:

> No one will dispute that the proposal means that women will be in the majority on the Parliamentary register. When I reach that point I cannot forget that that preponderance, whatever the exact figure may be, will have been largely due to, or at least greatly increased by, the fact that we lost 740,000 precious lives of men in the great war, and that War is still taking its toll among the ex-service men. Therefore, I cannot help thinking that I see that to propose a great extension of this kind looks like taking advantage of the heroic sacrifices of these men.[34]

As this quote clearly shows, the war worked against women as well as for them. There seems little doubt that the franchise for women was a secondary consideration for politicians. Most Conservatives who were hostile to the bill complained about other elements in it – notably the loss of some forms of plural voting. A report from Conservative constituency agencies showed that they favoured giving the vote to women by a ratio of two to one.[35]

Since it had been the party battle over this question that had blocked female suffrage for so long, once the major parties agreed on virtual universal manhood suffrage – once the fear of democracy was removed – the women's question was solved – although admittedly only temporarily – without too much difficulty.[36] In such a context most of the hostility to women's suffrage simply vanished. In fact, once the vote had been given to working-class men, it was clearly to the advantage of the Conservatives to counter that by adding female local government voters – who, after all, were richer and, therefore, more likely to vote Conservative – to the register. For another thing, if the WSPU was virtually quiescent during the war, so were the anti-suffrage sympathizers. Many of them, of course, were absent at the front, but those who remained sensed that the wind had changed. Mrs Ward, one of the leaders of the anti-suffrage movement, even wondered if they should not simply retreat with dignity and drop the whole thing.[37] The anti-suffragists decided, though, to fight to the end. But they were severely handicapped in that, once the party conflict over adult suffrage was removed they had few really convincing arguments to offer. There was, of course, the old argument about women's fitness for the vote – which was sounding less and less credible as time went by. Many anti-suffragists used the argument that women would tend towards pacifism. Lord Loreburn argued that:

> The limitation of the age of female voters to 30 was illusory and illogical. He did not see how it could be excluded when men of 21 were admitted. A woman of 21 was much older than a man of 21, as every one knew from his own experience. Within a very little time, therefore, the majority of the entire electorate would be women ... Was it desirable, in the interest of the Empire, that feminine influence should be very powerful at once, and most probably predominant in the very near future over questions of peace and war? Was it right that women should have the controlling voice in those things, when men would have to bear an indescribably greater share of the sufferings that would follow?[38]

Note that even an extremist like Loreburn realized that women's suffrage would have to come some day. In this speech he is simply asking to postpone the inevitable until the issues raised by the war could be settled. His point of view did not have much support, for the bill passed the House of Commons by a margin of seven to one. Its reception in the House of Lords, however, was another question. Of course, since the Parliament Act of 1911, the House of Lords no longer possessed an absolute veto, but they could at least delay any bill for two years. The anti-suffrage party then turned its attention to the House of Lords and to its leader, Lord Curzon, also president of the NSOWS. Curzon, however, from fear of a constitutional crisis between the two houses, simply collapsed and abstained from voting on the question. The bill passed the House of Lords without difficulty.

One cannot generalize easily about the role of the Conservative Party in the debate over women's suffrage. Like the Liberal Party, the Conservatives were divided over the question. In a sense, they were lucky not to be in power when the suffragette militancy was at its height. In any case, there was no inherent conflict between conservatism and women's suffrage. On the contrary, as we have seen, giving the vote to richer women was frequently viewed as a form of protection from the effects of too much democracy. Its supporters (and there were very few people in the Conservative Party who were in favour of universal suffrage) claimed that it would help put off the arrival of universal suffrage. Those who opposed it frequently did so simply because they feared it would reopen the reform debate and hasten the day when Britain would become a full democracy. Most Conservatives did not have strong feelings on the question, and primarily considered it from the point of view of party advantage. By the early twentieth century most people no longer believed that women were incapable of making intelligent political decisions – the Primrose League had been far too effective for all but the die-hard element to accept this. When the majority of Conservatives accepted universal manhood suffrage in most cases their objections to votes for women disappeared. In fact, as we have seen, the limited franchise for women actually worked to the advantage of the Conservatives. The party certainly had its heroes and its villains in the battle. Its pro-suffragist members were hardly as exciting as the Pankhursts (although it might be argued that after 1907 the Pankhursts themselves, except for Sylvia, were Conservative suffragists): their main tactics were letter writing and heated discussion during dinner parties. Still, they had their role in the breaking down of male politicians' attitudes on the question and of their final acceptance of women's suffrage. As we shall see in the next chapter, it would be a Conservative government, that of Stanley Baldwin, which would finally give women the vote on the same terms as men.

Part II
The Beginning of Overt
Political Power

4 The Party Mobilizes for Women

The Representation of the People Act was a watershed for now women had to be taken seriously by politicians. They had to be courted as voters, and the parties had to make room for them. In 1918 the Conservative Party, like all the other parties, was forced to adopt its structure to accommodate the newly enfranchised women. Unlike the other parties, though, the Conservatives already possessed a long tradition of female involvement through the Primrose League and, later, the Women's Amalgamated Unionist and Tariff Reform Association (WAUTRA).[1] In April 1918 the National Union changed its rules so that women could be admitted into the party organization. The most obvious way of incorporating women was simply to absorb the Primrose League (which was by now a predominantly female organization) and the WAUTRA. Most habitations of the Primrose League, however, refused incorporation.[2] The League thus steadily continued its decline, which, as far as the men's section was concerned, had already begun in Edwardian times. Now that it was possible for women to join the Conservative Party itself, they too fled the League in large numbers. It seemed an immense step forward to most of these women to be finally allowed into the party. The most active and politically aware women thus left, and the League faded into a refuge for those nostalgic for the Victorian era. The WAUTRA, on the other hand, agreed to incorporation and became the basis of the new party women's organization. The chairman of the WAUTRA, Caroline Bridgeman, oversaw its transformation. The National Union also established a women's staff and started work on the formation of women's branches throughout Britain.[3]

Before discussing the development of the women's branches, it is necessary first to examine the structure of the Conservative Party.[4] The party organization exists at the local, regional and national level and contains two different elements: the volunteers and the paid officials. The voluntary members form local groups in each constituency and these groups are organized into regional associations. At the very top of the pyramid is the central body, the National Union of Conservative and Unionist Associations, that links all the others together. The senior party officials are located at Central Office in

London, which is under the direct control of the party leader. Of course, the party leader – especially when he or she is also prime minister – has many other jobs to do and so the task of supervising the day-to-day working of Central Office and the party is given to a party chairman chosen by the leader. Central Office has a network of regional Area Agents, but the actual Conservative Party agents in each constituency are not employees of Central Office. They are paid by the local volunteer groups. They are thus not directly under the control of Central Office although there is obviously a close relationship between the two. Central Office has many resources and can provide the agents, either directly or through the Area Agents, with information, advice and practical help. It also keeps a list of approved candidates and organizes exams for those who wish to be party agents. Such a complicated structure may seem to be a recipe for disaster, but, in reality, the voluntary and professional sides of the party usually work well together. One major advantage of the system is that it offsets the autocratic tendencies of the strongly hierarchical system under the party leader. The rank-and-file members possess a great deal of influence and, thus, cannot be coerced.

The question that faced the party in 1918 was how best to fit the women into this structure. This, of course, was not the only issue before the party, for the mass increase of the electorate made it of vital importance for the Conservative Party to establish a truly popular base if it wanted to survive and grow in this new atmosphere of democratic politics. In 1917 Bonar Law had warned members of his party that it was absolutely necessary for them to adopt franchise reform. He explained that:

> And, gentlemen, I should like to say this also; our Party if it is properly conducted has no reason to fear that the mass of the people in this country will not support it ... If we cannot win that support, we may as well go out of business, and it is our duty now at all events to make the best of the situation which has arisen and to see that everything is done to make our Party what Disraeli called it – and what, if it is to have any existence, it must be – a truly national party.[5]

To make it 'a truly national party', it had to be democratized and formed into a mass organization.

Given the history of the Primrose League, it was entirely logical for the party to decide to base their existence as a mass organization on women's membership. The National Union decided to form its own department to deal with this issue, and by 1928 it was employing 29 staff members.[6] One thing that was heavily debated was whether there should be two separate organizations for men and women, which would of course be linked, or one united association. The women at Central Office, the Conservative Party headquarters, decided that the former alternative was preferable and sent out a circular, advising constituencies that: '... owing to differing circumstances of the various constituencies, it would be unwise to lay down any cast iron rule for the organisation, but it is recommended that, where possible, separate men's and women's associations shall be formed, with separate offices, members and funds, but united at the top in one joint executive on which women shall have proper representation.'[7] The constituencies then were given a certain degree of flexibility, but it appears that in most cases the advice in this circular was followed. Separate organizations for men and women were established in most areas. In 1927 Marjorie Maxse of Central Office commented that the most usual situation was to have an effectively male constituency organization and a women's branch that sent a representative to the Joint Executive Council.[8]

Most prominent women in the party believed strongly that it was much better for the women to have their own group. Marjorie Maxse, for example, felt women needed their own branches because this would give women more responsibility. Maxse considered that men did not want 'to give women the responsibility of organising women, and of providing them with a legitimate sphere for their aspiration'.[9] Her aim, and that of others, was to maximize as much as possible the role and the power of women in the party. Obviously, the establishment of distinct women's branches, to some extent, maintained the women on the fringes of party politics. However, there is no doubt that their position was now far stronger than it had been at the time of the Primrose League. Women now made up a substantial part of the electorate and no party could afford to ignore them. During this period they were also the most dynamic group within the Conservative Party, as we shall see. Maxse, Bridgeman and others were almost certainly right that in this early period, women profited from a separate organization.

Unlike Labour women, the Conservative women had substantial power in that they provided most of the party workers – vast numbers of whom were needed after the enormous increase in voters in 1918 – and raised a great deal of money. It would actually have been easier to ignore them in an integrated structure. The men would have almost certainly occupied the major positions and would thus have had control of the money raised by the women. This money was obviously one of the women's greatest strengths. It became even more important after the war for the traditional Conservative system of having candidates pay election expenses was coming even more under attack. Baldwin and many others felt, rightly, that this eliminated many excellent candidates and limited the party to often second-rate rich men. This period was one of determined modernization, as the Conservatives tried to make themselves appealing to the new, predominantly working-class, electorate. Both Baldwin and his party chairman, J. C. C. Davidson, wanted to show that success in their party was based on merit and not on aristocratic connections. Constituency associations were, therefore, more and more often expected to supply at least part of the campaign costs. By keeping women in their own branches and with their own funds, it became impossible to ignore them – they, and more particularly their money, were far too necessary. Maxse, at least, clearly realized that a united organization would have to develop one day, and she certainly did her best to ease tensions between the men and women, as we shall see. However, it was undoubtedly advantageous to women to remain separate until they were an accepted and firmly established part of the party.

This inevitably led to conflict, though, because the women had their own ideas and the men, inevitably, resented any challenge to their authority. Women, of course, had already proven themselves to be excellent fundraisers at the time of the Primrose League, and they continued to do so. Furthermore, not only did they have their own money, but they could decide how to spend it. One of the ways they spent their money was to hire their own women organizers to oversee the constituency.[10] This, of course, put them in conflict with the men's group who had their own paid constituency agent. Ultimately, the functions of the agent and the women's organizer overlapped. Each branch also had a separate office and communicated individually with Central Office. Such a situation was certain to result in confusion and duplication of effort. It is not surprising, therefore, to discover that the men often viewed the women with suspicion. They worried that the women were trying to build up a rival organization that would take away some of their power. In most cases the men simply refused to accept the women on equal terms. In particular there were battles between agents and women organizers. For example, the male agents belonged to the National Society of Conservative Agents which provided them with certain important benefits like pensions, and many men at Central Office felt that the women organizers should be admitted. They believed that it would go a long way towards ending the – as one official described it – 'petty jealousy' between the men and women.[11] Local societies, however, refused to accept this advice, and the women organizers were denied admittance until after the Second World War. In 1926 the women organizers gave up on their attempt to be integrated into the National Society and formed their own National Association of Conservative and Unionist Women Organizers. Central Office went to work to try to reach some kind of agreement. In October 1923, the Principal Agent published a letter explaining the different duties of the men and women agents. The women agents' work was limited to holding committee meetings, forming branches, and teaching organization to women. In April 1924 Marjorie Maxse tried to find a balance between the rival groups. She told the agents that the women's branches were not independent of the constituency groups, but, at the same time she emphasized, though, that they were to work with and not under the local agent.[12]

This, however, did not end the controversy, for women organizers suffered from severe disadvantages as opposed to male agents. Even those who had passed the agents' examination and effectively did the work of an agent received much lower pay than their male counterparts. This, of course, was not peculiar to the Conservative Party: equal pay for women was the rare exception at this time. It did, however, create bad feeling between the two, particularly since for a long time women were officially barred from promotion to agent. Maxse, once again, had to try to moderate this dispute. As before she tried to emphasize that both the men and the women had rights and duties in relation to each other. She told the women organizers:

> do not seek to usurp their [the men's] place or power; and do not work for feminism but for the Party. Nor do women wish to become Agents...On the other hand, it is unwise to drive the women or expect them to work 'under' the Agent. Like soldiers or anyone else, they will work their utmost when they are led and still keep some degree of freedom.[13]

Her message was clear: the women should not try to do the job of the men, while the men should accept that the women needed some degree of liberty. Maxse was strongly supported in her efforts to calm these disputes by J. C. C. Davidson, the party chairman. With the powerful support of Central Office she was able to overcome much of the jealousy and resentment between the two groups and make them realize that they had to work together.

Another of the goals of the women leaders and of Central Office itself was to make sure that women were highly visible in the party. As in everything else, they succeeded in doing this far better than the other parties did. The chairman, vice-chairman and three other members of WAUTRA became members of the Executive Committee of the National Union and women were assured of a continuing membership on it.[14] Furthermore, the rules were changed to ensure that women got at least one-third of the places in party organizations both in London and in the constituencies. In 1926 the Conservatives went further still, and Caroline Bridgeman became the first woman chairman of the National Union and, as such, chaired the annual conference. She was also the first woman chairman of any political party. In 1930 Lady Iveagh was appointed as the first woman vice-chairman of the party, and she was given special responsibility for the women's membership. In fact, the existence of a special vice-chairman concerned with women has continued until this day. One other obvious area where women had to be visible was at the annual party conference. In 1927 Caroline Bridgeman and another leading Conservative woman, Lady Elveden, proposed an amendment to the party rules for conference delegates. A delegation normally contained four members: the local chairman, the agent and two others. Bridgeman and Elveden asked that a rule be instituted making it mandatory that one of the four, at least, should be a woman. This amendment was accepted, and it ensured that large numbers of women were – and still are – present at party conferences.[15] In 1927 36 per cent of the delegates were women, while in 1930 it rose to 38 per cent.[16] The contrast with the Labour Party and its overwhelmingly masculine trade union membership, could hardly be more clear. Quite simply, the atmosphere of the Conservative Party was much more congenial socially for women than that of the Labour Party – at least during this period. Furthermore, a women's annual conference was also created in order to highlight the specific work of the women. It has met continually almost every year since 1920. An examination of the issues debated at these conferences, however, shows little real difference with the men's. Once again, Conservative women were less interested in women's issues than in Conservative ones.

Visibility, however, did not mean power. Women's role and women's work as members of the Conservative Party did not differ significantly from the days of the Primrose League. They were doing essentially the same things: organizing fundraising events, hosting teas, canvassing and propaganda. The other, more important, work was usually done by men. Most evidence points to the fact that the role of women in the selection of the local candidate was generally limited. They also appear to have been involved in making few other important decisions: the men determined campaign strategy and propaganda and the male agent was far more powerful than the women's organizer. Women also were generally limited to the National Union. Their role in the parliamentary dimension of the party and in the formation of policy was extremely limited. As we shall see, the women did take some initiative in this question and formed the Central Women's Advisory Committee, but, as its name implies, it was essentially consultative. Furthermore, it was only officially recognized by the party in 1928. Until then it was in a kind of limbo state. Nor were Conservative women particularly pushy about wanting to have power. Just being part of the party seemed exciting enough to many, and indeed it was a major advance. Women continued to accept, as they had in Primrose League days, the secondary role that was given to them. Most women had never previously tried to force their demands on the party, and they did not suddenly begin to do so in 1918.

There were, however, some important achievements for women in this period. One of the major figures in the integration of women in the party was undoubtedly J. C. C. Davidson, party chairman from 1926 to 1930. Davidson was convinced that the women were absolutely vital to the organization. He himself felt that: 'The dominant feature at this time was the rise in the importance of the women electors.'[17] Believing as he did, Davidson set out to increase the women's importance and to end the conflict between the men's and women's organizations in the country. As he explained it:

Again from the moment when I sat in the Chair at the Central Office I realised that there was a distinct antagonism running right through the Organisation in the Country between the men and the women, and I set myself the task of overcoming this evil, which, if it persisted, I was convinced would gradually undermine the essential unity of the Party. I took what was at the time considered a bold step in putting forward Lady Iveagh as Vice-Chairman of the National Union, and a still bolder step in appointing Miss Maxse Deputy Principal Agent of the Party. I treated the men and women

Area Agents as colleagues, entertained them together on equal terms, and met them in conference as one team instead of two. The appointment of Miss Maxse has been completely justified, and I believe that the co-operation between the men and women in the Party is greater to-day than it has ever been.[18]

His strategy was simple: to convince the men that the women were a permanent part of the landscape and one that could not be treated with disdain. His ultimate goal was to improve co-operation between the two branches.

Davidson, like Baldwin, wanted the modernization of the Conservative Party into a genuine mass movement, and women were one of the main elements in his strategy.[19] He was certainly immensely impressed by their energy and enthusiasm. As he told one friend: 'When I think of the sacrifice that some of our women have made and the incalculable services they have given the party – women like Lady Bridgeman – it is not surprising that I am moved to cheer them on to further efforts.'[20] A cynic would say that his choice of phrase – 'to cheer them on to further efforts' – is revealing. He does not insist on recognizing them as equals; he does not say he wants to promote them to more influential roles in the party, but rather he wants to encourage them to do still more work. Still, there is no doubt that the women's position improved during his tenure. One of his major actions was to ensure that the women had a proper headquarters in London near the Houses of Parliament.[21] It was under his leadership that Bridgeman became chairman of the National Union and that the number of women on the executive committee of the National Union was raised to between one-third and one-half. To a large extent he and Maxse succeeded in making the men's and women's branches work smoothly together. Under his direction, the men finally were forced to accept that the women were a major element in the party, and once this had been done, much of the bickering ended.

In any case, the women's branches grew quickly and by 1921 there were over 1300 of them in the country. By 1924 this figure had reached 4067.[22] The Countess of Iveagh asserted in 1928 that the women's organization in England and Wales had nearly a million members.[23] Martin Pugh estimated that the membership grew at a high rate in the 1920s but then levelled off in the 1930s.[24] In all of these things they were way in advance of the Liberal and Labour Parties' women organizations – even though the latter had been formed earlier. The Conservatives just had a better women's organization to build on.

Many women did, however, feel that they needed more than just local women's organizations. Very early on the decision was taken to form women's committees at the regional and national levels. Once again, the women feared that their needs might be ignored unless they had representatives present at every level of the party structure and specifically concerned with women's issues. The regional committees were first called Women's Parliamentary Councils because they were organized around the wives of Conservative MPs.[25] Their name was soon changed to Women's Advisory Councils or Committees because, as one Cornish member explained, the word 'Parliamentary' was not always well seen:

> In proposing this Resolution Lady Sanders said that she felt the word 'Parliamentary' was somewhat misunderstood. In certain parts of Cornwall she found that it was looked upon with suspicion, and a feeling that it might be a feminist movement within the Party. Although this was quite groundless she felt if it would in any way help to remove this feeling, that the Council would welcome the change, and further that by substituting the word 'Advisory' for 'Parliamentary' it brought us more into line with London.[26]

Once again we see the traditional deference of the Conservative woman. There is no desire that a committee – even one specifically founded to present the women's point of view – should appear to be feminist. This, of course, does not mean that the committee cannot lobby for feminist issues, but they do not want to appear as placing feminism over the party standard. At around the same time, the equivalent national level organization also changed its name to the Central Women's Advisory Committee and was officially recognized by the party in 1928.

As the above quote shows us, the change to the word 'advisory' was particularly significant of the anti-feminist tendency of the members. They wanted it clearly understood that they were not there to campaign for more women in Parliament but simply to advise the party on women's questions. It has always been fashionable to portray Conservative women as traditionalists and anti-feminists, and, indeed, there is a great deal of evidence for this point of view. But the anti-feminism of these women can be exaggerated for it was part of a general trend in Britain at the time. Feminism before 1918 had concentrated so strongly on the suffrage question that once the vote was won, interest in feminism faded for a long time. Of course, there was the problem that the vote had not been given to all women, and this anomaly cried out for rectification. Women also still suffered from many other legal disabilities. To meet these problems, the NUWSS reformed itself as the National Union of Societies for Equal Citizenship (NUSEC) in 1919, and prominent Conservatives like Maud Selborne and Lady Frances Balfour continued to be involved. However, most people seemed to think that after 1918 the great goal had been achieved, and it took them a while to realize that winning the vote did not end all the handicaps against women. One sign of this indifference was the financial troubles of NUSEC. Although women only received the vote on the same terms as men in 1928, already in 1923 NUSEC was destitute of funds.[27] The 1920s were essentially a period of consolidation, adaptation and acceptance with regard to women in politics. We have already seen how Davidson worked for precisely this among Conservatives. On the other hand, parallel to the decline in membership in the feminist organizations, there came the massive growth of women's membership in the political parties. The two were obviously related. Women were clearly abandoning the feminist organizations for the political parties.[28] Here they might feel closer to the centre of power and be able to bear more pressure directly on the party leaders. Other women seem to have believed that feminism was a distraction from the more important issues of the day – which, of course, could be best dealt with through the parties in any case.

To some extent, women were probably mistaken in placing so much confidence in male-dominated political parties, for very few women rose to the top during this period – particularly in the parliamentary domain. However, in the early 1920s political parties were paying close attention to this new and massive part of the electorate. The Conservatives, for example, published a magazine for women supporters called, perhaps significantly, *Home and Politics*. The order of words is important for the magazine's message was that politics would never take precedence over home for women.[29] Of course, on a higher level, politicians' new interest in women led to some important achievements at this time. Soon after the Representation of the People Act, in October 1918 – to the general surprise of feminists – Parliament voted the Parliamentary Qualification of Women Act which gave women the right to sit in the House of Commons. This created a panicked effort by feminists to find some women candidates for the December general election.[30] In all, seventeen women were candidates but only one, Christabel Pankhurst, got the coveted 'coupon' of coalition support. Pankhurst was standing, not as a candidate of any recognized political party, but had formed her own Women's Party. Surprisingly enough (or perhaps not too surprisingly given what we have already seen about Pankhurst) the Women's Party was not terribly concerned by women's issues. Pankhurst announced the goals of her party as 'Victory, National Security and Social Reform'.[31] Thanks to the 'coupon' Pankhurst came very close to winning for she only lost by 775 votes. Only one woman was elected, Constance Markiewicz who was a candidate for Sinn Féin and thus never took her seat at Westminster. It would take another year before a woman would actually reach Westminster, but that woman would certainly make an impression there and throughout the world.

In 1919 the American-born millionaire, Viscount Astor died, and his son, Waldorf inherited his title. Waldorf was the MP for Plymouth, and he certainly did not want to give up his House of Commons seat to go to the House of Lords. However, legally, he had no choice. His seat was declared vacant, and a by-election was called. Waldorf Astor suggested that his American wife Nancy should replace him as the Conservative candidate. The constituency committee immediately agreed because Nancy Astor was a well-known and well-liked figure in the district. This was obviously a case of 'male equivalence' but too much should not be made of this fact. A large number of male MPs at this time had got there simply because of their family connections. Elizabeth Vallance has argued that the candidacies of most of these early women MPs were 'the extension of their acceptable role as wives...Their husbands had, as it were, legitimized their political aspirations and this "halo effect" of male acceptability was perhaps at the time essential'.[32] The validity of this assessment is debatable. It can be argued that it is not particularly significant that many of the first women in Parliament got there because of family connections, since a large number of men did too. For example, after the 1929 election, the Conservatives controlled 260 seats in the House of Commons, but 59 of these MPs were related to peers – and thirteen were actually heirs of members of the House of Lords. Education also showed the male Conservative MPs to be primarily from upper-class or upper-middle-class backgrounds and to be continuing aristocratic traditions. 134 had gone to a major public school and 117 had been at Oxford or Cambridge.[33] It would be interesting to compare the proportions of men and women MPs who had entered Parliament during this period through 'male equivalence', but, of course, the number of women MPs was too small to allow for any kind of accurate conclusions. The inter-war period was one of transformation for the

Conservative Party from an oligarchy based on political dynasties to a modern mass organization. It is therefore difficult to view the women's experience as particularly unique.

In any case, the press was absolutely fascinated by this by-election, and they came in hordes to see the millionaire Yankee viscountess campaign among the poor of Plymouth. The result was an early form of media circus under which Nancy Astor bore up remarkably well. In many ways she was quite an extraordinary person. She was by no means an intellectual, but she possessed other qualities that made up for this fact: wit, humour, vitality, a vast capacity for work and a burning desire to help the disadvantaged. She made no attempt to hide what she was and went around Plymouth in an expensive carriage with a coachman in livery. Even when Astor went to the poorest areas of Plymouth she still dressed like a millionaire. The result was a triumph for her: she won with a majority of over five thousand votes and became the first woman MP. The papers went wild. *The Times,* in describing her arrival in Parliament, showed that some things, at least, had changed for women:

> When the moment for Lady Astor's introduction came, the House had an unfamiliar appearance. There seemed to be many more women than men in the Strangers' Gallery – another sign of the times, for it was reserved for men until a few months ago. At the other end of the Chamber the Ladies' Gallery,[34] with the hated grille removed for ever, was crowded with a company which included many of Lady Astor's personal friends ... Two women journalists, greatly daring, sought and secured admission to the Press Gallery for the first time in its history. The invasion was unexpected but the Serjeant-at-Arms held that, as the House and the public galleries were now open to women, he could not prevent duly accredited women representatives of newspapers having the *entrée* from engaging a similar privilege.[35]

Perhaps it is understandable that feminism became less active during this period. Women were busy savouring the results of suffrage, and, at least at first, barriers seemed to be falling all around them.

Lady Astor proved to be a very unorthodox Conservative, for her political views were usually way to the left of the average member. For example, she was strongly in favour of extending the suffrage to women on the same terms as men. Furthermore, Astor was not afraid to tell Baldwin how she felt on the question and even voted against the government on it. She supported then controversial issues like birth control, equal pay, employment of married women and nursery schools. She was also very much in favour of J. C. C. Davidson's policy of trying to make the local party, rather than the candidate, pay election expenses. She felt this would give the party candidates of a higher calibre and, in particular, encourage more women to stand for Parliament: 'They had splendid women who would be pleased to stand, and one reason why they could not was that they had not the money.' This, however, Astor recognized was not the only explanation for the limited number of women candidates. They simply were not being adopted by local associations, and, Astor stressed: 'Another sad thing was that it was not the men so much, in the local associations, as the women.'[36] Note that this will become a standard refrain in the Conservative Party until the present day: that the women are more opposed than the men to women candidates.[37] At this stage, as we have seen, women did not have an immense role in the selection of the local candidate, but there is no doubt that throughout this period their power was increasing, as Astor's quote shows. The Party leadership in general supported the goal of getting more women into Parliament. The National Union's conference of 1921 passed a resolution, moved by Astor, that called for more women candidates at the next election. Sir George Younger, party chairman at the time, observed that: 'I have tried my very best to get certain constituencies to accept a lady candidate, and one chairman wrote back saying I had given him the shock of his life.'[38] Central Office was trying so hard to get women candidates that the constituency associations began to complain about too much pressure being put on them.[39] As Astor pointed out, the resistance to women candidates did not come from the party leadership but from the local organization. The party leadership had staked its existence as a mass organization on attracting large numbers of women volunteers, but it took a while to convince the local associations that a greater role for women was necessary and even desirable.

Even Astor herself was extremely traditionalist in some ways. Although espousing mildly feminist positions, personally, however, Astor remained convinced that a woman's place was in the home with her children. She herself had six children but, in spite of this, still saw her membership in Parliament as reflecting her role of wife and mother. As she explained it: 'I feel someone ought to be looking after the more unfortunate children. My children are among the fortunate ones.'[40] Here, once again, we see the old doctrine of the separate spheres for men and women. Women's involvement in politics becomes acceptable when it is an extension of her domestic role.

Astor clearly saw her role as a woman MP as one that was primarily concerned with social questions and in this she did not go against the standards of the day. In her positions on social issues, however, she did differ significantly from her party. In many cases she was far closer to Labour members, and she did not hesitate to vote against her party on a question she felt strongly about. Astor summed up her views in the following way: 'The Government are entitled to general help and loyalty of their supporters, but it does no good to the country and no real good to the Government to give them blind submission.'[41] She herself felt a certain sense of isolation within her party for this reason. As she explained to a friend: 'I often feel under a great disability when I have to stand up to the party leaders, because on many issues I can produce so little evidence that other women of our party feel as I do. On the whole, you know, the progressive view on women's questions, though I know it to be held by hundreds of the rank-and-file women, does not always find expression among the leaders on the women's side.'[42] She was thus a maverick and born backbencher. On the other hand, she was also a celebrity, and Conservative Party members, even if they did not agree with her, were happy to have her come and speak for them during election campaigns.[43]

Of course she is best known – and unfairly so – for pro-appeasement views. Astor was not greatly interested in foreign policy and only 3 per cent of her speaking time in Parliament was devoted to it.[44] Like so many other people who had lived through the horrors of the First World War, she wished to avoid another war, but she was not particularly pacifist. She once summed up her views by saying:

> I do not think, however, that we can serve the cause of peace very effectively either by swearing 'No more war!' in mass meetings, or by putting the blame for war on other people. It is almost as if we were to attempt to abolish crime by shouting 'No more police!' I do not want to underestimate the psychological value of 'the will to peace' but it is not nearly enough.[45]

As this quotation shows, she was by no means an all-out appeaser. She did support the Munich Accords but primarily because of her deep respect for Neville Chamberlain. Nor was she alone in her sentiment for almost everyone in the country approved of Munich. On the other hand, in May 1940, after repeated disasters, Astor was one of those who realized that Chamberlain had to go and appears to have actually helped convince Labour members to force a division of the House on the question. In reality, her reputation as an arch-appeaser comes from a extremely unjust article by Aneurin Bevan. Bevan, who was not known for the gentleness of his speeches, went so far as to suggest that she was anti-democratic and quasi-fascist. It was an unfair attack that has sullied her reputation ever since.

Lady Astor was soon joined by other women in the House of Commons, including some Conservatives. By far the most important of these was the Duchess of Atholl who would become the first Conservative woman to hold ministerial position. From 1924 to 1929 she served as Parliamentary Secretary to the Board of Education. Ironically, Atholl had opposed women's suffrage and certainly could never be qualified as a feminist. For most of her career she faithfully followed the party line, even to the point of proposing the rejection of a bill to give women equal voting rights with men in 1924. In almost every way she contrasted greatly with Astor. Atholl was quiet, studied, intellectual and, until the end of her career, far to the right of Astor. She was not, however, totally against feminism or she would not have stood for Parliament. She explained her views just after her election:

> I think we have still to try to make the House of Commons and the nation realise what women can contribute to the work of Parliament... To do this, it seems to me, we have to use many of the qualities we find needed in our domestic life. Forty years ago, the ideal wife was one who said 'Amen' to her husband whenever he opened his mouth. To-day that idea has been abandoned, and we have instead an ideal of comradeship, of partnership in life's happiness and difficulties alike, which we recognise as much better.[46]

Here we do find one thing she had in common with Astor: they both believed that women's political role was an extension of their domestic role. The idea of separate spheres for men and women was maintained at this early period. Women now voted and sat in Parliament, but their concerns remained those of the home – of matters that directly touched on women and children. Of course, as we shall see, Atholl would, perhaps surprisingly, be one of the first women MPs to violate this rule by becoming heavily involved in foreign policy questions.

Strangely enough, it was Lloyd George who first suggested to her that she should stand for Parliament. He felt that a stronger female presence was needed there, and she seemed to him to have exactly the right qualifications.[47] She had been deeply involved in local government for years and knew a great deal about committee work. She was also well-known to her electors because, before her husband had inherited his title, he had sat for that constituency.[48] In many ways she did seem to be an ideal candidate. After consulting her husband, who was strongly in favour of the idea, and others, she decided to try. She was elected in 1923 recapturing the seat for the Conservatives by the tiny margin of 150 votes and became the first woman to represent Scotland. Since the short-lived Labour government of 1924 had appointed a woman as junior minister, Baldwin, when he returned to power at the end of the year, decided he should do the same. His choice almost inevitably fell on Atholl, who was, at this time, so much calmer and more obedient than Astor, and the duchess found herself a junior minister. Her time at the Board of Education was not particularly happy. She worked hard, but she found it exceedingly difficult (as did practically everyone else) to get along with her chief, Lord Eustace Percy. He was not at all friendly with her, gave her virtually no power, and had a tendency to ignore everything she said.[49] Being a good subordinate she generally grinned and bore it, but in one case she found herself strongly opposed to Percy. He was in favour of a government plan to make into block grants all central government funding given to local government, including for education. Up until then they had been in percentage grants. Atholl was totally against the idea and felt it would be a disaster for education in the country. She was so upset that she actually decided to go over the head of her minister and made an appointment to see the prime minister. Apparently she succeeded in convincing Baldwin for he agreed to keep the percentage grants system.[50]

Perhaps this episode was a sign that Atholl was changing, for in the late 1920s she began to take a more independent line. She never became a feminist, but she did start to have feminist friends. They, in turn, began to have some influence on her. In any case, the late 1920s and the 1930s saw Atholl take up a number of causes, and some of them were totally against her party's accepted policy. In 1929, for example, she first heard about female circumcision and discovered that it was practised in parts of Africa under British authority. She was horrified by the custom and decided that she had to do something to try to stop it. Atholl allied with the veteran feminist Eleanor Rathbone to bring the problem to the attention of the House. The response they received was hardly encouraging for no one seemed at all interested and, indeed, many MPs seemed to find the whole idea laughable.[51] Less to her credit was her decision to oppose, like Churchill, the India Bill of 1935. Here she was clearly in conflict with the party leadership. Even more controversial was her support for the Republicans in the Spanish Civil War. She wrote articles, gave speeches and even went to Spain to show her support. At the end of 1936 she even went so far as to establish with Eleanor Rathbone a National Joint Committee for Spanish Relief, and Atholl herself became its first chairman. This action was greatly resented by the Conservative Party leadership who viewed the organization as a front for the Republicans. Atholl was nicknamed the 'Red Duchess' at this time because of her hostility to Franco and the nationalists. At one point she even heard other Conservative MPs referring to her as a communist, for, from their point of view, by supporting the Republicans she was betraying her own class.[52] It was entirely logical, therefore, for her to take a strong position against Neville Chamberlain's policy of appeasement. She was so outspoken on these questions that Chamberlain ordered the Whip to be withdrawn from her in 1938. Once the Whip had been withdrawn she found that her constituency had started searching for another candidate. This decision and the Munich Accords, which she viewed as deeply immoral, caused her to resign her seat, and she stood for it again as an independent. Her only opponent was the official Conservative Party candidate, so the by-election was, in effect, a referendum on Munich. She, of course, had hoped to win, but, in the end, she lost by the margin of 1313 votes. That defeat ended her parliamentary career. Churchill had advised her to wait, and it seems clear that if she had done so for only a few more months she probably would have been triumphantly re-elected.

Of course during this period other Conservative women entered Parliament, but none of them equalled Astor and Atholl in importance. The number of women in Parliament slowly grew throughout this period, and fewer of them got in through their male connections – a fact which directly paralleled the situation for men. The period also saw a virtual avalanche of women's legislation which was passed either by the Conservative dominated coalition or by an entirely Conservative government. In 1919 there was the Sex Disqualification (Removal) Act which stated that 'a woman shall not be debarred by sex or marriage from the exercise of any public function, or from being appointed to or holding any civil or judicial office or post'. In theory this law opened up vast opportunities to women, especially married ones who very often were forced to resign their jobs when they got married. Unfortunately, legal decisions narrowed the scope of the law, and in many cases women continued to be forced to resign their jobs on marriage. However, it did have a major effect in certain areas. It opened the legal profession to women for the first time, as well as enabling women to become jurors and magistrates. Other laws required the registration of midwives and nurses, allowed husbands and wives to inherit equally from each other, gave women and children the right to maintenance payments, and provided pensions for widows and orphans.[53] This legislation did not, of course, end all of the legal disabilities from which women suffered, but they certainly were an important step forward. They proved that the vote was a powerful right.

Of course by this time these bills were no longer very controversial and could hardly be described as feminist. They could not be viewed as revolutionary either for, in most cases, they concerned woman in her traditional role as wife and mother. This was one point on which the Labour and Conservative parties could agree, for there was virtually no difference between the two parties in their presentation of women. The woman's domain was her house, and her job was limited to that of wife and mother.[54] Since these bills fitted in with this philosophy, they enjoyed support from all the major parties. Controversial issues were avoided, and controversial here means anything that departed from these accepted roles. Issues that concerned women in the workforce, like equal pay or the employment of married women, were pushed to the side. Birth control was also a subject that was generally ignored, perhaps from fear of a reaction among Catholic voters. The Restoration of Pre-War Practices Act of 1920 was a classic example of a law that worked against women but was supported by all three parties – and most notably, perhaps, by the Labour Party. This act gave the trade unions the power to force employers to restore practices that had existed before the law and applied, not only to pre-war industries, but also to any new industry that might have developed during the war. Obviously, one of the major changes the war had caused was that women had been employed in large numbers in order to replace men absent at the front. This act effectively sanctioned the firing of women workers and their replacement by men. Of course, there were other factors at work too. The economic situation – for Britain had been in a more or less continuous depression since the end of the First World War – made it practically impossible to put into effect something as costly as equal pay. Nor can the Conservatives be particularly blamed for these deficits, since Labour's policy was not fundamentally different. There was a general consensus between the three major parties on women's role and women's legislation, and none of them seriously departed from it during this period. Even an issue like family allowances was resisted by both Labour and the Conservatives at this time. There is no doubt that if much was achieved, there still remained a great deal to do.

One particular women's issue hung over Parliament at that time and that was the question of equal voting rights for women. We have already seen that Astor was strongly in favour of this, even to the point of defying her party, while Atholl was, at best, indifferent. On 18 October 1924, a few days before the general election, Stanley Baldwin, leader of the Conservative Party, had committed his party to 'equal political rights for men and women' and promised an all-party conference to decide the question.[55] The Conservatives won the election, but for a long time nothing was done about the promise. This should not reflect too badly against Baldwin for it was traditional to wait until near the end of a parliament before instituting a major electoral reform. After the election the Home Secretary repeated the pledge, insisting that: 'I will say quite definitely that means that no difference will take place in the ages at which men and women will go to the poll at the next election.' In 1927 when a special cabinet committee met to consider how to put the promise into action, one member announced that: 'It was safe to say that the Party had formed no definite opinions as yet on the subject and would support the Government in any proposals which might be formulated provided that these proposals were not unduly delayed.'[56] Davidson, Conservative Party chairman, supported this view and went even further, saying that 'if possible, public opinion in the country was even less interested in this subject than was the House of Commons'. He believed that: 'the supporters of equal franchise were a very small if very vocal minority and commanded no general support.' There could hardly be a clearer statement of the indifference towards feminism during this period. Neither side – at least in the Conservative Party – felt very strongly about the question. They did agree, though, that the all-party conference should be abandoned, probably from fear that Labour would push for the most democratic result possible. Whatever bill would be introduced – if such a bill were introduced – would be a Conservative one, although it was expected that it would enjoy bipartisan support.

Since the general feeling in the country seemed to be one of apathy, Central Office saw no urgent necessity in fulfilling the promise. In fact, Davidson advised waiting because expanding the number of younger voters would almost certainly hurt the Conservatives. He prepared a report which, among other things stated that:

It must I suppose be accepted as certain that the Government are committed to the introduction of a Bill to equalise the franchise for men and women. If this is not so, and there is still room for argument on the political question, we are decidedly of opinion that the reduction of the franchise age in the case of women to 21 would have a detrimental effect on the fortunes of the Party. In the agricultural districts it is not considered that such a reduction would make any difference – in fact it might be favourable, but in the industrial areas, particularly in those districts where women work in the mills, it is believed that such a measure would bring on to the electoral rolls a large majority of votes for the Labour Party, by reason of their being under the influence of the Trade Union officials. This, at any rate, is the general view of our constituency Agents in the industrial areas whenever they might have been consulted.

Here again we see the same phenomenon as in the earlier struggle over the vote. The primary question most politicians were asking was not: 'Should women be given the vote because it is their natural right?' but rather 'If women are given the vote, will it work to the advantage of my party?' As in the pre-war period, most people show little concern for anything but party advantage. Davidson, for example, can hardly be considered a misogynist. We have already seen that he strongly supported a number of reforms in order to give women more power within the party. The main objection of Central Office was simply that young people were believed to be more likely to vote for Labour. Questions of principle were subordinated to questions of political advantage.

A number of ingenious ways were thought up in order to try to fulfil the pledge without hurting the party too much. It was suggested that both men and women should be given the right to vote at the age of 25 with existing rights being protected, but there was no denying that this would create an uproar since there was a centuries-old tradition in England of enfranchising at least some men at age 21. Then Eustace Percy, the Duchess of Atholl's antagonist, suggested that both men and women should have the vote at 21 if they had an occupation qualification, and that they should both get it at 25 if they only had a residence qualification.[57] This, however, was returning to an earlier period of fancy franchises and was certain to be heavily criticized. Another possibility that was discussed was to give everyone over 30 two votes and everyone between 21 and 29 only one vote. The Home Secretary, Joynson-Hicks, however, objected to this saying that:

I do not think it would be wise for the Government to take up such a scheme. It would involve an experiment in a direction which, so far as politics are concerned, has never been tried before in this country, nor, so far as I know, even discussed. It is impossible to foresee how the proposal would be taken by the country generally, but it would not be popular with the under-30's, who already regard the scales as too heavily weighted in favour of middle age, and it would certainly give rise to much controversy of a kind which I believe would be embarrassing to the Government.[58]

He was undoubtedly right. Davidson was thinking only in terms of fulfilling the promise while trying to ensure the maximum number of Conservative votes. Joynson-Hicks had to think of the wider political implications, and, in fact, none of these proposals was likely to be very popular. It was far more likely that they would provoke a great deal of controversy and negative publicity. The trend of the time was towards greater democracy and not less.

Finally, with strong support from Baldwin, the decision was made to take the simplest course and to equalize male and female voting rights. Both men and women were given the right to vote at 21. Most Conservatives had understood the lesson of the 1924 general election, where women had made up 40 per cent of the electorate and where the party had triumphed with 48 per cent of the vote. There seemed little reason for Conservatives to fear an increase in the number of female voters. The most complicated question was that of voting based on business premises. At this time, men who owned businesses were allowed to vote both in their constituency of residence and in the one where their business was located. Since this measure obviously benefited the Conservatives, there was no chance of this second business vote being eliminated.[59] The simplest way of changing the law would have been to give the vote to women who owned businesses, but this involved only a tiny number. The Conservatives finally decided to give women whose husbands owned businesses the right to vote in the business constituencies as well. In some ways this was a brilliant stroke for it pleased the feminists and increased the number of Conservative votes. The bill, although it would create a majority of two million women voters, met with very little opposition. Four Conservative members moved its rejection on the grounds that the measure would 'endow women with permanent political supremacy', but even they did not believe equal voting rights could be put off interminably. They simply called for the issue to be placed before the electorate before enacting the bill. Their protests were considered nothing short of ridiculous by their fellow MPs of all parties. The years since 1918 had destroyed whatever fear of women voters had existed before. It was clear that women would not vote as a bloc and dictate to men. Like men, they conformed to traditional political parties. *The Times* felt that: 'only those who are foolish enough to be impressed by raw statistics will start up in panic-stricken animosity against the "monstrous regiment"'. The women's vote, *The Times* assured its readers, was simply a 'myth'. Women would not vote as one but, like men, for different parties.[60] The debate in Parliament was along the same lines. Almost no one voted against it, and the bill easily passed.

Furthermore, in 1928 all women were allowed to vote and to be candidates on the same terms as men in local government elections. Women were now in theory equal citizens but they still possessed a number of handicaps: they did not have the right to full guardianship of their children; if they married a foreigner, they lost their British citizenship and their children were not recognized as British citizens; they could still be legally forced to resign their job when they got married and equal pay was the rare exception rather than the rule. On the other hand, women finally had equal voting rights with men, women were beginning to enter Westminster, and a number of professions and universities had been forced to open to women. Women had truly become a force in politics, although one that still lacked clout. We take for granted these achievements today, but women at the time did not. The very fact of being able to vote, to be members of a political party and to take university degrees seemed to most women at the time to be enormous advances – as indeed they were. The immediate effects of women's suffrage were impressive. It is not perhaps surprising that after a long period of agitation a reaction should set in. Women had been demanding the right to vote for a long time and – at one stage at least – in a very militant fashion. It was normal that, after 1928, feminism – although not the presence of women in politics – would fade for a while.

The Conservative Party's record during this time was no worse than Labour's or the Liberals'. More than any other party, they had given women a visible role in the party structure. Visible, of course, does not mean vocal, but, throughout this period, there is no doubt that their role was increasingly important. Davidson and other enlightened members of the leadership worked to incorporate women and to convince the men to accept them. Even if the women remained in separate branches, they were still achieving recognition. By 1928 women had become an integral part of the Conservative Party: the Central Women's Advisory Committee and the Area Advisory Women's Committees had received official recognition; women organizers were an important, if exploited, part of the party bureaucracy, and women were employed by Central Office. Furthermore, the Conservatives had enacted or helped to enact a number of laws to improve women's position. The first woman MP had been a Conservative, and the party had followed Labour's footsteps by appointing a woman minister. It would be going much too far to say that the Conservative Party supported feminism – it certainly did not – but neither did any other party. At the same time, the Conservative Party was markedly more feminine than the Labour Party. It was very often a traditional femininity, but it had an undoubted appeal to women. For whatever reason, the Conservatives tempted women in far larger numbers than did the other parties, both as voters and members – and they were able to find a place for them. The party leadership at least understood the importance of attracting women for they realized that women were the necessary base on which to build a truly mass party structure. Unfortunately, they very often met with resistance in the constituency associations. Still, women now were a majority of the electorate and had established for themselves an important base in the party. It was now up to them to expand on it.

5 From Domesticity to War, 1928–45

In 1928 feminists finally achieved what they had dreamed of for decades: the vote on the same terms as men. The strange thing is, though, that instead of transforming the situation – as many people had predicted – it seemed to make very little difference. Baldwin had warned NUSEC that this would probably be the case. He felt that the immediate results would be modest: 'I have been too long in politics to take the Apocalyptic view.'[1] Of course, that is why Baldwin went against the advice of the party leadership and insisted on giving the vote to women on the same terms as men – because he knew it would make little difference. This had, in fact, been the lesson of all past reform acts. We have already seen how Salisbury had been stunned to discover that the vastly more democratic Britain that came into being after the Third Reform Act was more likely to vote Conservative than before.[2] Baldwin was certainly right when he perceived that women's position would be improved, not so much through the vote, as through changing attitudes in society. He told women's suffrage supporters that: '...it is...by a mere procession of time, ideas, customs, and conditions perfectly natural to our great grandfathers became perfectly absurd to us.'[3] There is a great deal of truth in this typically Conservative argument. Throughout this book we have seen – and will see – that politicians generally wait for major reforms until they are sure that most people – male and female – support them, and that, in any case, they will not cause any revolutionary change in society. Social attitudes had modified enough to give women the vote, but they had not gone much further. Women's involvement in politics actually declined during this period, and this change went far beyond feminist organizations. Certainly, the women's branches of the Conservative Party declined in numbers at this time, although to a less marked extent than the men's branches.

Of course, the period from 1928 to 1945 was one of great crisis and change, and the events in the nation – the depression and the Second World War – inevitably took precedence in people's consciousness. Against developments of such magnitude, feminist demands, or even simply everyday political give and take, might, indeed, seem trivial to many people. It is important to remember that most women in the country were not feminist or even much interested in feminism. Most people were simply preoccupied with the everyday business of living, which could be very difficult during this period, particularly for the unemployed. In a time of great crisis any nation is tempted to focus on the immediate problem. Inevitably, in the 1930s, the economic situation took precedence over every other issue. In 1929 the New York stock market had crashed bringing on a worldwide depression. A few months before this, in Britain, Labour had formed its second minority government with Ramsay MacDonald as prime minister. After the crash unemployment soared to two and a half million by the end of 1930. By the summer of 1931 the depression had fractured the Labour Party over the question of cutting unemployment benefit to control the budget deficit. Most of the Labour Party held unemployment benefit to be sacred and so refused to sanction any such cut. A governmental crisis occurred that had as its strange result the formation of a National Government between MacDonald and a few Labour supporters and the Conservatives. Until 1945 the Conservatives would be continually in power as the dominant (and sometimes virtually the only) member of a coalition government. It is not really surprising to discover that during a period of economic, and to a lesser extent political, crisis, women's issues were pushed to the side. The 1931 election was essentially a one-topic campaign and, as such, was almost completely focused on the appeal of the National Government. What is perhaps stranger is that women's issues did not play a larger role in the 1935 election. A study of both parties' manifestos shows that they were marginalized and that if any question did pertain to women it was inevitably in their roles as wives and mothers. Furthermore, at such a time of economic crisis, issues like career advancement for women or equal pay were immediately dismissed. The strength of the trade unions, the weakness of working women, the severity of the depression all worked against women. There was also the moral claim of the ex-soldier. Many people argued that he was owed something by society because of what he had suffered at the front and that, in a time of job scarcity, he should have priority. It was generally felt that women had a duty to resign their jobs so that the returning men could have them. In such a climate it was difficult for women to make many advances.

What was true in politics was also true in culture during this period. For example, the period saw the growth and development of women's magazines. Weeklies like *Woman's Own*, *Woman's Illustrated* and *Woman* were all founded in the 1930s and grew at a phenomenal rate until well into the postwar period. By the late 1950s *Woman* was enjoying a circulation of over three and a half million.[4] None of these magazines could be even remotely qualified as feminist. They gloried in domesticity and focused on subjects like dress, cooking, home decorating, and, almost inevitably on how to get and keep a man. On the surface, at least, these magazines seemed to be the antithesis of feminism, and, when taken in conjunction with the marginalization of women's issues in politics at the time, they could easily lead one to believe that feminism was virtually dead throughout these years.

This is only one side of the picture, though, because if organized feminism was in decline, it did not mean that women made no progress at all at this time. There is no doubt that traditional feminist issues like birth control were becoming more and more accepted by society. Attitudes to sex were changing in the 1930s and, for this reason, sexual double standards were clearly beginning to fade. More and more women were also joining the workforce, and some of these, at least, were married. The trend towards married women's employment can be traced to this period, although, admittedly the numbers remained small. There were undoubted legislative gains for women, in particular, as we shall see, during the war – although, as before, most of these concerned woman in her roles as wife and mother. To some extent, also, feminism benefited from the electoral truce during the war, for the lifting of party conflict allowed women from all parties to work together in Parliament on certain issues of particular interest to women. The number of women MPs also continued to grow during this time, and for the first time in the Conservative Party, women were elected to Parliament not through their family connections but by working their way up through local government or the party hierarchy.

On the other hand, membership in the women's branches, although remaining high, declined somewhat at this time. The women's branches, however, continued to be the backbone of Conservative Party strength in the constituencies. In fact, during this period there were more and more complaints about the men's branches and their relative inefficiency. Conservative constituency organizations had always had a tendency to be more social than political. To some extent this worked to the party's advantage because it ensured a large number of volunteers, but, on the other hand, it did not mean that these volunteers were very dedicated. This was particularly a problem with the men's organization, whose members often viewed the club as an opportunity to get away from home and enjoy a drink with friends.

In one analysis by the Women's Advisory Council in the Western Area, several members complained about the lack of dedication of the men. One woman went so far as to say that: 'Men [were] not particularly helpful between elections due to the fact that they support their political club merely as a means of playing billiards.'[5] This point of view was echoed throughout the party, from the rank-and-file to Central Office. Lady Iveagh, a leading figure in the Conservative women's organization and an MP, felt that the party's organization was defective because it was 'not fully developed all around'. From her point of view, the problem was that the 'women [were] inclined to work too hard which tended to put off the men'. This had to be remedied as 'women cannot reach every type of man'. She insisted that the 'men's clubs must be reorganized and run on more educational lines.'[6] The constant complaints about the men's clubs led at least one agent to warn that the party needed to see to it 'that the men are not sickened by always hearing that they do nothing'.[7] The problem was that no one was able to think of any successful way of improving the situation, and so, inevitably, the party became more and more dependent on women.

This fact was certain to increase the power of women, even if many of them were reluctant to push themselves forward. The most obvious changes were seen in the professional part of the party structure. During this period, for example, women finally won the right to become agents. In the late 1920s it was decided that women organizers should first pass an exam in order to qualify. This undeniably increased the stature of women organizers for now they could say that they had similar qualifications to the men. There remained, however, the serious problem of a shortage of women organizers. There were several reasons for this. For one thing, other fields of work were becoming increasingly open to women, and they were taking advantage of it. It was felt that the job of woman organizer demanded long work hours, especially during an election, for very little pay. To make matters worse, the pay and benefits varied considerably from one constituency to another, which led to calls by the National Society of Women Organizers for the payment of agents and organizers from a central fund.[8] This was strongly resisted by the constituency associations who liked to maintain a certain control and authority over their agents and organizers. This led to suggestions that Central Office should at least draw up a list of terms on which women organizers could be employed: minimum salary, holidays, etc.[9] The lack of promotion possibilities was also considered to be a major handicap in recruiting qualified women organizers.[10] The obvious remedy to this problem was to allow women the chance to pass the agents' exam. This started first in Scotland where the Conservative Party was weaker and financially poorer and where, therefore, it was often difficult to attract qualified agents. The first woman agent was apparently Miss A. Curtis of Chelmsford who became an agent in 1936. She was soon followed by other women, although during the 1930s very few of them qualified outside Scotland.[11] This was, then, only a very slight opening of the door to promotion. The situation would remain like this until after the Second World War when Lord Woolton would undertake a complete reorganization of the party.

On the other hand, the number of Conservative women in Parliament increased substantially at this time. In 1927 Lady Iveagh had been returned in a by-election. In many ways she was the classic example of the transition figure for she represents both the old conservatism and the new. Typically, like so many other Conservative women MPs, she had inherited the seat from her husband. On the other hand, she was highly qualified in her own right. She had a long tradition of political work and had risen through the party hierarchy. She was vice-chairman of the Central Women's Advisory Committee. She had been deeply involved in all aspects of the women's organization in the party since it had started in 1918. As such she represented a new sort of woman MP who was reaching her position by climbing the party hierarchy, although her husband, of course, had helped. She came from a family of politicians and three of her ancestors had been Speakers of the House of Commons.[12] Such a bloodline was in no way peculiar to women Conservatives. As we saw in the last chapter, the interwar period was one of modernization for the party. The power of the aristocracy declined, and the party was inexorably becoming more professional and democratic and less oligarchic at every level. At the same time, the aristocracy did not leave politics overnight, and many Conservatives still had a noble lineage: Lady Iveagh cannot be considered as very different from many male members. Fewer women were getting there through their male relatives, but this was also true of men.

The great victory of the National Government in 1931 had caused all Labour women to lose their seats and had brought a relatively large group of thirteen Conservative women to Westminster. Among this group were the first Conservative women to reach Parliament without inheriting their seats from their husbands. Of course, a large number of these new women MPs had not been expected to win, for they represented constituencies that had been considered virtually hopeless. Women, in both the Conservative and the Labour Parties, were very often chosen to represent such constituencies. Their seats were – and still are – therefore, more precarious than the average man's. A fairly large number of women tend to enter Parliament each time that one party has a landslide victory, but as soon as things become more equal between the parties, women are the first casualties.[13] This tendency actually increased after the Second World War and, to this day, there are relatively few women who represent absolutely safe constituencies. The new women included Thelma Cazalet who was a convinced feminist and had worked her way up through local government. She would later become the first woman MP to marry and, adding her husband's name to her own, would be known as Thelma Cazalet-Keir. Irene Ward was another Conservative woman to enter Parliament at this time. She had defeated the first woman minister, the Labour member Margaret Bondfield. Ward had worked her way up through the party having done volunteer work for years. Mavis Tate, who was elected from West Willesden, was younger than the traditional woman MP and had married into the Tate sugar family. She was also quite interested in feminist questions, and she, Ward and Cazalet-Keir would form a group who would try to force the Conservative Party to take a more progressive stand on such issues.

The most notable of the new women MPs was undoubtedly Florence Horsbrugh from Dundee. She had been active in war work, for which she had won the MBE, and in the Conservative Party in Scotland. She too had reached Parliament unexpectedly for no Conservative candidate had won Dundee in a hundred years. Horsbrugh would later become the first Conservative woman to belong to the cabinet, serving as Minister of Education from 1951–4. She impressed the party leaders with her ability from the moment she entered Parliament. By 1937, for example, Horsbrugh had already scored a notable achievement by becoming the first woman to move the reply to the Speech from the Throne on the opening of Parliament. She received a great deal of praise for this. The irreverent Conservative millionaire, Sir Henry Channon, said of her performance: 'She used simple, but magnificent prose, and scored a great success; she was wearing a dark-brown, flowing dress and fawn gloves.'[14] She had apparently spent quite a long time deciding how to dress for the occasion, and, as this quote shows, there is no doubt that MPs paid attention to her clothes.[15]

One of the oddest stories about a Conservative woman in this period was that of the secret mission of the actress, Lady Diana Cooper, wife of the anti-appeasement Conservative politician Duff Cooper. She was used by leading political figures to bring a message to Mussolini in the hopes of dissuading him from attacking Ethiopia. The whole idea began at a dinner party. As Diana Cooper described it:

> Amongst others sat Duff, Winston Churchill and Lord Tyrrell, former ambassador and Head of the Foreign Office, all of them heated and anxious about Italy's coming violation of Ethiopia. Methods were discussed of encouraging Mussolini's unnecessary resolve. They could think, at dawn, of no better way than to depute me, due for Rome two days later, to inform those in dictatorial power how strongly England was against the aggression. This journey can be called the real Failure of Mission – just as well send a tramp.[16]

The mission was a fiasco as Cooper had difficulty reaching anyone in authority, and the few people she did see did not take her seriously. They could not believe that a true government message could come in such a way. In this they were right, for the whole episode simply shows the weakness of the anti-appeasement group. With most of the government disapproving of their point of view, they were forced to result to such escapades.

One sometimes has the feeling, when studying the archives of the period, that, more than anything else, Conservative women were preoccupied by the lack of domestic workers. They seemed particularly irritated by the fact that many women received unemployment benefit when there were so many openings for servants. Evelyn Emmet, later a leading figure in the Conservative Party organization, spoke for many when she wrote that:

> We wish to put before you, on behalf of an interested group of women, our views with regard to the domestic servant problem. We consider it requires urgent investigation and would disclose widespread interest. In support of this statement we would like to point out that the shortage of domestic servants is acute, especially in the country and is clearly getting worse. Small households employing one or two maids find it quite impossible to obtain them. Yet it is common knowledge that there are a large number of unemployed women supported by the taxpayer on unemployment pay.[17]

Numerous resolutions on this subject were submitted to the Central Women's Advisory Committee. There is no doubt that domestic work was falling into disfavour at this time because it limited women's freedom. Attitudes towards women were obviously changing, and, at least before marriage, girls wanted to enjoy some liberty. Working in a factory or shop gave them more free time and independence

One should not be too harsh on these Conservative women, though, because, in an age before most labour-saving devices existed, keeping house was an onerous and time-consuming task. Since many of these women had children and were heavily involved in political or philanthropic activities during the day, they carried an immense burden. Evelyn Emmet, for example, was a member of the London County Council and spent a great deal of her time on unpaid council work:

> Most morning meetings of the Council start at 11 o'clock and afternoon committees are, as a rule, over by five. The only day Council work is likely to be prolonged indefinitely is on Tuesday when the full Council meets at 2.30. It is owing to the fact that there is hardly any evening work and that one can arrange to serve on committees which fit in with home duties that it is possible for a number of women to serve on the Council who could not consider standing for Parliament.[18]

Local government was, to a considerable degree, based on the support of large numbers of unpaid women members. Such a system could only continue if women could be freed, to some extent at least, from their duties as housekeepers and mothers. Conservative women's complaints on the subject of domestic servants were not realistic, but nor were they, in most cases, simply the whining complaints of a highly spoiled element of society. They were the complaints of very overworked women.

One of the most interesting efforts of the Conservative Party during this period was to establish branches, known as the Optimist Clubs, among young women working in factories. The mid to late 1930s saw a concentrated attempt in the Lancashire, Cheshire and Westmorland Provincial Area to organize such clubs. It is somewhat amazing that Conservative women's groups grew up in factories during the Depression, and there is no doubt that much of their attraction was that they were a respectable way for young women to have fun. As the organizer explained: there were 'fewer outlets' for the 'youthful spirits' of girls than for boys.[19] The Optimist Clubs, like the Primrose League before them, filled a gap. In 1936 it was estimated that these clubs numbered about 150 to 200 girls.[20] These girls were invariably quite young – some were not even old enough to vote – and not particularly interested in politics. What made at least some of these clubs successful was undeniably the personal and social element. Very early on they established good relations with the National 'Keep Fit' movement for women and, among other things, organized weekly gymnastics classes with them.[21] As one organizer commented: 'At the beginning, girls are raw material and suspicious of efforts to help them, and only unfailing personal interest breaks down this attitude and teaches them to be "clubbable".'[22] Another report showed the essentially unpolitical nature of these branches, for the Leigh club specialized in talks about foreign countries. For the year from 1936 to 1937 they had organized talks on subjects like Palestine and Austria – with the emphasis on tourist attractions rather than political developments. Their success was ascribed by the report to a great extent to the ability of the lecturers: 'Our panels speakers have known just how to interest and educate the girls without being too obviously instructive.'[23] Other activities organized by these clubs included Christmas parties, rambles, jumble sales and lessons in dressmaking and handicrafts. More than anything else, this resembles the Primrose League in its Victorian heyday. Once again we see working-class membership of a Conservative organization, although on a much smaller scale than in the League, and once again the primary interest is not political but social.

The 1938 report on the clubs showed them to be steadily growing and analysed the membership of these clubs. The Leigh club was particularly successful and focused on social evenings and talks. Along with general travel talks occasional political subjects were introduced like 'World Politics'. Other activities included hospital and library visits as well as rambles. The Bolton club was somewhat different in that it included a number of older, married women who often brought their children with them to club meetings. According to the organizer, their interests were somewhat different: 'They like handicrafts, games and sewing, and rather less of the formal talks than Leigh.'[24] The social events were particularly successful there with over sixty women present on each occasion. These were the two largest of the factory groups. The others were more problematic concerns. The Hindley branch, for example, was much more affected by the depression. As the organizer explained:

The Hindley girls have had some successful musical evenings singing and dancing, but they are much younger than at the other branches and either out-of-work or unable to find even the necessary weekly 2d. or, in some cases, overworked and too tired to attend regularly. Speakers find Hindley much less get-at-able than the other branches. Altogether there seems to be an 'inferiority complex' about this small town, making it self-centred and difficult to work. With all these disadvantages, we are still in existence.[25]

Even in Hindley, though, the membership was increasing, primarily, it would seem, because of the attraction of its social programmes. There were two other of these clubs. The first, the Heyrod Street club was a relatively old society which seemed to be particularly interested in dramatic productions. They seemed to have spent most of their time either on an elocution class or on preparing and presenting plays. The final group, that of Radcliffe, had only been established in April 1938 and included about fifteen girls. Once again, social events dominated for they had produced a successful social evening with singing, dancing and other musical events.

The following year's report continued to show growth in these clubs. The Leigh and Bolton groups continued to perform well with increased membership and high attendance at meetings. The social events continued to predominate, but the organizer was delighted to notice that the girls were becoming more and more interested in politics:

A most encouraging feature is the increased demand for talks on political questions. When asking the girls which programmes they preferred, these Clubs mentioned the panel speakers who had addressed them as the most popular. The girls would not have listened to a political address a few years ago, but our panel speakers have shown such tact and ability in knowing just how to address them that their interest has been aroused. We have also had 'Socials' which bring in new members.[26]

It is certainly extraordinary to hear that members of a Conservative Party branch disliked hearing political talks, but it clearly shows the essentially social element of these women's groups.

The other clubs also continued during this period. The Radcliffe and Hindley branches also showed growth. The report on the Radcliffe club is particularly interesting for its description of the members:

These girls are of ages from 15 to 17 and it is really an achievement that they have attended regularly each week to listen to travel talks, careers for girls and public affairs, for which they themselves provide the funds, and arrange for refreshments. Only very rare financial help is given, and an odd half-crown to tide over a difficult patch, so that they are self-supporting and are developing a corporate spirit and a wish for public service. In each Club, if a member is ill, we visit and send flowers from the Club.

It was this personal element and particularly the devotion of women organizers, that allowed Conservatism to get a foothold in industrial districts during the depression. Furthermore, this was not the only attempt to interest the working class in conservatism. The depression preoccupied society and so the Conservative Party. Conservative women already had a long tradition of philanthropic as well as political volunteer work. For this reason, it seems almost obvious that they would try to organize relief for those suffering from the depression. The Central Women's Advisory Committee, for example, recommended in 1932 that each area should form National Emergency Working Parties in order 'to provide clothing and other necessaries to relieve abnormal distress in the Industrial Areas'.[27] To many this seemed to be an excellent idea: it was at the same time humane and politically intelligent. Of course, it did provoke complaints, for such activities skated very close to the edge of the corruption laws. In the end, the women decided to transfer the task to a non-political organization, and the specifically Conservative organizations were disbanded. In many cases, though, the actual volunteers remained the same.[28]

The Optimist Clubs, however, appear to have died out after the Second World War. Many of the girls, of course, were called up for war work and left the area. As elsewhere, the Conservative Party mobilized in a big way for the war. This was particularly true after May 1940 when the formation of a coalition government caused the establishment of an electoral truce. Freed from ordinary political duties, Conservative branches, and particularly Conservative women (since many of the men were serving with the armed forces) devoted themselves to war work. The activities of the Northwest Provincial Area were repeated throughout the country; they dealt with the evacuation of children from the cities and their settlement in safer rural areas, with the care of refugees. They manned canteens for servicemen, the home guard and other vital war workers, and, in some cases, even organized and ran canteens themselves.[29] In Somerset and Bristol, Conservative women were involved in sewing parties to make clothes for the troops, and in salvage activities, among other things.[30] These examples were repeated throughout the country. Pre-occupation with the war effort undoubtedly meant that many branches effectively disappeared under such conditions. At this period the Labour Party obviously had an advantage, since many of their members were factory workers who, because their work was indis-pensable to the war effort, could not be moved. In spite of efforts by the Central Women's Advisory Committee, the Conservative Party's local organizations undeniably declined during this period, and this was an important reason for their election defeat in 1945.

Of course, a great deal of blame for this must be laid at the door-step of the Conservative Party leadership. As party leader, Churchill could hardly be termed a success – in fact, some might argue that he could hardly be termed a Conservative. Churchill had been an outcast for most of the 1930s and undoubtedly harboured resentment against the party. He quite rightly devoted all his energy to the conduct of the war. At the same time, he made no attempt to halt the nation-wide decay in the party nor even to find someone capable of doing so. He felt that everything should be sacrificed to the war effort, and, as we have seen, many other Conservatives obviously agreed with him. The result was that in many parts of the country the party virtually dis-appeared.[31] The women's organization, for example, did not even hold its annual conference from 1939 to 1946. Not only did the volunteer branch of the party wither during the war, but the profes-sional part did too. In March 1945, when it was clear that an election would probably be held soon, Central Office estimated that 155 women organizers had been employed in 1939. Of these, three had since died, 18 had retired or resigned, 21 were no longer available, and 80 were engaged in war service. This left only a tiny number still in place in the constituencies.[32] The situation was apparently similar for agents. Maxse was convinced that these facts would greatly increase the position of women organizers after the war. It would certainly open the possibility of promotion to agents' jobs for many more women than before. Given how critical the need was, the Party did not have much choice.

While the war may not have been a good period for the Conservat-ive Party, it did see notable advances for women. If the 1930s has traditionally been viewed as a period in which feminism was in serious decline, the Second World War has stood out as one when women – at least for a brief time – made important strides. There is a great deal of truth in these assertions. With the war the situation changed, for women were necessary to replace male workers now in the army. In 1941 the government reluctantly came to the conclusion that it was necessary to mobilize women. The National Service (No. 2) Act gave the government the right to conscript women into the women's branches of the armed services, into munitions factories and for civil defence. Women were thus forced into traditionally masculine roles, but, for all that, they still found themselves severely limited. In the armed forces, women basically only occupied non-combatant jobs like cooking, driving or secretarial work, and there was virtually no room for advancement. Almost inevitably, and to a large extent because of trade union demands, women were excluded from any positions of responsibility. Women's uniforms tell us a great deal about their own and the government's perception of them. Fashion designers were hired to make attractive uniforms and cinema personalities were shown modelling them. The very strong emphasis on femininity, so apparent in the 1930s, continued during the war. To some extent it may even have increased, for men were most obviously in their traditional role as protector of the home. As in the First World War, the very risks run by men pointed up the difference between the sexes.

There is no doubt, however, that this wholesale entry of women into the workforce caused a certain re-evaluation of women's role. For one thing, men discovered that women worked more efficiently than they had expected. No less a figure than Ernest Bevin, Minister of Labour, said in 1944 that: 'We thought it would need three women for the output of two men, but by the help of our production engineers, new devices, and Labour aids in one way or another, I am glad to say that the output is almost equal one for one.'[33] There is undeniably a certain pettiness about the comment for he never credits the women themselves with being responsible for their own efficiency – probably because he does not want to give ammunition to those in favour of equal pay. However, the point is still clear: women can do work as efficiently as men, which was something of a revolutionary discovery in and of itself. Of course, women continued to be paid, in most cases, at two-thirds the salary of a man, and most employers considered them to be temporary workers only. They thus had no security of keeping their job after the war. There is strong evidence, however, that the women also considered themselves to be temporary workers. The Central Women's Advisory Committee, for example, were told by a woman who worked as a welfare advisor to a large group of factories that: 'About 70 per cent of women in industry to-day want to return to their homes after the war.'[34] Mass Observation confirmed this, estimating in 1944 that less than one quarter of working women wished to remain in their job after the war.[35] Single women generally expected to stop working when they married, while married women with small children found the whole experience exhausting. The one truly significant thing that Mass Observation found was that 29 per cent of married women wanted to continue working after the war, although most of these were older women with grown children.

One of the most remarkable facts about the war is the unity achieved between women of different parties in Parliament in pursuit of feminist goals. The electoral truce limited party hostility and, for the first time, allowed women from all parties to co-ordinate their activities. Florence Horsbrugh and Ellen Wilkinson both had government posts and so remained to some extent separate from the other women. However, Thelma Cazalet-Keir, Irene Ward, Lady Astor and Mavis Tate formed an able group of Conservatives who were deeply interested in women's questions. In many cases they were joined by Megan Lloyd George of the Liberal Party, Eleanor Rathbone, an Independent, and Edith Summerskill, Agnes Hardie and Jennie Adamson of the Labour Party. When they acted together, as they very often did, they formed a redoubtable group. Ernest Bevin of the Labour Party, who was Minister of Labour, was obviously one of their main targets, and Labour as well as Conservative women participated in the attack. The wholesale entry of women in the workforce served to dramatize the injustices from which they suffered. Parliament, for the first time, began to take a sustained interest in the question of women's employment. Several debates were held on the question, and many important issues were discussed: wages, working conditions, day nurseries and training facilities, for example. The women MPs did win some victories: probably the formation of the Women Power Committee to advise the Ministry of Labour on the employment of women was one of the most important. The very fact that many women were forced to work who might otherwise never have done so made women's employment problems more generally known.

It was clear though that male politicians continued to see women as second-class citizens. In one of the more shocking decisions of the war, the 1939 Personal Injuries (Emergency Provisions) Act provided for women to be compensated for wartime injuries at two-thirds the rate for men. This provoked protests from women MPs, feminist groups and perhaps most importantly from women working in civil defence. It also broke from the traditions of British law, for, until then, compensation had been based on the suffering of the individual and not on any loss of earnings they might have sustained.[36] Mavis Tate, a Conservative MP, led the attack in the House of Commons, although she was strongly supported by women MPs from all parties. In November 1942 Tate secured the support of 200 colleagues for an amendment to introduce equal compensation. The Labour Party was, in theory, committed to equal compensation, and would almost certainly vote against the government if the issue were forced to a division. By this time it had also become clear that public opinion was strongly in favour of equal compensation, so the government decided that it was time to do something about the question. A Select Committee was formed, and in 1943 it pronounced in favour of equal compensation. To some extent, this can be viewed as the first step towards equal pay.

Indeed, it became more and more evident that there was support for such a policy in the country. The Equal Pay Campaign Committee (EPCC) was formed in 1943 and counted among its leaders Tate from the Conservative Party and Summerskill from Labour. The group focused on teaching and the civil service as the most likely possibilities for the introduction of equal pay. One obvious result came in 1944 when Thelma Cazalet-Keir, a Conservative MP, moved an amendment to the Butler Education Act that would have given equal pay to women teachers. She warned the chief whip about her intention, which, according to her, he did not take seriously: 'he received [the threat] with a sort of pitying nonchalance natural enough when the odds seemed so heavily on the Government's winning'.[37] In the resulting division the government was actually defeated by 117 to 116. The reaction from the government – from both Conservative and Labour members – was harsh. Churchill forced a vote to delete the amendment and made it an issue of confidence in the government. Under such conditions he obviously won the vote, but it had shown the strength of feeling over the question. Churchill's main objection to equal pay was that, given the enormous expense of the war, the country quite simply could not afford it. What is particularly interesting about this episode was that the main opposition to equal pay did not come from Churchill but from Ernest Bevin. He refused to make any concession on the question because he feared it would cause unrest among the trade unions, and he apparently even threatened to resign over it. His actions caused some bitterness among the women in Parliament, and he was harassed throughout the war by Irene Ward, Conservative MP and chairman of the Woman Power Committee. The government, however, remained firm to the end.

The war had many other effects on women too. There is no doubt, for example, that the sexual double standard continued to erode during this period, and women, particularly those in the services, enjoyed a greater degree of sexual freedom. Immorality was a charge that was frequently brought against the women's services. This was true to such an extent that the government decided to form a committee to investigate the situation. Strangely enough, this committee, as proposed, would have only consisted of the Parliamentary Secretaries of the three Services departments – all of whom were men. The women MPs protested against this and eventually the government gave in. The committee was formed with a majority of female members. Complaints were also heard about women who had been conscripted to work in munitions factories and about the Women's Land Army. These women were often quite young and, for many of them, it was their first time away from home. The work they did was also generally arduous and physically exhausting. It is not surprising, therefore, to discover that many of them used their new freedom in pub-crawling and flirting with soldiers. One result of this greater sexual freedom was soaring venereal disease rates. To try to curb this serious problem the government introduced Regulation 33B which gave the authorities the right to force someone to be examined and treated for venereal disease if they had been named by at least two other persons as responsible for giving them the disease. While, in theory, the regulation applied to both men and women, in reality it was almost only used against women. Understandably, this caused a great deal of resentment, and a number of feminist groups protested against the regulation. At the same time as pre-marital and extra-marital sex increased, marriage rates were going up dramatically – which is a common phenomenon in time of war. Fewer and fewer women remained single. Of course most of these younger married women had to do without their husbands, who were usually in the army. This was certain to inspire new confidence in women for most of them discovered that they could manage quite well without their husbands. On the whole the wartime period increased women's expectations while not markedly improving their legal position. This could only have important consequences in the postwar period.

The period of the depression and the war also saw a growing infatuation with welfare reform which would culminate in 1942 with the Beveridge Report. Feminist thought was undeniably influenced by this trend and much feminist activity then was turned towards the achievement of the welfare state. There were demands for improved child care, family allowances, and better maternity leave, among other things. The problem with linking feminism with increased welfare benefits was that it threatened to split the movement along party lines. It obviously appealed to Labour Party supporters while getting a tepid response from many Conservatives. It would, however, be wrong to view the Beveridge Report as in any way feminist for, on the contrary, it was in many ways reactionary. Upon marriage women lost any benefits they had accumulated, for, as the report stated:

> Every woman on marriage will become a new person, acquiring new rights and not carrying on into marriage claims to unemployment or disability benefit in respect of contribution made before marriage. Some new rights, as for marriage grant and maternity grant, apply to all married women; all women also during marriage will continue to acquire qualifications for pensions in old age through contributions made by their husbands.[38]

Women were clearly viewed as subordinate to men under the Beveridge Report, as this quotation shows.

The war also saw a number of changes which were designed to improve health care for mothers and children and which lowered maternal and infant mortality rates considerably. To a large extent, this was linked more to a concern over falling birth-rates than to feminism. These bills were all put into effect by the Conservative-dominated coalition government. In June 1940 the National Milk Scheme was introduced that provided free or inexpensive milk to all pregnant and nursing mothers. Evacuation also made necessary the introduction of certain acts to give free milk and meals to a number of schoolchildren. The 1942 Vitamin Welfare Scheme gave pregnant and nursing mothers, as well as children under five, free or subsidized vitamin A or D, cod liver oil or orange juice. There is no doubt that for the working class the wartime period saw an improvement in diet. Great strides were also made towards eliminating maternal and infant mortality. Perhaps the most important change during this period was the introduction of family allowances in 1945 by the Conservative caretaker government. Eleanor Rathbone, the Independent MP, had long demanded their introduction as a recognition by the state of the importance of a mother's work. However, the bill as prepared in 1945 could hardly be less feminist. It had been introduced primarily because of concern over the falling birth-rate and because many Conservatives thought it might work against inflation by keeping down demands for pay raises. The bill, in fact, provoked an outcry from feminists because the money was to be paid to the father rather than to the mother. Under pressure from feminist groups, it was finally decided to pay it to the mother.

Welfare feminism then was a double-edged sword: while it caused women to make some important gains, it also encouraged male politicians to continue to think of women primarily in their roles as wife and mother. It encouraged both parties to treat women's questions as essentially limited to social security. Furthermore, it must be admitted that, to some extent, the preoccupation with welfarism weakened the feminist movement for it divided it along party lines. Not surprisingly, the Conservative women's branches sometimes found it difficult to accept this preoccupation with welfare. Many of them viewed the Beveridge Report with deep suspicion. The major exception to this trend was the Tory Reform Group which was a band of Conservative MPs who strongly supported Beveridge's ideas. They feared that the Conservative Party was losing touch with the trends in popular thought and wanted to push it in a more progressive direction. Two of these MPs, Thelma Cazalet-Keir and Irene Ward, had helped form the Conservative Women's Reform Group and as such were committed to support certain feminist points of view. The fact that these women were also members of the Woman Power Committee only added to their influence. In 1945 they wrote a pamphlet called 'When Peace Comes' which considered the position of women after the war. Their goal was to push the Conservative Party to adopt a more advanced stand on women. Cazalet-Keir felt that: 'During visits to different parts of the country contacts had been made with considerable numbers of women holding important posts. These women had a new idealism and high hopes for the future, but very few were interested in politics or party alignment.'[39] They wanted to capture these women for the Conservative Party but felt that to do so the party needed a more progressive policy. There is no doubt that many women in the Conservative Party felt that the party was not making a determined enough attempt to attract professional women. The Central Women's Advisory Committee believed that few members of professional women's clubs were Conservative and that they represented a potentially influential group. They felt that some effort should be made, first, to get Conservatives involved in these clubs, and, then, to introduce these women to Conservative ideas.[40] Given the importance of both women and the professional classes to the Conservative Party, the loss of professional women, even if their numbers were still small, would obviously be a blow.

As the war neared its end and a general election loomed, there were growing calls for increasing the number of women MPs. This led to the foundation of a new organization, Women for Westminster. In theory, this group was non-political and worked for the election of women from any party. They tried to encourage women in local party organizations to insist upon the nomination of women candidates. To a large extent they failed for the movement was based on support from women in the constituency organizations – which was very often not the case. It also failed because the war had totally disorganized the party structure, and, therefore, when a general election was called, both parties – but especially the Conservatives – were taken unprepared. They tended to nominate what candidates they could find quickly. The Conservative Women's Advisory Committee had a mixed reaction to Women for Westminster. They refused to become officially involved in the organization but kept a close watch on its activities and allowed individual Conservatives to join it. There was a Conservative Committee of the Women for Westminster movement and its leader, a Miss Bowker, informed party leaders about their activities and consulted with them regularly.[41] As time went on, though, the CWAC became more hostile to Women for Westminster:

> At that time [January 1943] it was becoming apparent that 'Women for Westminster' was far from being a democratic organization, and that, while under the control of its present officers, its tendency would always be left wing and there could be little hope of a fair deal for those holding Conservative views... They therefore asked all Area Chairmen to keep watch in their Areas and if it was found that members of our Associations were taking active part in the formation of branches to dissuade them from so doing.[42]

Of course, since the Conservative women's organization had held themselves aloof from Women for Westminster from the start, it was only natural that a left-wing bias should form. In any case, the group very largely failed in its goals and had very little influence in any party. The 1945 election saw a total of 87 women candidates (14 Conservatives, 38 for Labour, 18 Liberals and 17 others), which was a tremendous increase over the 1935 figure of 67. However, only five of these held safe seats (two Conservatives, one Liberal and two Labour members). A full fifty of those standing for the three major parties were contesting safe seats held by the opposing party which meant almost certain defeat.[43] In the end, a record total of twenty-three women were elected to parliament, but twenty of these were from the Labour Party. This remarkable figure, however, appears to have been due to the unexpectedly large victory of the Labour Party which caused them to win constituencies they had previously considered hopeless. It does not mean that the party had a more progressive policy in relation to women. The Conservative results were predictably disastrous since so many women held marginal seats. Only Lady Davidson managed to keep her seat, and she was a fairly inactive figure in Parliament. The wartime co-operation between women of different parties in Parliament over women's issues ended abruptly in 1945.

This period, then, was one that saw mixed results. On the surface the feminist movement lacked numbers and popularity, but in reality there were important advances for women. On the legislative level, there were many notable gains for women, although these laws developed from a spirit of welfarism rather than feminism, and the Conservative Party's record on these questions was not terribly different from Labour's. Growing numbers of women were also entering the professions, and new educational and employment opportunities were developing. On a personal level, the double standard was eroding, and women were experiencing greater sexual freedom, although a significant stigma was still attached. The number of women in politics was also increasing, although the women's branches of the Conservative Party declined during this period – as did the Conservative Party organization itself. However, the number of women in Parliament had grown, and the war period showed exactly how much could be gained if women from all parties acted together on feminist questions. The 1945 general election, however, put an end to this experiment, and most Conservative women lost their seats. The unexpectedly large Labour victory shook the Conservative Party to its foundations and forced the leadership to reassess their past actions. Churchill appointed Lord Woolton as party chairman with a brief to reorganize and reinvigorate the party.

Part III
Women and the Postwar
Conservative Party

6 The Conservative Party and Women Voters, 1945–75

This period began with the Conservatives' surprise election defeat in 1945 and ended with the selection of a woman party leader for the first time in British history. These thirty years saw amazing changes in Britain as it developed from postwar austerity towards the 'affluent society' only to return to serious economic problems in the 1970s. It was also the only period of twentieth-century history when the alternation between the Conservatives and Labour in power was fairly equal. For the first time the gender gap, although long suspected, was proven to exist, since polls now introduced a certain scientific element into political campaigns. Women were shown to be slightly more favourable to the Conservatives than were men. For this reason, the party targeted them in particular and made special efforts to attract their votes. To a large extent, though, they focused on issues which agreed with the traditional vision of women in their role of wife and mother and tended to spend less time addressing more controversial questions like equal pay. In this, there was little difference between the Conservatives and Labour. The welfare state that Labour instituted worked to the benefit of women, obviously, but it was based on the fundamentally sexist view of women as dependants. This period was also one of great upheaval in women's roles in society and the economy. In the immediate aftermath to the Second World War, domesticity was the fashion of the day, and feminism was clearly out of style. On the other hand, certain long-term trends distinctly showed that women's role was in full evolution. The most important of these was the one towards greater numbers of women in the workforce. This was caused by a postwar shortage of workers and helped along by the desire of many families to supplement their income. By 1951 it was clear that the government would have to come to grips with this evolution and would, indeed, given the shortage of workers, have to encourage women to accept a new role in society. The rebirth of feminism in the 1960s, then, was not an isolated phenomenon but one that developed logically from the trends of the previous period.

During the Attlee governments, the Conservatives made important efforts to gain the women's vote and especially that of the housewife. Although more and more women were entering the workforce, most people saw this as the era of the housewife, and the Conservative Party made a determined effort to attract their vote. They were an obvious target since it was believed that women were more likely to vote Conservative in higher numbers than men. Studies by the Public Opinion Research Department (PORD) of the Conservative Party, founded after the war, confirmed that women tended to vote Conservative and that Labour's strength was greatest among men in the 30 to 49 age group. There was, however, one major exception to this trend and that was in the middle class where no gender gap appeared to exist.[1] The Gallup Poll only confirmed what the Conservatives had already discovered. A 1950 poll showed that 46 per cent of men and 36 per cent of women were satisfied with the government's performance.[2] The PORD also estimated that women were more likely than men to be floating voters by a ratio of six to four.[3] Women then were the most volatile element in the electorate, but one that, on the whole, tended towards Conservatism. They showed this in 1951 when, largely because of their votes, the Conservatives returned to power. First, under Winston Churchill and then successively under Anthony Eden, Harold Macmillan and Sir Alec Douglas-Home, they stayed in power until 1964. It has been estimated that, all other things being equal, if only men had had the right to vote in the period from 1945 to 1979, Labour would have been continuously in power. The gender gap obviously worked in favour of the Conservatives and made them, for much of the postwar period, the natural party of government.

One of the major reasons for women's disproportionate support for the Conservatives in the immediate postwar period was undoubtedly the fact that housewives experienced the privations of the so-called 'age of austerity'. From analysing a number of polls and studies, PORD came to precisely this conclusion:

> In so far as there is a sex difference, it is clear that there must be some factor of dissatisfaction with the government which is peculiar to women. This is unlikely to be, for example, losses on nationalised industry, while housing difficulties are common to both sexes. The probability is that it has something to do with food, which means that it may vary with variations in the government's food policy.[4]

Rationing continued in the postwar period and, in fact, got worse: bread, for example, had never been rationed during the war but it was now, and the meat ration was further reduced. The Conservatives hoped to take advantage of this dissatisfaction to convince house-wives, and particularly working-class housewives, to vote Conservative. Thus, a great deal of their activity during this period was concentrated on capturing the women's vote. In this they appear to have succeeded to a large extent because the gender gap between men's and women's voting reached an all-time high in the 1951 and 1955 elections. In 1951 an estimated 54 per cent of women and 46 per cent of men voted Conservative. The difference remained the same in 1955 with 47 per cent of men and 55 per cent of women supporting the Tories.[5] All available information points to one conclusion: that the Conservatives would not have won either of these elections if women had not had the vote. A Conservative Research Department report of 1969 summed up the position rather well: 'Certainly since the war, and probably since the late nineteen-twenties, a majority of men have voted Labour and it is only because women have the vote and are both more numerous and more likely to vote Conservative that we have ever been able to win a General Election during this time.'[6]

It was thus absolutely logical for the Conservatives to decide to concentrate their attention on the women: their dissatisfaction with the Attlee government was greater, they were more likely to vote Conservative, and, perhaps most important, they were less likely to vote than were men. If the Conservatives could achieve a higher turn-out in women voters, then they might very well ensure their return to power. It is not surprising, given the results of the PORD studies, to see that, on the whole, the Conservatives responded to the need to cultivate the women's vote by trying to capitalize on issues like food rationing and not with any overtly feminist rhetoric. Like Labour, their policy for women was oriented towards family life and domest-icity, although there were a few exceptions. Conservative policy did include proposals to introduce equal pay in the civil service (although when was not clearly stated), to admit women to the House of Lords, and to force divorced and separated husbands to pay maintenance.

Given the need to attract women voters, party literature for women was an important subject. Party policy was to avoid writing campaign literature specifically for women but rather to devote a large amount of space in general publications to issues believed to be of particular interest to women like rationing. Certainly many high-ranking women in the party found that Central Office was not making a sufficient effort to woo women voters and that the publicity department had no understanding of women or of their interests. There were complaints from the WNAC's[7] sub-committee on Party Literature for Women that 'the staff of the Publicity Department of the Central Office is inadequate for the purpose', and they strongly advised the appointment of a woman. They further criticized the masculine bias of Central Office by saying that: 'It is agreed that the information provided in our Party literature is excellent, but that what the Publicity Department lacks is someone with a big enough mind to grasp the potentialities of publicity, especially with regard to the women electors.'[8] The WNAC felt that women were, in general, less well-educated than men – particularly with regard to politics – and that the literature produced by Central Office was too complicated for most of them to understand.[9] The sub-committee wanted simpler and more direct literature with good illustrations, so that it could be easily understood by the ordinary housewife.[10] Their criticism appears to have had an effect for the publicity department at Central Office was reorganized and a woman officer added in order to 'look after publicity matters of special interest to women and to consider how questions would strike women electors'.[11]

The goal of the Conservatives in the immediate postwar period, then was to rejuvenate their party organization which had nearly disappeared in some places during the war and to take advantage of the discontent caused by austerity in order to attract voters – and, in particular, women voters. There were many reasons for this postwar austerity, for the war had caused Britain to develop huge debts and, at the same time, to lose much of her traditional market overseas. The expense of introducing Beveridge's recommendations and establishing the welfare state was also enormous, and Labour was only able to do so thanks to a loan from the United States and the Marshall Plan. The economic situation after the war, thus, was precarious, and it should not come as a surprise to discover that a severe balance of payments crisis struck in 1947. From our point of view it had two major consequences. First, as we have seen, it forced the government to adopt a policy of extreme austerity. Second, and perhaps more important, the government had to accept the need for large numbers of women workers in the country. The end of the Second World War had seen the demobilization of many women and their return to the home. This was, in fact, the policy of the Attlee government, which maintained a sharply traditional view of the role of women – although there is no doubt that a Conservative government would have behaved in exactly the same way. The Labour government was still thinking in terms of the First World War, and their basic idea was that women should step aside and let the returning men have the jobs. In 1946, for example, they cut subsidies to day nurseries thus forcing local governments to close them. This was in keeping with the mentality of the day which glorified family life and made it one of the cornerstones of the welfare state. The postwar period saw a soaring marriage rate and a baby boom, which seemed to confirm what most politicians already believed: that the woman's place was clearly in the home.

The 1946 National Insurance Act reflected this point of view. It wholly adopted Beveridge's idea that married women were dependent creatures. They normally paid no contributions and were entitled to benefit only through their husbands. However, those who continued to work had the choice of contributing or not, but if they did contribute, they received benefit at a lower rate. The single woman did contribute but her contributions and benefits were lower than for men since it was assumed that she had no dependants to support. On the other hand, any unmarried woman living with a man was also denied benefit and considered to be his dependant, since the government feared that any other possibility would discourage marriage. Welfarism then was a two-edged sword for women. It undeniably helped many women to make ends meet through family allowances, compensation and other forms of assistance. It also provided them with valuable services like medical care. All available evidence points to the fact that, before the establishment of the National Health Service, women received less medical treatment than men. This was partly because male workers often had medical insurance which their families were not entitled to and partly because women deprived themselves of medical care when finances were limited. On the other hand, the welfare state was created by men, and it was thus designed to respond to male needs or to male perceptions of female needs. As such, welfare legislation assumed that women were completely dependent on men, and they were relatively disadvantaged in relation to men for benefits. The welfare state reflected the prejudices of its time.

When the Conservatives returned to power in 1951, there was little change in this policy and, in fact, little demand in the nation for such a change. The government, popular psychologists and women's magazines all concurred that the most desirable role for women was that of stay-at-home wife and mother. Only in this way could the future generations be assured of a healthy start in life. Of course, to a large extent, this attitude was a response to the upheavals of the Second World War. Men had been absent in the army, women in the factories and children evacuated to the countryside. For a brief period of time, the war had, in many cases, destroyed the family unit, and it was perfectly normal that in the immediate aftermath a renewed emphasis should be placed on the traditional view of the family. Few voices were raised against this mentality. One of the few was a young Conservative housewife named Margaret Thatcher. In a 1954 article, she defended the working mother:

> What is the effect on the family when the mother goes out to work each day? If she has a powerful and dominant personality her personal influence is there the whole time... Of course she still sees a good deal of the children. The time she spends away from them is a time which the average housewife spends in doing the housework and shopping, not in being with the children assiduously. From my own experience I feel there is much to be said for being away from the family for part of the day. When looking after them without a break, it is sometimes difficult not to get a little impatient and very easy only to give part of one's attention to their incessant demands. Whereas, having been out, every moment spent with them is a pleasure to anticipate... Later on there will not be that awful gap which many women find in their lives when their children go away to school.[12]

While few people at the time agreed with Thatcher, economic conditions were forcing attitudes about married women to change.

Everybody had been wrong about the postwar economic climate, for it turned out that it was not at all like what had occurred after the First World War. Britain in the late 1940s was faced with an economic crisis, but one that was caused, not by unemployment, but by a shortage of workers.[13] The Labour government had to re-evaluate its position on women and employment for they quickly discovered that they needed to keep large numbers of women in employment. The Women's Land Army, for example, was maintained until 1950. This crisis had obvious social consequences as well, for it also revolutionized attitudes to married women and employment because the need for them in the workforce was so clear. Furthermore, it opened new fields to women. The main reason why there had been so many legal limitations to women's work had quite simply been the fear of unemployment. Trade unions had tried to block women from holding jobs in traditionally male industries because, since women were paid less than men, they feared that employers would prefer to hire women. In a period in which workers rather than work were in short supply, this attitude was certain to change – although obviously, given the pervading views of society, it would take time for women to gain anything close to full equality.

By 1951 more women were at work than during the war. It was estimated that one-third of the working population were women, and one-fifth of all married women were in employment.[14] By 1971 over nine million women were working which meant that they made up over 36 per cent of the total working population.[15] More and more women were staying at home for only a few years, until their children entered school, and then returning to the job market. There are, of course, a number of qualifying points that need to be made here. First, women were primarily concentrated in low-paying, unskilled jobs that held little possibility of promotion. Many of them were also employed part-time or held only temporary positions. The number of women in the professions had not increased significantly since the 1920s. They had made up 5 per cent in 1921 but only 9 per cent in 1966.[16] This reflected the limited in-roads women had made at the universities, for the number of places open to women had barely increased since the 1920s. Opportunity for women, then, was extremely limited, and the most desirable professions remained overwhelmingly in the hands of men. In spite of these obvious criticisms, an important barrier had been crossed. Before the war, working women had been frowned upon and accused of taking jobs from men. In the postwar world, women's employment became increasingly encouraged by the government and socially acceptable. People began to believe that working women could help the economy of the nation and provide a valuable supplement to the income of the individual family.

Nor was this phenomenon limited to one class or income group, as had been the case in the past. Married women from all social classes were entering the workforce at this time.[17] There were many reasons for this. The welfare state and the postwar baby boom certainly caused an increased demand for nurses, teachers, secretaries and typists. The consumer boom of the time also resulted in new openings in industry, which, given the continued shortage of male workers, could only be filled by women. Education in particular was in a period of great expansion because of the vast increase in secondary schooling under the Butler Act and because of the baby boom. It was nearly impossible, however, to provide adequate staffing for the schools. To further complicate matters, more women were getting married and at a younger age. The single woman, who had provided the bulk of women workers in the prewar period, was a disappearing species, and it was believed that they would make up no more than 5 per cent of women in the near future. It was also found that, although at the start of the century, only 81 girls in a thousand got married before the age of 21, in the period from 1951–55 this figure rose to 186 and by 1960 it had reached 264.[18] Since the school-leaving age had also risen during this period, this meant that there was expected to be very few single women in the workforce in the future. When added to a continuing and chronic labour shortage in the country, the obvious conclusion to draw from this demographic information was that married women would have to enter the workforce in large numbers or British society would face a crisis of the first order.

The Ministry of Labour estimated that in 1900 only 20 per cent of working women were married compared to 44 per cent in 1951 and 53 per cent in 1963. By 1971 the figure had jumped to 63.9 per cent and showed no sign of stopping.[19] Furthermore, the growth in married women's employment had occurred primarily since the Second World War, for only 10 per cent of married women had worked in 1941. By 1952 this number had more than doubled, reaching 26 per cent, and by 1963 the figure was at 33 per cent. It was clear from this that the role of married women in the economy would not disappear in the years to come but was likely to grow and become more important. There were, however, several problems that resulted from this trend. The first was that most girls were not receiving a sufficient education or training to enable them to take on the better paid or more difficult jobs in the future. These girls survived by working in low paid jobs that demanded little training and then quit working after they got married. After this, they almost inevitably stayed home for five to fifteen years until their children reached school age. This phenomenon was called 'wastage' through marriage and affected almost all women, even those in the professions. At this period it was proving to be a serious economic handicap. The number of students deciding to become teachers was continually increasing, but, since most of these were women, large numbers of them later left in order to get married. It was estimated that in 1962, 19 000 women became teachers but 17 000 also left the profession. The situation was similar in the hospitals. The establishment of the NHS had caused new openings for nurses but large numbers of these were leaving the profession to get married. The result was constant shortages in a critical field.[20] Of course, many of these women returned to the job market after their children started school, but they were at a serious disadvantage. They would have little recent training and since medicine in particular was changing at a rapid pace, they would need to retrain. The need for refresher courses existed in other fields too, and the government would have to see that programmes to do this were established. Even so, this would not solve the tremendous needs in professional and technical jobs. The only way to change this would be to modify the education that girls received from the earliest age. The Ministry of Labour came to the conclusion that the only way to ensure the future of the country was to keep girls in school as long as possible and to make sure that they received a better education in mathematics and science. The Ministry believed that basic ideas about women had to be changed: 'Girls must be discouraged by educational and financial policy, and by public opinion, from settling at the earliest possible age for a job far below their potential capacity.'[21]

Of course, this was only one part of the problem. Girls had to be given a better education and taught to aim higher, but, at the same time, discrimination against them had to be ended. Discrimination was particularly bad against women in universities. At many universities, there were considerably fewer places for women than for men, Oxford and Cambridge being the classic examples. At both these universities, the vast majority of the colleges were open to men only, and women could study at only a handful of colleges especially for their sex. By the nature of things, then, women could have only a fraction of places available at both these universities. The situation remained like this until the late 1970s and early 1980s when public pressure finally forced Oxford and Cambridge to gradually allow women into the men's colleges. Of course, the result of this discrimination against women students was that entry exams demanded a far higher level from women than from men. It is easy to understand the bitterness felt by women who found themselves rejected by a university when men friends with lower exam results got in. The situation at medical schools was particularly bad. Medical schools, in general, were supposed to have a minimum intake of 15 per cent women in order to receive government grants. In reality this was usually the maximum, and, as late as 1966–7, one-fifth of all the medical schools in Britain were found to have an intake below that amount.[22] To make matters worse, the figures for the most prestigious medical schools, those of Oxford and Cambridge and London (with the exception of the Royal Free which had been founded for women only), were even lower than for the rest of the country. This occurred during a period of extreme shortage in doctors – which reached such a point that the

NHS was becoming increasingly dependent on immigrants to fill vacancies. Of course, the medical schools justified their discrimination, as did the universities, on 'wastage' through marriage. However, as the WNAC's parliamentary sub-committee pointed out, there was also a significant proportion of male 'wastage' which no one ever talked about. Many male doctors found it far more profitable to go abroad and establish practices in countries like the United States where they could earn more money.[23]

The political parties were already fully aware of this phenomenon and accepted that better education was necessary for girls and that married women were a permanent part of the job market. When presenting these facts to the general public – and more particularly to their supporters – however, the Conservative Party took care to justify these changes by showing how they would help women in their traditional role as wives and mothers. For example, one pamphlet on the question stressed that: 'By broadening our girls' education and giving them responsibilities as wage earners and citizens with a stake in the country's future we shall make them better mothers also.'[24] The WNAC established a working party to analyse this problem. Although insisting that women with young children should not be working full-time (they did admit that part-time work might be acceptable), the working party did come to some important conclusions:

> It appears that while the basic problem is an acute shortage of labour arising from full employment, the earlier and very high marriage rate and the imminent disappearance of the single woman, there is some variation of outlook in different localities. Taking the country as a whole the solution of the problem is of immense and immediate importance for the future growth and prosperity of the nation whether it be in the Social Services or in the fields of the professions, industry or commerce. A situation has developed which, except in the spheres of Teaching and Nursing, has not been recognised by the general public, yet it has reached such dangerous proportions that it would seem that shock tactics are necessary.[25]

The country obviously needed married women to return to work, and the government was awakening to the fact that they needed to do something to encourage them to do so or face a severe economic crisis.

Furthermore, the character of women workers was changing. Before the war most of them had been young and unmarried. But in

1951 it was estimated that only one-third of employed women were under 25 and that 22 per cent of married women had a job outside the home. This latter figure rose to 30 per cent in 1961.[26] One study done at the time estimated that approximately one-third of wives went to work from necessity but that the rest did so merely to earn extra money.[27] One reason why married women were returning to work was that they were getting married at an earlier age and having children younger too. Since birth control was becoming more effective and more popular, this meant that, when the youngest child entered school, most women still had a long period of life in front of them. Since labour-saving devices were also making housework much easier, the temptation to go back to work and escape the boredom of staying at home, was frequently great. Women, however, still faced formidable obstacles at work. Approximately three million women were employed in industry but virtually all training opportunities that would allow them to advance to higher paid positions were denied to them. The better jobs, then, were almost invariably held by men. Women were also far less likely to join trade unions: only 24 per cent of those employed in industry did so as against 55 per cent of men.[28] It was thus very difficult for women to voice their point of view and have it taken into account. Women continued to be paid three-quarters of men's wages, and there were virtually no apprenticeship schemes for them. Furthermore, the retirement age for women was 60 while for men it was 65. This meant that senior positions, which were usually reached at the end of a career, went almost invariably to men since they were expected to remain on the job for more years. Even more important, the earlier retirement age affected women's pensions, which were already considerably lower than men's because their pay was lower. This could often have serious repercussions for elderly women, especially since they tended to live longer than men.

As a result of this, the question of equal pay did not disappear after the war as many politicians had hoped. It continued to grow in importance and to claim more converts. The non-party Equal Pay Campaign Committee (EPCC) continued its work under the successive leadership of Mavis Tate and Thelma Cazalet-Keir, both former Conservative MPs, and with the support of a number of women from all parties in Parliament. Some members of the WNAC were certainly trying to push the party to take a firmer stand on the issue. Evelyn Emmet argued, in a report for the WNAC parliamentary sub-committee, that:

In view of the experience of the war years, any appeal for the return of large numbers of women to industry at the present time would be greatly assisted by the knowledge that the government had itself given a lead by establishing equal pay within its own services. It is here that we should press for the implementation of the principle as soon as possible.[29]

Emmet reasoned that equal pay was becoming necessary because men and women were more frequently doing the same jobs and because women had been shown to be as productive as men. Women resented being paid less than men, and this acted as an incentive for them to remain at home. They would be more likely to return to work if they were assured of a fair wage, and, since the country desperately needed more workers, this could only be advantageous.

The grassroots membership of the women's section were not always in agreement with this argument, and many of the rank-and-file women in the Conservative Party were against equal pay. In the South-east Area, for example, discussions on the subject had shown that two branches were in favour of equal pay, two unable to come to a conclusion, four against and one had voted in favour of equal pay for single women but not for married women. This contrasted with the Area Women's Advisory Committee where eight members supported it and five were against.[30] The usual argument given against equal pay was that men, in general, had dependants to support while women did not. In some cases, irrational arguments and scare tactics were also used against equal pay. One representative of the Schoolmasters' Association, for example, announced on the BBC's *Woman's Hour* that equal pay would mean that men's wages would be reduced to those of women – an event which was unlikely but which could incite hostility to the concept.[31] When this fact was combined with the economic crisis and the lack of interest of senior male politicians in the party, the WNAC had to move cautiously on the question. Instead of presenting the case for equal pay as one of simple justice, they tried to show how it would work to the advantage of the country and the party. We have seen already how Emmet argued that it would encourage more women to work and thus help ease the financial crisis. Lady Davidson used a different tactic. She emphasized that an announcement in support of equal pay could gain the Conservatives the support of large numbers of professional women – a group that they found difficult to reach: 'The present women members of the Conservative Party may not be strongly in favour of equal pay, but the women *whose support the Party also needs,* industrial, business and professional women, *are* strongly in favour of it.'[32] This was a recurring theme among women in the higher ranks of the party: that the Conservatives were losing touch with professional women and that special efforts should be made to attract their interest and support. Lady Davidson also feared that Cazalet-Keir, who was strongly involved in the movement, would embarrass the party by telling outside organizations that the Conservative Party had no intention of acting on the question.

The issue was given a further immediacy by the formation of a Royal Commission in 1944 under the coalition government to consider the question of equal pay. In November 1946 this Commission published its report. It noted a number of difficulties with instituting equal pay: defining equal work, the fact that men usually had more family obligations than women, and the fear that women would be forced out of employment if equal pay were instituted. The Royal Commission saw no major difficulty, however, in introducing equal pay in the civil service and considered that it would have a positive effect on recruitment. On the other hand, they feared that, if introduced in teaching, it would have the negative effect of driving men from the profession.[33] The Commission could not agree on the question of introducing equal pay in private industry, and most argued that if it were introduced, employers would always prefer men, and women would be driven out of employment. The Commission also emphasized that introducing equal pay would be an enormous financial burden for the country. It was generally believed that, for this reason, it was unwise to introduce equal pay at a moment of economic crisis such as was occurring in postwar Britain. Following this lead, the Attlee government decided that the best thing to do was to ignore the whole question.

Irene Ward, who returned to Parliament in 1950, however, refused to let the matter die and pestered the government continually on the question. Other women also felt that the Conservatives should issue a statement on equal pay. Maxse argued that the Labour Party might try to adopt the issue in order to secure support from women, and since the Conservatives were desperately trying to win women's votes in order to return to power, the argument carried a certain force.[34] Emmet searched for evidence to attack one of the major arguments against equal pay: that men had greater family commitments than women. Her discovery was that the welfare state had ended much of the justification for this line of argument by introducing children's allowances, reducing the cost of education and instituting other benefits for the family.[35] It was being more and more suggested that income tax deductions for dependants rather than higher wages for men was the answer to this problem. The 1950 election caused the question to receive more attention. Continuing their efforts to attract women, more Conservative than Labour candidates had endorsed equal pay during the campaign. Since Labour and the Conservatives had nearly the same number of members, it was obvious that another general election would occur at any time. Given the perception that the women's vote was the key to victory, the two parties began a rivalry to capture it. All three parties included equal pay in their manifestos. In November 1950, Irene Ward proposed an amendment criticizing the absence of equal pay from the King's Speech of that year. She secured large Tory support for this amendment. The Conservative leadership, however, was as wary as that of Labour to committing their party to an immediate enactment of equal pay, even if it were only limited to the civil service. Essentially Churchill and Attlee played the same game on the issue – that of waiting until the economic situation improved. Furthermore, once the Conservatives had returned to power, the WNAC found it difficult to pester the government – at least publicly – on the question because of party loyalty. They did not, for example, participate in a deputation which demanded equal pay for teachers.[36] Some progress, however, was made. An important victory was won in 1955 when the government agreed to introduce equal pay in much of the civil service. Women's salaries were brought up to those of men through seven equal annual instalments. By 1961 large numbers of civil servants and all teachers received equal rates of pay. In 1957, the Women's Annual Conference called on the government to examine the legislation relating to women's employment and to update it.[37]

There the matter rested until the women's liberation movement rebrought feminism into the political discourse and until the Conservatives, having lost to Labour in 1964, felt that the wind was once again blowing in their favour. Realizing the importance of the female vote, their new leader Edward Heath made important efforts to capture it. For example, the Conservatives moved an amendment to the 1968 Prices and Incomes Act which would have exempted pay raises designed to implement equality from the wage freeze. This was rejected by Wilson's government, who did, however, promise to start negotiations with the trade unions to introduce equal pay in the near future. Part of Wilson's motivation undoubtedly came from a Ministry of Labour report – which the government apparently tried to suppress – which showed that most of Britain's working women were grotesquely underpaid: one-half, seemingly, were paid under five shillings an hour. The Ministry of Health was particularly criticized in the report.[38] By this time the Conservative Party had given a full commitment to equal pay, and Wilson decided to introduce it in 1970 just before another election was due. Barbara Castle, Secretary of State for Employment and Productivity, had the honour of introducing the bill, and it easily passed both houses. The debate took place against a background in which both parties bent over backwards to try to show that they had done more for equal pay than the other side.

This did not mean, of course, that the party's attitude towards women's employment had undergone a revolution. Like most other people at the period, Conservatives viewed women's employment with ambivalence. The Conservative Party reflected the views of society at the time in that, while women's work was accepted, domesticity was still glorified. Their brochure 'A Woman's Place' has this to say about women in the workforce:

> And if women form an essential part of our manpower resources, they also 'constitute a *distinctive* manpower resource because the structure and the substance of the lives of most women are fundamentally determined by their functions as wives, mothers and home makers'. Widespread recognition of this marks the change in attitude towards women and work from the older egalitarian feminism. Most girls expect to marry – and most do – so that their attitude to their work is quite different from that of a man. Few think of a lifelong 'career'; they see themselves working until they have children, or have enough money to set up home. When as married women they come back to work, they do so not as part of a planned pattern but in response to circumstances.

In and of itself, all of this was quite true. Most young women thought in terms of getting married, having children, and staying at home, rather than of having a career. In most cases, when married women returned to the workforce they did so not because they had planned on doing it. They came back either because they had to do so, or because they wanted extras, or because they were bored at home. This in turn contributed to the precarity of women's employment and was frequently used to justify their exploitation. The pamphlet has this to say about the attitude of employers and the lack of promotion for women:

The employment of women has, therefore, disadvantages for employers: the cost of training is relatively higher because the likelihood of a girl staying on when trained is so much less; there is a high rate of absenteeism, especially among married women, usually associated with illness and difficulties in the family, and a high turnover. All this has to be borne in mind when considering the sort of work women do, the pay they receive for it and their chances of getting the better paid and more responsible positions.

The vicious circle we have already seen in women's education was repeated in women's employment: women had low career expectations and so settled for lesser positions. Employers, in turn, used these low expectations to justify keeping women out of the better jobs. The pamphlet sees little hope for large numbers of women making it to senior positions because of the years spent at home looking after children. It insists that few women can have the top jobs, but states that it is still vital to have these few. However, the pamphlet is quite clear that these women were not there to challenge men. 'A Woman's Place' then can hardly be considered as a revolutionary document, for it clearly accepts the status quo. It is thus in every sense of the word, a conservative publication.

Undoubtedly, one of the effects of married women working, and of full employment in general, was a rising prosperity in the country – a prosperity that only began to reveal itself in the mid-1950s after the Conservatives had returned to power. If women had voted earlier for the Conservatives because they wanted the end of austerity, they now continued to vote for the Conservatives because they felt this was the best way of keeping the gains they had made. A working party established to study the role of women in the Conservative Party found that, in 1959, most women who voted Conservative had done so because they felt it had brought them prosperity. The report argued that: 'Intuitively they [women] felt they could secure what was best for their families by voting Conservative. Best, in these terms, meant good jobs for their husbands, good schools for their children, shiny domestic appliances for their household use, if possible a family car; in fact generally "keeping up with the Jones".'[39] This was, of course, the period of the 'affluent society' when Macmillan was quoted as saying, 'You never had it so good' and when materialism was the order of the day. Women appear to have been as much – if not more – affected by this materialism as men. After the war and the austerity of the Labour government, the wide variety of choice that was becoming available to them – as well as the restfulness of not having to queue for hours to buy a small piece of meat – must have seemed like paradise to them.

Of course the situation for the Conservatives began to degenerate in the early 1960s as problems developed. First, there were a number of scandals in the government, of which the most important was undeniably the Profumo affair. The economy also worsened, and Macmillan, trying to give an image of activity, fired a large number of his ministers in July 1962. He certainly did not achieve what he wanted, for the severity of the purge worked against Macmillan's image, who became known as 'Mac the Knife' in the popular press. The Conservatives were also hurt by General de Gaulle's veto of British membership in the European Common Market. This had been Macmillan's major initiative to improve Britain's economic performance, and he had planned to base the next election campaign on the benefits of membership. With de Gaulle's veto, Macmillan lost much of his credibility as well as his only major issue for the election. Finally, Macmillan's sudden resignation in 1963, and the circus that ensued as various Conservative leaders jockeyed to replace him further hurt the party. The 1964 campaign, then, was virtually lost even before it began. Added to this, the new Tory leader, Sir Alec Douglas-Home, was not at all telegenic and came across as an out of touch aristocrat. It is not surprising, therefore, to discover that the Conservatives lost the election, although by a fairly small margin. The gender gap, however, continued. A Conservative poll showed that Douglas-Home had a 9 per cent lead in popularity among women voters, while Harold Wilson enjoyed an 18 per cent lead among male voters.[40] There were clear signs, however, at this time that the gender gap was on the decline. One study showed that, in the working class at least, by the 1960s a correlation existed between age and sex: the older the woman the more likely she was to vote Conservative. There was no noticeable difference in voting habits between men and women in the 23–34 age group – a fact which could lead to the conclusion that women were becoming less Conservative.[41]

After the loss of 1964, Douglas-Home was replaced by Edward Heath, who had risen from a lower class background. He immediately embarked on a programme of modernization of the party and paid particular attention to the needs of women. He set up the Cripps Committee in order to investigate legal disadvantages faced by women and to propose legislation for remedying them.[42] In 1968 the

Conservative Research Department undertook a study of women voters and of issues of particular interest to them. The results of this study showed that social attitudes were continuing to change and that women's role in the community and the economy remained in full flux. The study showed, for example, that two-thirds of both men and women believed that women with small children should stay at home and take care of them. However, only 50 per cent of women under age 34 held this view – a clear sign that further change would occur. Furthermore, half of both men and women felt that married women with children were too tied to the home, and over 40 per cent felt that women needed to be more than just housewives or mothers in order to lead a happy life. Also, most people were in favour of establishing government programmes to assist women with small children who were trained as nurses or teachers to return to work. Only 31 per cent of men and 25 per cent of women felt that it was not a good thing for men and women to compete at work. Attitudes were also evolving towards accepting that housewives deserved an equal share in the couple's property, although only 40 per cent supported equal ownership in all cases. The study also showed that most people, both male and female, wanted to see more women MPs and more women in other important positions. Still, it was notable that one-third to one-quarter of men remained hostile to such suggestions. Furthermore, the general public still viewed acceptable government positions for women in traditional terms. Most people felt that the best ministries for women to hold office in were Pensions, Social Security, Health and Education. Attitudes were changing but they had not yet been completely transformed: people still saw women in terms of their domestic and family interests. Finally, the study showed that the great majority of both men and women were in favour of equal pay – a fact which obviously contributed to both parties supporting it at this time.[43]

The study also revealed that, in spite of repeated proof that more women than men voted Conservative, most people did not see either party as particularly sympathetic to women:

> There is strong reluctance to think that any political party is sympathetic towards women and their problems. Amongst women themselves there appears to be a very slight tendency to think that the Conservatives may be more sympathetic, but the relative popularity at this moment in time (with all the polls showing substantial Tory leads) is not reflected in the answers. In other

words, increasing support for the Conservative Party amongst women is not based on any feeling of mutual sympathy.[44]

Even in 1968, when women's liberation had become an important movement once again, most people based their voting decisions on other criteria – most notably on the economic situation.

This discovery normally would not have encouraged the party to take a more progressive point of view on women's issues. However, Edward Heath was personally sympathetic, and the decline in the gender gap and the electoral misfortunes of the Conservatives at this time meant that the party was willing to make unusual efforts to win voter support. Many people viewed the Conservative Party as being out of touch with the times, and the leadership was determined to change this. They felt that improving the party's image with regards to women would go a long way towards doing this:

Our attitude to women is also relevant to our 'out of date' image. Nowhere is the difference in attitudes between the generations more marked than in attitudes towards sex. This difference is due, amongst other things, to some fairly fundamental changes that have taken place in the last twenty years in the social context and in the structure of the population. A man in his forties grew up when, as since prehistoric times, more women than men were reaching marriageable age; a man in his twenties when more men than women. In the formative years of the older generation the norm was still for the women's sphere to be sharply divided from the man's; on marriage the husband would generally be the only bread-winner and the wife would be occupied looking after him, the children and the household, helping him in his work and career but – except in certain industrial areas – not normally contributing independently to the family's earnings. Today 45 per cent of married women work; the younger generation of women – helped no doubt by family planning and the mechanisation of housework – regard it as quite normal to have a separate and independent job or career and sometimes are under some financial pressure to do so.[45]

In 1969, Geoffrey Howe and Beryl Cooper were commissioned to investigate the situation of women and write a series of recommendations. Their report basically accepted many of the observations made in earlier studies on the situation of women in the workforce. Among other things, they emphasized that more part-time work was necessary in order to accommodate women with young families and that more retraining schemes should be developed to allow married women to acquire or refresh their skills and professions. Furthermore, the deficiencies in the education of girls were recognized, and it was emphasized that equal opportunity should be introduced at every level of education. Howe and Cooper also came out in favour of ending restrictions on the employment of women, and particularly of married women and announced their support for equal pay. Finally, they insisted that greater effort had to be made to ensure that women reached prominent positions in the Conservative Party.[46] Their report was one of several made by the party on the women's question at this time. When the Conservatives returned to power from 1970 to 1974, many of these recommendations were put into effect, and a significant body of legislation with regard to women was modernized.[47] This phenomenon, however, was not limited to the Conservative Party, for Labour also had realized what way public opinion was blowing and also introduced important legislation of its own. As in the earlier period, there was little difference in the two parties' attitude towards women.

The postwar period had been one of paradox in relation to women's role: domesticity was extolled by psychologists and women's magazines and society in general while, at the same time, the number of women in employment did not stop increasing and the fact of their being employed became more socially acceptable. This trend continued after the Conservatives returned to power. The rebirth of the feminist movement in the late 1960s did not suddenly spring from nowhere but was rather a normal reaction to the tension engendered by this paradox and to the changes taking place in society. It is clear that it had a great deal to do with the demographic trends which were opening up the universities and the professions to women. By 1968 a new generation of women were reaching adulthood, and they, unlike their mothers, had grown up in a period of prosperity and increasing opportunities for women. Entering the workforce with high ambitions, they were rudely returned to earth by the strong discrimination against women. It is easy to imagine the response of these highly educated, middle-class women who, after leaving university, discovered a working world in which they probably made two-thirds of a man's salary, in which their opportunities for promotion were small, and in which they were expected to give up their jobs upon marriage. Such disappointment was almost certain to call forth protest. Changing attitudes in society meant that politicians felt that it would be beneficial to act upon their demands – at least to some extent. This was true of politicians in both major parties, and it may even be argued that the Conservatives had a better record during this period than the Labour Party.

7 Women in the Conservative Party Organization, 1945–75

The 1945 election defeat was one of the worst in the Conservative Party's history, and, for this very reason it galvanized the party to undertake needed reforms. Churchill named Lord Woolton, the popular Minister of Food during the war, to the position of Party Chairman: he began a major reassessment of the party and undertook to modernize it. Under his leadership constituency branches, which, in some cases, had practically ceased to exist during the war, were rejuvenated, and women's membership, in particular, started to grow. The old structure of separate men's and women's branches was abolished. Joint branches for both women and men were established as the basis of the party organization but separate women's sections continued to exist. These women's sections were co-ordinated by women's advisory committees whose task was to take care of the special interests of women within the party. The hope was to integrate the women more fully into the mainstream organization of the party in order to avoid the competition and overlapping that had existed between the separate branches, while allowing them to retain an important degree of autonomy. By the 1960s these women's sections were simply being called constituency women's advisory committees and membership in them was optional.

Of course, the establishment of joint branches did not necessarily improve the position of women, although it did certainly give them more room for advancement in the National Union. In many cases it may actually have hurt the women's organization. As had been feared when the party was first opened to women after the First World War, the men very often simply ignored the women – or, worse still, expected them to do all the menial work with few of the rewards. Not infrequently, men refused to allow women to enter their traditionally masculine clubs, and in some cases women's activities and committees had quite simply been eliminated. As late as 1967 it was observed that:

It must be recognized, however, that the women of the Party feel very strongly that although the official attitude of the Party as a whole is one of benevolence and goodwill, when it comes to the realities of power and patronage and the selection of candidates, reasons will usually be found for excluding rather than including women. In some Areas and constituencies the Chairmen and Agents tend to form a closed shop and there is neither consultation nor the provision of information to the woman chairman and her committee.[1]

The WNAC observed that in many constituencies, particularly rural ones, regular women's meetings had ceased and that, as a result, the party organization had declined in these areas, causing the Conservatives to lose votes. The WNAC felt that women needed to be given more encouragement and called the attention of the party chairman and the agents to the importance of women's groups.[2] Marjorie Maxse, now party vice-chairman and forthright as usual, insisted that they should 'not let the existence of joint organization be the cause of a falling-off on the women's side, for a falling-off had undoubtedly taken place'.[3] She stressed that women's afternoon meetings should be retained as they had proved to be of value. Statements from Central Office, however, were not always followed in the constituencies.

Conflict between the women's sections and the men's, then, did not disappear with the creation of an integrated organization, and, in some ways, perhaps, they worsened. The WNAC was concerned by the small numbers of men doing party work in the local government elections. Throughout the country the bulk of the work, whether committee room, canvassing or simply passing out literature, was done by women. The WNAC felt that the Area Chairmen, who were almost always men, should do more to encourage male Conservatives to get out and work in the local government elections.[4] Evidence was found that in the North-West Area, the women's sections still considered themselves to be quite separate from the constituency association. In other areas, several instances were found of women's sections resenting the, as they termed it, 'interference' of the agent, even if he or she were only trying to make the group more effective.[5] It was found that, in many cases, the main function of the woman's section was to provide social activity – which essentially meant food and drink – for the other sections of the party organization. Although the women were, in general, quite happy to do this, they frequently issued the complaint that 'Women do all the work'. The working party criticized this situation and insisted that it was harmful for the party: 'When used by the women themselves, it bred complacency and prejudice; when used by men or Y.C.s [Young Conservatives], it implied the worst kind of flattery bestowed with a lively sense of securing favours to come in the shape of tea and sandwiches, coffee and even hot dogs!'[6] The working party came to the conclusion that the women's sections needed to be more politically oriented and that their social roles should be given less prominence. As the report emphasized: 'Any tendency to regard them as "hewers of bread and drawers of tea" should be condemned.' The working party also felt that women organizers should be appointed in marginal seats so that the crucial women's vote would receive more attention. As late as 1973, the WNAC found repeated complaints among women in the constituency associations that they had neither been consulted about or informed of the Chelmer Committee's investigation into the party organization. It was found that:

There has been strong criticism that many constituency women chairmen were neither offered the report nor consulted by constituency chairmen and agents. In most cases they had to ask if they could borrow a copy of the report and some were quite unaware of its existence. Considering the size of the women membership in constituencies we consider this to be most unsatisfactory.[7]

In spite of their major contribution to the party organization, women were still taken for granted by the constituency associations and often left out of major developments.

One important reform instituted by Lord Woolton was to re-evaluate totally the roles of organizers and agents. Under the new system, both men and women started their careers as organizers and worked their way up to being agents. This new arrangement led to the integration of the organizers in the National Society of Conservative and Unionist Agents which now added 'and Organizers' to its title. However, an important distinction remained, for agents had full membership in the society while organizers were only associate members. Furthermore, the sex differentiation did not disappear overnight, for women were still more likely to be organizers while most agents were men. Women also could still meet with considerable hostility when they tried to exercise the function of agent. One woman agent, Nancy Matthews, described her first meeting as agent for the hopeless constituency of Barnsley, with the candidate, Gordon Spencer: 'Refusing to shake his new agent's hand, Spencer warned her at their first meeting; "I must tell you that I disapprove of women as executives in politics. If I had been around when they appointed you, I would have objected.'" Later, when Spencer came last, he told Matthews on the platform: 'It's all your fault. I'd have done better without you.'[8] The situation of women organizers and agents, therefore, clearly remained unsatisfactory, but equally obviously it was improving. There were fewer and fewer rules blocking women from promotion although prejudice continued and had a highly negative effect in many cases.

At the national level, a woman vice-chairman continued to exist at Central Office with a large number of duties, which included: liaison with the women's organization at all levels throughout the country; appointments of JPs; organization of Royal Garden Parties; responsibilities with regard to the women's conference and to the organization of certain receptions during it; among other things.[9] The Central Women's Advisory Committee continued to function, although, as we have seen, it changed its name to the Women's National Advisory Committee (WNAC) during this period. The WNAC consisted of the chairmen of the Area Women's Advisory Committees and women members of the National Executive Committee. It had three subcommittees. First, there was the General Purposes Committee which was responsible for the everyday business of the committee. Second, there was the Outside Organizations Sub-Committee which was in contact with every national women's organization in the country. Finally, there was the Parliamentary Sub-Committee which consisted of the chairman of the WNAC, a specific number of members chosen by the WNAC and the National Union and all women members of both Houses of Parliament.[10]

The 1945 election defeat had so devastated the Conservatives and the party was so desperate that they were willing to put into effect almost any reasonable suggestion. In 1949, for example, ideas for women's meetings were drawn up by the WNAC and sent out to the constituency associations. One suggestion was to organize a quiz: the chairman would divide the participants into two groups and have each group quiz the other. Lest this should become too serious and high-powered, the WNAC felt it necessary to warn members that: 'As well as having serious political questions, it has been found of value to ask some rather more frivolous ones, in order to lighten the afternoon.'[11] Another suggestion was to organize fancy dress parties for small children in order to attract the mothers. Most of the activity would be social but a little propaganda play or 'very short speech' could be given in order to bring home the political point in an entertaining or at least not too tiresome way. The WNAC had found that children's activities were often extremely valuable and noted that: 'In certain places, the Conservative organization has given a children's party to the whole village, including Socialists. These have resulted in an increase in membership and the conversion of certain Socialists and floating voters.' Other recommended activities included: jumble sales, cookery demonstrations, dress shows, box suppers, and plant meetings.

In all of these suggestions, we see that the political dimension, while obviously important, was hidden behind a social veneer. These activities were fully in keeping with the history of local Conservative associations and showed that the party, in this domain at least, had not really changed much since the days of the Primrose League. The premium was placed on entertainment with the presentation of a relatively painless political message. The East Fulham constituency was particularly successful with its 'Young Mothers' meetings. Here we see once again the remarkable ability of the Conservatives to fulfil a social need within the community:

> Experience in East Fulham has shown that the majority of young married women have had very little political experience or education and, in general, have accepted the political outlook of their husbands. As it was difficult for young married women with children to attend political meetings or even social functions organised by the Conservative Party, the East Fulham Women's Branch formed a Young Mothers Circle in the late autumn of 1950 which served the double purpose of allowing young mothers, who otherwise were confined to the house, to have an afternoon out, and at the same time gave Conservative workers an opportunity of propagating Conservative policy.[12]

The Conservative Party owed its success among women to a large extent because it was, on the local level at least, primarily a social organization. Women could feel at home here in a way they could not in the far more masculine Labour Party associations. This had, of course, been the situation all along.

One important suggestion for reorganizing the party that Central Office viewed with approval was to form housewives committees in each constituency association in order to organize and give voice to criticisms against the Labour government's policy of austerity. There was, however, one major problem with this idea, for there already existed a non-party group known as the Housewives' League, and there was some fear that the Conservative housewives committees would be confused with this organization. The Housewives' League had been formed after the war to protest the continuation of rationing and food shortages, and, at first at least, it appeared to strike a response among British women. The end of the war had led many people to hope for the end of its hardships as well. What followed, however, as we have seen, was the 'age of austerity', and the British Housewives' League had arisen almost spontaneously because of dissatisfaction with rationing. Its leading figure was Dorothy Crisp who hoped to use it as a vehicle to get herself into Parliament. The British Housewives' League, however, peaked quickly for it soon established a reputation for reactionary extremism. Their meetings not infrequently degenerated into scuffles between their supporters and communist hecklers – all of which attracted a great deal of negative publicity for the League and ensured membership would fall off promptly.

The League was officially non-party, but because of its extreme right-wing mentality many left-wing groups believed it to be a front for the Conservative Party. In reality it was not, for the Conservative Party leadership repeatedly refused to have anything to do with it. In fact, it was deeply resented by the official party's women's organization and most particularly by the powerful Marjorie Maxse. Maxse, in fact, warned Conservative women from joining the League, which she felt was organized for 'personal motives'. She explained to the wife of one Conservative candidate that the party's objective in that constituency was to elect her husband. Therefore, Maxse reasoned: 'Any association which tends to drain membership and funds from the local association is not furthering the interests of the party in any particular district.'[13] From Maxse's point of view, and from that of most other leading Conservatives, the British Housewives' League had little going for it: it drew members and funds away from the regular party organization which they were so desperately trying to rebuild and it attracted unwanted controversy. It also drew attention to extreme right-wing opinions from which mainstream Conservatism wanted to dissociate itself. The League, according to Maxse's reasoning, worked against the long-term interests of the party and therefore was to be avoided.

Given what we have just learned, it is not surprising to discover that, after its first initial success, the British Housewives' League began a steady decline. By mid-1947 it was already attracting much smaller numbers to its rallies and meetings. By late 1947 it was clear that the organization was beginning to suffer from serious financial problems and that it could not long continue without a major infusion of money. This led its moving spirit, Dorothy Crisp, to apply to Central Office for funding. The Party reacted by refusing to have anything to do with her. When she telephoned in December to ask for an interview with Woolton, she was told that he was too busy to see her.[14] When she then wrote to ask for assistance, Woolton was unequivocal in his refusal to give any money to the League. He insisted that all money raised by the party had to go to the party and that he could not ask anyone to contribute to an outside organization.[15] If Woolton himself may have had some regrets about the demise of the Housewives' League, Maxse and other figures at Central Office ensured that he should not show them. Maxse was unequivocal in her belief that the League should be allowed to die as quickly as possible. Crisp, realizing that without Conservative support the organization could not survive, decided to extricate herself from it as gracefully as she could. In February 1948 she resigned the chairmanship of the League on the grounds that she was expecting her second child and that she had to accompany her husband to the Far East. After her departure the organization simply fell to pieces. It continued to exist for another year or so, but its functions attracted only a small number of people. One Conservative report insisted that a major fundraising activity had attracted only around 150 persons, and soon after the League effectively ceased to exist.[16]

Although the party was hostile to the Housewives' League, this does not mean that they were hostile to all non-party organizations. Its objections to the League did not apply to other groups. In fact, as part of the rejuvenation of the party, Conservative women were actually encouraged to join outside organizations and to use every opportunity to address them. It was emphasized that they were not to talk in direct political terms but with subtlety to make the Conservative viewpoint apparent.[17] It was also suggested that Conservative women should join old people's clubs, since studies showed that one-sixth of the population would be elderly by 1961. Conservatives had to show that they were interested in them and in their problems in order to win their votes.[18] Other recommended areas for volunteer work were: hospitals, parents-teachers associations and societies that dealt with housing and children's problems. Once again, we see that nineteenth-century link between political activism and philanthropy. Conservative women were even told to engage people in conversation in trains and to leave literature in hotels. Any method was acceptable if it was not illegal and if it presented the Conservative viewpoint to voters.

One problem, however, continued and had to be cured: that of Conservative volunteers who were not sufficiently prepared to answer questions. One of the major necessities facing branches was to provide adequate information to their members so that they would be able to present the Conservative case in an intelligent fashion. One of the more interesting attempts to do this was the decision in 1948 to prepare a 'Women's Charter' which was intended to modernize the Conservative position on women – particularly with reference to social questions – in the way that the 'Industrial Charter' had updated economic policy. Its basic audience, however, was not to be the general public but party activists. It was designed to serve 'as ammunition for canvassers and also a guide-book for our own supporters'.[19] Under Rab Butler's initiative, a committee was established to write the charter under the chairmanship of Malcolm McCorquodale of the shadow cabinet. Its vice-chairman was Evelyn Emmet and its members included Lady Tweedsmuir, MP and Marjorie Maxse. Its terms of reference were 'to undertake an investigation into legal, economic and social conditions affecting women in the home, in industry, and in government service, and to make a report'.[20] Two sub-committees were formed to deal with the legal and industrial position of women while the full committee considered the economic position. The party's 1948 annual conference tabled a resolution expressing warm support to the 'Women's Charter' committee, but it was – in what is not a very common occurrence at Conservative Party annual conferences – defeated. Many women at the conference, in fact, had shown themselves to be against the charter for a number of reasons. They argued that the charter itself was not a good idea and could simply become a 'vote-catching stunt'; that it was not a good thing to consider women's problems separately from everything else; and that, therefore, it would be much better to pronounce on these problems in general policy statements.[21] The conference defeat did not destroy the committee, but it did change the name of its document. In March 1949 the 'charter' was published under the name of *A True Balance* and presented to the women's annual conference of that year, where it was enthusiastically approved. The document attacked discrimination against women and insisted that 'women should play an equal part with men as citizens'. The most controversial element of *A True Balance* was undoubtedly its call for the introduction of equal pay for men and women in at least some parts of the economy. It also listed important examples of legal discrimination against women and called for their reform. The report received the unanimous support of the

WNAC and sold around 250 000 copies in the nation.[22] Little, though, was done in the immediate future, and the report was not presented to the party's annual conference. Leading Conservative women, however, refused to let the report die and continued to lobby the party's front bench about its recommendations, although they would not receive much satisfaction until Edward Heath's premiership.

In any event, all of this activity undoubtedly rejuvenated the party and particularly the women's part of it. Total party membership for England and Wales had declined to 911 600 during the war, but it made a rapid recovery afterwards. In 1948 party membership was estimated at 2 249 031 in England and Wales, and women made up slightly more than 50 per cent of that total.[23] Of course, many of these women joined the party more for social reasons than for political ones. Their interest in and understanding of politics thus were often limited. All evidence points to the fact that these women had virtually no interest in feminism and that they were generally, on social questions at least, to the right of the party leadership. An analysis of available documents also shows that there was a noticeable difference between the rank-and-file Conservative women and their leaders. The WNAC appears to have taken a more progressive view on most questions and to have been far more interested in feminist objectives. Many of their members strongly supported equal pay, and the committee as a whole worked to increase the number of women MPs.

During this period, there were clear signs too that the gap between the grassroots members and their leadership was growing, and this applied to men as well as women. The women's conference of 1956 saw an emergency motion against the Conservative government's decision to end capital punishment. The resolution, although seconded by Florence Horsbrugh, was pushed through by overwhelming demand from the rank-and-file. The women made quite a spectacle of themselves at the conference through their vociferous opposition to ending hanging and received a great deal of press coverage. The whole episode gave the women's movement a reputation for reactionary extremism.[24] A 1964 resolution showed how behind the times their attitude on women's role could be. A majority of the women's conference carried a resolution which, while recognizing the need for more teachers and nurses, regretted the opening of crèches to allow young mothers to return to work. Young mothers, it was felt, needed 'to do the most important job in life – to bring up and care for their babies in their most formative years'.[25] Of course, the leadership also was capable of resistance to change, as when they opposed raising the school leaving age, insisting that: 'Delinquency begins by keeping unwilling children too long at school.' The women went on to argue that: 'They just sit and do nothing and get used to being idle.'[26] The danger, of course, was that the Conservative Party at its base would become totally out of touch with the political trends of the day and with the average voter. Even the look of Conservative women, as shown through the women's sections, seemed totally out of contact with the times. As Gerald O'Brien of Central Office wrote to his chairman in 1967:

> There is, however, one major impediment to the use of the Women's Conference as a medium for projecting the Party image and that is the women themselves. At the Festival Hall this year they once again provided a striking and splendid display of summer fashions. They could, in fact, have been transferred en masse to the enclosure at Ascot and no one could have said that they were not suitably dressed for the occasion... [In a report] it was said that the average man in the street does not identify himself (or herself) with those holding office in constituency associations. If the female of the species as seen at the Women's Conference was taken as an example of our constituency representatives it is not difficult to understand why.[27]

Conservative women, then, were becoming an embarrassment to the party. The Conservative Party was trying to project a modern, popular image of a party no longer defined by its upper-class membership. Heath and Thatcher both reflected this trend, being from lower class origins, and certainly Thatcher had little to do with the women's organization and showed little sympathy for them.

Given all this, it should not, therefore, be surprising to learn that, in spite of the immediate postwar rejuvenation, the Conservative Party increasingly found it difficult to recruit younger women. The women's leadership was decidedly not happy with this situation. In 1957 a working party was set up under the leadership of Barbara Brooke, vice-chairman of the party, to investigate the situation of the women's organization and to make recommendations to strengthen it. The WNAC desperately wanted to renew the organization and add new women to it but found this extremely difficult for two main reasons. First, the older members resented younger women being brought in and refused to make way for them. A meeting of the leaders of Area Women's Advisory Committees observed that, while efforts were being made, they were insufficient and not enough was being done to attract new members: 'The temptation obviously exists even for strong and successful branches to try new forms of meetings with existing members rather than to attempt to double the achievement of new methods and meetings for new potential members.'[28] The older women were causing problems because they were too inflexible and found it difficult both to change their methods or to give up their leadership positions in favour of a younger generation.[29] If it was not always easy to find young women ready to take leadership responsibilities in the organization, it was sometimes even more difficult to get older women to resign their positions and allow younger ones to take over.

The second reason was that younger women did not find the Conservative Party organization very attractive in and of itself, and, for the most part, did not wish to join it.[30] In a period in which women's role in society was being constantly changed and re-evaluated, the Conservative Party women's sections seemed to many people to be increasingly out of touch with reality. A poll taken by the WNAC in 1960 showed that politics was still not the primary interest of most Conservative women. It discovered, for example, that their favourite subjects of conversation were (in order): children, homes, and standards of living. The preferred magazines were *Good Housekeeping* and *Vogue*. *The Economist* ranked third from the bottom and was read by only 7 per cent of the women. Favourite activities had hardly changed from the nineteenth century. The preferred type of meeting continued to be the afternoon tea party with a speaker. Other popular functions included: coffee, lunch or dinner meetings. In some areas wine and cheese receptions or cocktail parties were also held. Canvassing was the major political activity undertaken by women – as it had been in the Primrose League's heyday. Activities which gave a more public role to women, like public meetings, interview sessions and audience participation meetings were, generally, not well viewed.[31] Surprisingly enough, one of the most important findings of the working party was that the new generation of women who were then rising to important positions in the party, lacked the political experience of their elders. The problem facing the party, then, was to attract young women and educate them politically so as to provide new and more modern leaders. At the same time, elderly women who found themselves unable to adapt to the modern world had to be gently pushed aside.

The working party decided that modernization of the women's sections should take place in three phases. In the first phase, a series of conferences were organized by Area committees in England and Wales on the theme of leadership, and at a later period conferences and meetings were organized at constituency level on the same theme. The working party found many serious problems with the local associations and, in particular discovered that many members knew very little about the party organization:

> There was evidence that many of the women attending had a very limited idea or no idea at all of the scope and duty of branch committees. It was clear that this type of ignorance was by no means exclusive to women. It appeared to emerge from the poverty of standards apparently accepted as normal in the working of many joint branches. This situation gives further emphasis to the need for constant endeavour throughout the Party to find good leaders and to guide, to inform and to distinguish them by every possible means at every level within constituency associations and particularly within the branches.[32]

The leadership sessions had, apparently, convinced some elderly officers to retire and allow younger and more dynamic women to take over. Some new recruits were also added to the party membership, although on a relatively small scale, and some areas in which women's work in the party could be extended were also put in place. The gains were moderate from these leadership conferences, but they were still felt to be important. Barbara Brooke believed that, at the very least, the conferences had shown how much work remained to be done in the women's sections, since they had served to illustrate the poor standards – and even absence – of Women's Advisory Committees in constituencies.

The results of phase 1 showed the importance of leadership from the centre. The working party came to the conclusion that the local Conservative organizations would only keep pace with the great social and economic changes of the time if they were under constant pressure to do so from London.[33] Pressure was kept up through a second phase of meetings and conferences. Phase 2 had two parts: first, 'Operation Handshake' to recruit new women to the organization and make them feel welcome, and another series of conferences, this time on the theme of 'Change and Challenge'. A booklet was produced for the occasion, called 'A Woman's Place' which provided information on the changes that were occurring in society and their effect on women and their role. This led the working party to plan phase 3 which was on the theme of 'Progress and Responsibility' and took place in 1962. These conferences were by no means unsuccessful, and the idea of a uniting theme to be studied at one specific time by associations throughout the country reappeared periodically. In 1968, for example, the theme of 'the family in the community' was chosen and was discussed by women's organizations throughout the country. The WNAC briefed the chairmen and secretaries of the Area Women's Advisory Committees and provided them with other necessary information so that they could assist the constituency associations in this task.[34]

These modernization efforts, however, did not solve the crisis in recruitment, particularly among younger women. In 1963 the New Groups were introduced by Joan Varley and aimed at the 25–40 age group, but their success was unequal.[35] New schemes were developed during the late 1960s and early 1970s. A meeting held between leading women in 1972 came to the conclusion that the women's organization in the constituencies had become too 'inward looking' and concerned with only a small number of 'dedicated supporters'. The danger of this was clear: 'There was far too little contact with women outside the traditional Conservative circles which were becoming increasingly unrepresentative of the electorate as a whole.'[36] The conclusions they came to did not differ significantly from what had already been noted after the war. First, there was a definite need to attract younger women and to establish communication between the local party association and other members of the community – notably through volunteer work. More visits to the constituencies by the party leadership were also necessary, although with a precise purpose such as persuading women's sections to seek new members or to get into closer touch with charitable organizations.

Joan Varley of the WNAC felt that younger women's branches should be formed in marginal seats in order to secure needed support. The problem was that she wanted such groups to be started by women and, at that time, very few women organizers were left. Varley felt that the party should make an effort to train new women organizers – perhaps married women working part-time – and then proceed to found younger women's branches.[37] In 1971, another attempt to attract younger women was made by Sara Morrison, party vice-chairman. She decided to hold a conference for younger women in early 1972 and to make it significantly different from other party conferences. As she explained in her letter to Geoffrey Howe and other young ministers (perhaps significantly, Margaret Thatcher did not receive this letter):

Success is dependent on breaking away from the traditional Women's Conference format into a more informal participatory type of gathering more suited to the younger element, including husbands, if they so wish. I need not add that we felt that it is immensely important in Party political terms to capture the attention and enlist the goodwill and energy of just such younger women as we hope will attend this kind of day; a day angled specifically towards their interests and with particular emphasis on giving them opportunities to air their views. None of the existing, more institutional Party Conferences are achieving this objective and after much consideration this seems a suitable way to attempt it.[38]

The result was a great success for Morrison. The informality appeared to work and it attracted a large number of younger women.[39]

The grassroots of the party, and particularly the women, went against the party image that the leadership wished to give, and obviously there were fears that this could work against the party in the ballot box. It was for this reason that the leadership tried so hard to attract younger women and people from other groups into the party. As a confidential report on women's rights explained:

There is no doubt that this Party contains members, some in exalted positions, whose attitude on 'Women's legislation' is unfavourable. And some staunchly Conservative women may be out of sympathy with reforms which favour, for example, the married earning woman. But it is important to remember that the women whose support we most need to win are precisely those who would benefit most from a policy of educational, legal and financial reform.[40]

The report warned against reflecting in party propaganda the anti-feminine bias of the civil service, which still conceived women as dependants – even though fewer and fewer women thought of themselves in this way. The report came to the conclusion that it would not be a bad thing for the government to introduce a sex discrimination bill and to publicize their sympathy with women's rights through a speech campaign.

Part of the reason why the Conservative women leadership was so desperate to reinvigorate the women's sections was that the Labour Party was making a major and sustained effort to attract women both into their party and into the trade unions. The results of the 1950 and 1951 elections, as we have seen, had shown a large gender gap, and it was clear that the Conservatives had won the 1951 election primarily because of the women's vote. After their defeat, Labour decided that they would have to reduce the gender gap if they wanted to return to office and find some way of attracting women voters. They set up a National Women's Advisory Committee similar to the one that already existed in the Conservative Party and they appointed a woman as Assistant National Agent. Labour also had twice the number of women MPs as the Conservatives. Trade unions also were trying to appear less masculine. In February 1952, a special issue of the *Transport and General Workers Union Record* had been devoted to women's questions and they had even managed to get Eleanor Roosevelt to contribute an article that called for all women to join trade unions. Conservative women leaders repeatedly lamented the fact that the Labour Party seemed to make more efforts to give women a visible position in their party. Labour frequently sent women to represent them at international conferences while the Conservative Party rarely did so – a fact which obviously greatly annoyed the WNAC.[41] The WNAC felt that Labour, by giving a more visible role to women, might steal the weaker women supporters of the Conservative Party.

One important decision made by the WNAC during this period was to constitute a parliamentary sub-committee. This came about because the WNAC felt that they were not in close enough contact with the parliamentary party. Maxse justified such a decision in the following terms:

> She felt that the women in the Conservative Party were lagging behind the Socialists and Liberals in recommendations put forward on matters of social service and of interest to women. They discussed bills etc., but the Central Women's Advisory Committee had at no time expressed its views on these. There was room for the Committee to make their views known and to play a part in the formulation of policy of special interest to women. There was the Secretariat dealing with the day-to-day policy and matters in the House. There was no special section of it dealing with women's questions and the Advisory Committee could supplement this work.[42]

The WNAC felt that it was absolutely necessary for them to be in contact with what was happening in the House and to be able to have regular consultations with MPs. The parliamentary sub-committee was founded in November 1946, and its defined function was: 'To consider proposed legislation of special interest to women and to report and advise on the passage of Bills through the House, having ascertained the views of the women members of the Party.'[43] Further-more, each Area Women's Advisory Committee was to appoint its own standing committee in order to advise the parliamentary sub-committee on the point of view of women in all parts of Britain. Obviously, during this period the parliamentary sub-committee's role was of limited importance, since the Conservatives were not in power. However, as we shall see, the party's return to office in 1951 would stimulate the sub-committee to take a more active role.

The parliamentary sub-committee consisted of the Conservative women MPs and Life Peeresses plus the women officers of the National Union and three representatives of the WNAC. It was chaired by the vice-chairman of the WNAC and met six to seven times a year during parliamentary sessions. Its functions were to discuss any legislation before Parliament that concerned women and to examine the advisability of introducing any new legislation. It also heard reports from outside groups about what issues were preoccupy-ing women in the country. It took up several issues, including equal pay. It prepared a bill, for example, which the members asked the government to support, to enable tenancy of a house to be transferred to the wife in certain cases of separation where the wife had custody of the children. The solicitation laws were also another target of the parliamentary sub-committee since they were considerably more harsh with regards to women than to men. Here the question was likely to be more controversial so the women recommended the establishment of a Royal Commission on the subject which could then recommend legislation.[44] Another subject raised by Evelyn Emmet in the parliamentary sub-committee was that of the joint signature of husband and wife on the income tax return. It appeared that many wives did not know their husbands' income. In many cases, men gave only a relatively small part of their pay packet to their wives who then found it extremely difficult to make ends meet.[45] Some members of the sub-committee felt that this was not a realistic pro-position and so there was not unanimous support for the idea. It was decided instead to popularize it through the BBC and the press and try to see what the reaction to it was.[46]

Another issue which the WNAC took up was that of women and jury duty. In 1963 the Home Secretary invited the WNAC to write a memorandum for the department on that question. The WNAC came to the conclusion that women were unfairly being excluded from jury service, which continued to be based on a property qualification. Since, for most married couples, only the man was listed as owning the house, most wives were automatically excluded from being called for jury service. Furthermore, even when husbands and wives jointly owned the property, it was discovered that Under Sheriffs very often would not call the wives. The result was that there were rarely more than one or two women on any jury in the country. The WNAC, in true Conservative fashion, did not go so far as to recommend that the franchise be used as the basis for selecting jurors, for they felt that a property qualification signified permanence and some financial responsibility. The WNAC did, however, feel that more women were necessary on juries, especially when sexual offences or crimes against children were being considered. The committee came up with three recommendations to ease the situation:

(i) That joint householders should always be eligible.
(ii) That the husband and wife of a householder would also be on the Jury list and eligible for service.
(iii) That the reasons for exemption as regards women should be standardized. At present they seem to depend on the kind or stony heart of the Under Sheriff or his office.[47]

Prejudice was undeniably a factor in women's frequent exclusion from juries. It was not uncommon for women jurors to be challenged simply because they were women and replaced by men.[48] One woman on the parliamentary sub-committee of the WNAC had discovered the case of a lunatic who was out on licence and who had, therefore, been noted down as a juror. To use such people as jurors and to ignore so many competent women seemed to most to be nothing short of a crime. The WNAC repeatedly called on the government to change the laws relating to jury service. They argued that, since Labour had already announced their decision to change the laws, the Conservatives should beat them to it and show how truly progressive they were. As a result of efforts by various women's groups, including the WNAC, the Home Secretary agreed in 1963 to set up a departmental committee to study the reform of jury service. The situation was finally resolved in 1972, under the Heath government, when the Criminal Justice Act made qualification to serve on juries depend on voter registration and not property holding.

The Conservative Research Department also launched itself into a report on national insurance benefits for married women which exposed a number of problems. Married women received a lower level of sickness and unemployment benefit than did unmarried women or men. This, in fact, had been one of the recommendations of the Beveridge Report and had been accepted by both the Conservative and Labour Parties during the coalition government. This difference in benefit rate was justified by its supporters on three main grounds. First they argued that married women had the right to choose whether or not to make contributions and could, therefore, qualify for her husband's pension. The second reason was that sickness and unemployment benefit were supposed to compensate for lost earnings and it was assumed that all married women had their husbands' earnings. Therefore, they did not need as much benefit as other people. Finally, lower rates for married women were justified on the grounds that any increase in their benefits would make the whole scheme much more expensive and, therefore, increase everyone's contributions.[49]

A Women's Policy Group was also set up in March 1962 on the initiative of the Party Chairman in order to study policy and how it affected women. It was hoped that the group's findings would have an impact on future party policy. They found several areas in which women were at a legal disadvantage. The first of these concerned passports. Women were themselves handicapped with regard to passports for they were forced to get a new one when they married – which, of course, was not the case for a man. Furthermore, divorced women also found it objectionable that on a passport application – although no longer on the passport itself – she was always identified as 'the divorced wife of her former husband'.[50] Women did not enjoy equal guardianship of their children with their husbands. The result was that the father's signature was necessary in order for a child under 21 to get a passport. In cases where the father had disappeared, and the mother had never got a court injunction giving her full custody, this meant that her children could not leave the country until they were adults. They were thus unable to take a holiday abroad or go on a school trip to another country. Emmet led a delegation on the subject and, although received with courtesy by passport officials, received little encouragement from them. The passport officials insisted that this concerned only a tiny number of passport applications and averaged only about four a week. Emmet did not think that 200 a year was a small number, especially since there were obviously other cases that did not come to the attention of passport officials. She and the other women felt that there were enough cases to justify something being done about it.[51] They decided to send a delegation to the Home Office to ask for a reform of the Guardianship of Infants

Act. The Home Office, however, proved to be unreceptive to such suggestions, for they felt that giving the mother and father equal guardianship over the child would lead to conflict if the mother wanted one thing and the father another.[52] The women themselves were divided over the question. Some of their members, notably Margaret Thatcher, felt that all that was needed was an alteration in the passport laws and were against giving mothers equal guardianship over their children.[53] When Miss Vickers, a Conservative MP, introduced a bill on the subject in 1963, it did not receive government support and was defeated.

The WNAC and its parliamentary sub-committee repeatedly tried to alert the Conservative leadership to this problem and to convince them to take a more feminist stance on the issues. They also made a concentrated effort to publicize some of the things the Conservative Party had done for women and to try to show that the party had a progressive viewpoint on the question. Evelyn Emmet, for example, complained in 1963 that, in spite of repeated approaches by herself and Irene Ward, the party leadership had done little to deal with the very serious problem of widows' pensions. They argued that the pensions of widowed mothers should not be based on the regulations governing retirement pensions since that effectively meant that no widow could improve her standard of living – which, of course, would not have been the case if her husband had remained alive. Emmet advised the Conservative leaders to set up a committee to investigate the question since the Labour Party had already promised to deal with it if they were returned to power at the next election. She believed that taking up the issue could only help the Conservatives and cause the Labour Party to lose a popular campaign issue.[54] The fact that, until Heath became leader, few people seemed to listen to this and similar suggestions only made the women feel more depressed. The WNAC's parliamentary sub-committee repeatedly insisted that something had to be done to counteract this depression. They argued that:

Concern was felt by members of the Committee that there were too many people at the present time within our own ranks spreading despondency. It was felt that this was mainly because they had not got a real grasp of the situation. This was considered to be extremely dangerous as it made our weaker supporters fall prey to Socialist propaganda, and every effort must be made to make them realise what the Government had achieved in a short time and in difficult circumstances.[55]

To prevent this, it was argued, the Conservative Party had to show its concern for women's issues. A confidential report on women's rights insisted that: 'Research has demonstrated the Conservatism of women voters – particularly among the working class.' The Conservative Research Department argued that the party might lose this support unless some action was taken to show their support for equal rights: 'This good-will could be eroded by the stronger association of the Opposition Parties with anti-discrimination measures.'[56]

It was perhaps for this reason that the decision was made under Edward Heath's leadership to form a special committee to investigate legal discrimination faced by women. This committee, called the Cripps Committee after its chairman Anthony Cripps, was formed in January 1968, while the Conservatives were out of power, at the request of the WNAC and its parliamentary sub-committee. It was given the following terms of reference:

To examine existing legislation on the statute book in order to determine –
(a) What changes are desirable in the law and in administration in order to enable women to participate equally with men in the political, economic and social life of the community;
(b) What changes are desirable in the law relating to their rights and obligations within the family;
and to report.[57]

The Cripps Committee, thus dealt entirely with the legal disabilities suffered by women. Since women obviously had to endure other types of discrimination, a supplementary report by two members of the committee, Geoffrey Howe and Beryl Cooper, called 'Opportunity for Women' appeared at the same time and made recommendations on improving the situation for women in education, employment and public service. One of the peculiarities of the Cripps Committee was that it was established without either a representative of the shadow cabinet among its members or the assistance of the Research Department. To some extent, therefore, it was outside the usual paths used to establish party policy. Thus the danger was real that the Cripps Committee could become little more than a publicity gimmick and that the party would make little effort to act on its recommendations. This, however, was clearly not Edward Heath's intentions.

The Cripps Committee's report, called 'Fair Share for the Fair Sex' was published in February 1969 and proposed alterations in certain particularly discriminatory laws. It dealt, for example, with the question of domicile which is the place where a person has his or her legal permanent home. Under British law, a married woman could not have her own domicile, and it always had to be that of her husband. This law applied even if they were legally separated, and this sometimes led to absurd situations. If a husband left his wife to move to Australia, her legal domicile would become Australia even if she had never been there. If while living in Australia he divorced his wife, this would be recognized by a British court but if the reverse happened, if a woman moved to Australia and got a divorce, no British court would recognize it since she would not have been in her legal domicile. Nationality was another question greatly in need of change. Only a father could pass on his nationality. If a man moved to France and married a French woman, his children would be entitled to British citizenship. However, if a woman moved to France and married a Frenchman, their children would not be. This could obviously cause a great deal of hardship if the marriage broke up and the woman wished to return to Britain, since her child, even if he or she had arrived there as a baby, would not be a British citizen. The assessment of 'marriageability' was another issue considered by the Cripps Committee. The Fatal Accidents Act undoubtedly provided a valuable service by providing financial compensation to widows whose husbands had died in an accident, but the amount of this compensation was, to a large extent, based on the judge's assessment of her 'marriageability'. If a woman was deemed to be likely to remarry then she was given less money. The determination of 'marriageability' was based on the woman's age, physical appearance, ability to have children, housekeeping ability and other factors. To make matters worse, the judgement was published in local newspapers, so the whole town could know how a woman had been rated. 'Marriageability' clearly could become a humiliation of the first order for a woman, but, strangely enough, no major figure in either party had so far protested against it. The Cripps Committee, however, recommended its elimination.

The Cripps Committee also studied the matrimonial property laws, since they too needed updating. In this they were helped by the Finer Committee on One-Parent Families and the report of a working party of the WNAC, under the chairmanship of Diana Elles who was also a member of the Cripps Committee, entitled 'Unhappy Families'. Under British law, anything bought by one spouse belonged only to that spouse – including the matrimonial home. Basically, if a wife had no earnings and no money of her own, she had no rights to any property bought by her husband. This rule was followed so strictly by the courts that even money that a wife saved from housekeeping was deemed to be her husband's property until the 1965 Married Women's Property Act had made it that savings from housekeeping were the joint property of the husband and wife. Serious problems still remained, however, particularly where the matrimonial home was concerned, for, in some cases, courts had ruled that, even if the husband had put his wife's name down as co-owner, she had no right to the property since she had no earnings of her own. This had obviously led to great hardship in some cases for the husband, if he left his wife and children and if he were sole owner of the house, could sell it without any need for her consent. It was not unheard of to find such cases where the husband disappeared with the money he had made on the matrimonial home and, therefore, could not be found to pay maintenance or child support. The wife's situation in such a case could be desperate: without a home, perhaps with small children and, not infrequently, with little training or work experience. The Cripps Committee proposed recognizing that indirect contributions (such as in housekeeping) were as important as direct contributions and, therefore, that family property should, with certain exceptions, be divided equally. In particular, the indirect contribution of the housewife to the marital home gave her an equal interest in it.

After the Conservatives returned to power in 1970 most of the recommendations of the Cripps Committee were put into effect. The government supported a Labour MP's private member's bill which, using the wording of the Cripps Report, ended marriageability in assessing damages for widows. The Lord Chancellor also introduced a bill to allow widows with young children receiving damages to control their share, for previously the court controlled both the widow's and the children's share if there were young children since it was believed that otherwise the widow would fall victim to fortune hunters. The Attachment of Earnings Act of 1971 made progress towards remedying another injustice – that of men who refused to make maintenance payments. This act forced husbands in arrears and their employers to inform the court of any job change and for the maintenance order to be transferred from job to job. Another bill made it easier for women to get maintenance payments when their husband or ex-husband left the country. The 1973 Guardianship Act finally gave mothers equal guardianship of their children. The separate taxation of a husband's and wife's income if they so desired it was another change made by the Heath government. Conservative women had long argued that husband and wife should be taxed separately. As the situation stood, the husband's and wife's incomes were combined which, if both spouses were working, very often made them eligible for surtax and destroyed any extra earnings they might make. Evelyn Emmet, for example, argued that this prevented many married professional women – whose services the country desperately needed – from returning to work. Emmet felt that the Treasury was all too ready to deny to women a separate existence: 'It really is time that the Treasury were shaken out of this complaisant view that once a woman marries she really ceases to exist and for them the husband is the only one who counts.'[58]

This was by no means the end of the changes introduced by Heath, for funding for nursery school places was increased, married women were given the right to have their own domicile, and certain elements of the law that discriminated against the mothers of illegitimate children were removed.[59] Perhaps one of the most important changes was in relation to matrimonial property as women were now given a much greater share. For the first time, the Matrimonial Proceedings and Property Act of 1970 recognized the non-financial contribution of a housewife to a marriage. While not in and of themselves major changes in women's condition, these acts were, nonetheless, important steps towards male and female equality before the law. The Heath government also accepted the need for more general anti-discrimination legislation and set up select committees in both Houses of Parliament to investigate the question. In September 1973 a consultative document was published 'Equal Opportunities for Men and Women' which used the reports of these select committees. This document proposed making it illegal to restrict women's employment (notably by advertising for persons of one sex) and to limit their opportunities for training. The document also proposed the establishment of an Equal Opportunities Commission to investigate the educational and employment possibilities of men and women. While the Conservatives did not have time to act on these proposals before they lost office, many of them were picked up by the Labour Party and later became law in the 1975 Sex Discrimination Act – although it must be admitted that this law went considerably further than the original Conservative plans. As a follow up to the Cripps Committee, a new Committee on Women's Rights was formed in 1973 which was chaired by Lord Jellicoe and included among its members Margaret Thatcher, Anthony Cripps, Joan Varley and Sara Morrison. This commission continued to consider the question of how the law affected women and demonstrated Heath's continuing commitment to the issue. Besides these reforms, Heath's government also achieved something else: they gave a new feeling of importance to the WNAC. Its members had for years been insisting that the party should show its support for women's rights and were gratified to think that someone was finally listening to them.

This period then saw a growing commitment of the party towards equal rights for women – a commitment which reached its peak under Heath's leadership and which, paradoxically, would decline later when a woman actually became the party leader. This commitment was very clearly based on pragmatic considerations: the proposed reforms were shown to be widely accepted by the general public, and, while some of their own members might be hostile to them, the party calculated they had more to gain by endorsing them. Furthermore, the Conservatives realized that they were dependent on women's votes to win elections and the decline in support for the party among working-class women in the 1960s obviously made them afraid. They were, therefore, determined not to lose the initiative on women's questions to the Labour Party. At the same time, a divergence was growing between the party leadership and the grassroots – particularly the women. After the 1945 defeat, Lord Woolton had attempted to rejuvenate the party organization, including the women's branches, and to a large extent he succeeded. But after that initial burst of energy, it became clear that the party was simply not attracting enough younger women. In the 1960s the WNAC made numerous attempts to do so but these generally met with little success. As time went on, the women's sections appeared to be more and more out of touch with their times and received more and more criticism both within and outside the party. The importance of women in the party continued – about two-thirds of active party workers during this period were women – but it was clear that these women were getting older and not being replaced. This fact, especially when taken in combination with the decline of the gender gap, had ominous overtones for the party's future.

8 Conservative Women in Parliament, 1945–75

This period saw women's participation in politics slowly growing at both the national and the local level. Barriers were clearly breaking down for women, but only a tiny fraction of them was able to benefit from this. Everywhere the story was the same. Women were getting increasingly involved in local government and other civic bodies, but the proportion remained low. The House of Lords was also reformed, and for the first time in its history, women were admitted to that august and reactionary body. Their numbers, however, could hardly be considered to be overwhelming. The amount of women candidates increased significantly during this period from 76 in 1945 – all parties included – to 138 in the second election of 1974, which meant that women went from being 4.9 per cent of candidates to 7 per cent.[1] This did not, however, mean that their number of seats increased proportionately, for women appear to have been given a high number of unwinnable seats or to have been chosen by minor political parties with less chance of winning. In 1945, 21 Labour women were elected to Parliament in the landslide victory in that year, while only one Conservative woman managed to hold on to her seat, and no new ones were elected. A total of 24 women sat in Parliament in that year. By the second election of 1974, this number had climbed only slightly, to 27, of whom 7 were Conservatives and 18 were Labour. Percentage wise this translates into a progress from 3.8 per cent of all MPs in 1945 to 4.3 per cent in October 1974. This can hardly be considered a major advance, to put it mildly. Furthermore, it was obvious that women had greater prospects for advancement in the Labour Party than in the Conservative Party. In spite of their smaller numbers, women were far more visible in the Labour Party and, in general, given more responsible positions. In spite of this, 1975 saw an event of the first magnitude: the election of the first woman to head a British political party, and she was, of course, a Conservative.

To begin with, let us consider the situation of women in local government. It was estimated that about 4000 women served on civic bodies, and another 4000 were magistrates in 1957.[2] In spite of clear progress women still made up only a tiny fraction of public bodies. The WNAC's working party on local government found that:

164

'It was ascertained through the Local Government Department at Central Office that there is no evidence on the whole that women are not welcomed – it is safe to say that they are sought, but very frequently given the worst seats.'[3] This, of course, was not very different from the situation with regard to women and parliamentary seats. The working party found that in the county, borough and urban district council elections of 1952, 600 Conservative women had been candidates, as opposed to 877 Labour, 47 Liberals, 245 independents with support and 213 independents without support. Many of these, of course, had not been elected. The WNAC decided that a concerted effort should be made to find suitable women candidates for local government. The working party made as its recommendation:

> That all women's committees should be constantly on the watch for Conservative women with ability. These are often found at work in non-political organizations. Conservative members on these outside bodies, as well as the Constituency Organization, should be consulted with a view to finding able people who may not yet be prominent in the Association, and so widen the choice.[4]

The WNAC, then, was actively looking for good women candidates, but they were often difficult to find or uninterested in serving. Even when they were willing to try it, it was not always easy to get them accepted for seats. The situation then was difficult although showing signs of improvement. This was clearly shown by the results of the 1968 local government elections and particularly in the greater London area. In these elections there had been 351 Conservative women candidates and 310 of these had been elected. To some extent, however, this had backfired on the Conservatives, for these women now had much less time to devote to their local associations.[5] Still, by the early 1970s it was estimated that only 12 per cent of the nation's local government councillors were women.[6] Women had enjoyed their greatest success in London and Oxford where they made up 20 per cent of the total. Furthermore, few women were getting top positions in local authorities. The Conservative Party's major woman figure in local government was undoubtedly Shelagh Roberts from the Greater London Council (GLC) who became the first woman to sit on the Conservative front benches there. She was also an active figure in the WNAC and became its chairman in 1975.

Certainly one of the major events of this period was the admission of the first women in the House of Lords. In 1958, Harold Macmillan's government reformed the House of Lords and created Life

Peeresses. Peeresses in their own right (those who received the title through inheritance), however, remained ineligible to take their seats. Since women had first been admitted into the House of Commons, pressure had been repeatedly applied to admit them also to the House of Lords. In fact, Lord Astor, the husband of the first woman MP, had introduced three bills in the 1920s to allow peeresses in their own right to sit there. These bills were all defeated in the overwhelmingly reactionary atmosphere of the Lords. Preoccupied by other concerns, the question was placed on the back burner in the 1930s and during the war. After the war a petition was circulated throughout the country and signed by thousands of people in favour of the admission of women to the House of Lords. Finally in 1949 the Lords agreed to admit women, but this was postponed until a general reform of the house could be undertaken. In 1957 the Conservative government announced the creation of Life Peers for which women would be eligible. The bill became law in 1958, and a few months later the first four women entered the Lords. Lady Astor had hoped to be the first woman to sit in the House of Lords as she had been in the House of Commons, but, for whatever reason, the government denied her this privilege. Lord Reading then managed to score a notable coup against the Conservative government by getting the Lords to vote in favour of admitting peeresses in their own right. Macmillan, however, simply ignored this and refused to let the ladies take their seats. They only did so four years later when a further reform of the House of Lords was introduced which also allowed peers to renounce their peerages.

Meanwhile, the situation with regard to Conservative women in Parliament had become nothing short of catastrophic. The 1945 election had seen only one Conservative woman return to Parliament, Lady Davidson. Central Office was certainly very keen to end this situation and to increase the number of women MPs. They instituted a policy whereby at least one woman's name figured on every list submitted to constituency organizations. The WNAC also decided to put pressure on Area chairmen to assist women candidates in any way possible – notably by inviting them to speak and by giving them publicity.[7] The problem was, first, that they did not have enough good women candidates: in November 1946, for example, they had only seven prospective women candidates and two of them had already been MPs in previous parliaments. From the very start of the selection process there simply were very few women, and thus an even smaller number could be expected to actually make it into Parliament. The second problem was that local associations often refused to consider women candidates – a complaint which had been repeatedly made since the 1920s. The WNAC, with Lord Woolton present and expressing his agreement, analysed the situation as follows:

> Among the points covered in the discussion were: the prejudice still existing against women candidates; the reluctance, in some instances, of women members of Association Committees to support women candidates; the financial difficulties if a woman candidate was expected to contribute £100 to the Association, there being a tendency for Associations to regard this recommended maximum as a minimum; the urgent need for Associations and Association Chairmen to realise and fulfil their financial responsibilities by increasing their incomes; the need for young working women candidates, the need for a definite lead on the question of women candidates to be given from the top; the desirability of increasing the number of women candidates for election to local authorities which give valuable experience.[8]

The Maxwell Fyfe reforms of 1948 ended the requirement that parliamentary candidates should contribute to their own campaign costs, and the constituency association was made responsible. This opened the Conservative Party to large numbers of working-class and middle-class candidates for the first time. It did not, however, open it to large numbers of women candidates. The reason why these reforms failed to achieve this goal has often been debated.

An article written by a prospective woman candidate in 1964 detailed some of the indignities women faced in their attempts to secure selection by a Conservative constituency association. She discovered that married women were asked about their husband, children and homes and whether they would be neglected if she entered Parliament. Unmarried women were bluntly asked: 'Why aren't you married? Isn't it rather odd?'[9] Women appear to have been particularly hostile as the WNAC quote cited above illustrates. This accusation had already been voiced by Astor in the 1920s: that the real reason why there were so few women Conservative MPs was that the local selection committees would not consider them and that the most hostile of these local members were other women themselves.[10] This criticism has been repeatedly given to the present day. A motion at the 1947 women's conference, for example, asked 'that attention to problems particularly affecting women should be prominent in the party programme and that it should be the aim of branches throughout the country to ensure the return of a reasonable number of representative Conservative women at the next election'. The debate that followed called forth major criticisms of their own women members. Some delegates spoke of the 'lazy-mindedness of women, their unwillingness to think, and their lack of support for each other, culminating in their support for male candidates'.[11] Given the independence of the constituency associations, there was little the WNAC or its parliamentary sub-committee could do about such a situation except make every effort to popularize the issue and try to create public opinion in favour of more women MPs.[12] The WNAC did manage to prepare a resolution for a party conference on the subject and have it approved.[13] The issue caused some bitterness among those at the WNAC, however, as can be seen by the Chairman's memorandum which clearly stated that many good women were in danger of being lost to the Labour Party: 'An intelligent woman, desirous of taking up a political career, has more chance of realising her ambitions under the Socialist banner, than under the Conservative, because our party, for some obscure reason, is apathetic, if not slightly hostile towards the efforts of women to enter Public life.'[14] Once again we see the WNAC's obsessive fear of losing women supporters to the Labour Party. As we saw in the last chapter, this preoccupied the WNAC at this period since it was clear that the gender gap was declining, and it was widely feared in the party that if they lost the support of women, the party would be unelectable at least in the near future.

Many attempts have been made to explain why Conservative women in local committees have been and are so hostile to women MPs. Jealousy, of course, probably plays a role, for many of them seem to resent the success of other women in traditionally male activities. A socially conservative attitude to the role of the mother is another explanation, for many of these women clearly view the role of a mother of small children as being in the home and that anything else is, at best, irresponsible. Others appear to see women candidates as vote losers – an opinion that no study has ever found the least support for.[15] Finally, many local Conservatives, including men, prefer married male MPs on the theory that they will get two persons to work in the constituency rather than one. The wife of an MP has an expected role to perform in the constituency and in the campaign. In 1971, Geoffrey Howe's wife wrote a memorandum on what constituency associations expected from the candidate's wife:

Constituency expectations of an MP's wife's role have been growing for some time. Right from the moment a candidate is selected, the wife – if willing – will be asked to play a considerable part in the Constituency. Apart from attending with her husband, she may well have engagements of her own to fulfil, is expected to be fairly knowledgeable on political matters, and generally to act as a sort of mini-ambassador for husband and Party.[16]

This role has rarely been adopted by the husbands of MPs, who, of course, usually have their own, full-time jobs, and, certainly, no one in the constituency association expects husbands of candidates to do as much work for the party as wives of candidates.

In any case, even if women are more hostile than men, the fact remains that men generally have more power on the selection committees. The antipathy of local women is, in and of itself, an insufficient explanation for the lack of women candidates, although it is undoubtedly a factor.[17] It is interesting to see how a woman like Evelyn Emmet, when presenting herself as a candidate to constituency committees, tried to make a virtue of her sex in order to counter any prejudice. She told one constituency committee in 1945:

One of the principal reasons I am offering you my services is that I am a Woman. I know this may sound a strange reason to those who still object to women Members of parliament. But I would ask them, if there are any here tonight, just to consider the situation from the point of our Party as it stands at present. On the Socialist side there are 19 women, on our side two only. These two gallant ladies are being killed by the work that is being put upon them and it is no secret that the Leaders of the Party are very seriously concerned and desperately anxious to get a few more well qualified women in the House to relieve the pressure.[18]

The fact that Emmet felt it necessary to defend her candidacy in such a way shows the extent to which prejudice against women in politics still remained and, as we shall see, continues to this day.

In spite of this, though, the number of Conservative women candidates continued to increase although at a slower rate than for the Labour Party. It was clear, however, that in both major parties, while more women were being chosen as candidates, they were frequently doing so for hopeless or near hopeless constituencies. For this reason, the number of women in Parliament has tended to increase significantly each time that one party or the other wins a landslide victory – women candidates who represented constituencies normally held by the other side made it to Parliament almost by accident. In 1945 14 women had been candidates but only Lady Davidson was actually elected. On the other hand, the Labour Party had 41 candidates of whom 21 made it into Parliament. Here we see the earlier-stated phenomenon very clearly for many of these Labour women had stood for traditionally Conservative constituencies and entered Parliament only because Labour's victory was exceptionally large. In 1950 the figure for the Conservatives was 29 candidates of whom 6 were elected, while for Labour there were 42 candidates of whom 14 were elected. The 1950 election, in fact, saw a record number of women candidates with a total of 126 in all parties. It would be many years before this figure would be surpassed or even equalled. This was certainly linked to the importance given to women's issues – notably food questions – and showed to what extent all of the parties hoped to gain the vote of women. Irene Ward and Florence Horsbrugh both returned to Parliament in this election. The most important of the new Conservative women was undoubtedly Patricia Hornsby-Smith. She had risen from poverty to become private secretary of Lord Selborne. Although only 35 at the time she had been active for years in Conservative Party politics and had already impressed the party with her potential before she even made it into Parliament. Hornsby-Smith, with Lady Davidson, was also a member of the WNAC and helped to keep it abreast of events in Parliament. On the other hand, in 1951 there was a slight decline with 25 Conservative candidates of whom 6 were elected, and 41 Labour candidates of whom 11 were elected.[19] None of the elected members was new, however, and, in spite of the Conservative majority in Parliament, Labour women MPs still outnumbered Conservatives by nearly two to one.

Churchill's return to power also saw the first Conservative woman to become a senior minister. When Churchill formed his cabinet in 1951, following the example of Attlee, he appointed Florence Horsbrugh as Minister of Education – although unlike Attlee he did not give her cabinet rank. Churchill insisted that he excluded her from the cabinet only because he wanted a small cabinet, but many people felt that he simply could not abide the idea of a woman at the cabinet table. Pat Hornsby-Smith was also made a junior minister and took over Horsbrugh's old job as Parliamentary Secretary to the Ministry of Health. She also became the youngest woman so far to receive ministerial appointment. Horsbrugh, at least, had a very unhappy time at Education. She was minister during a period of austerity and was forced to cut spending. Unfortunately, this also coincided with the first children of the postwar baby boom reaching school age, and the number of buildings and teachers was clearly inadequate for the demand. To make matters worse, being outside the cabinet, she could not effectively argue the needs of her department. Obviously, she was subject to a great deal of criticism, and very often through no fault of her own. In 1953 Churchill finally gave in and allowed her to enter the cabinet, but he made it clear that he did not enjoy her presence. Whenever she dared to voice an opinion on foreign affairs, Churchill apparently commented: 'Fancy the Minister of *Education* taking an interest in foreign affairs.'[20] Her ministerial career ended unhappily as well when Churchill forced her to resign in order to make room for Sir David Eccles whom the prime minister wished to reward for his organization of the coronation. Horsbrugh was made a Dame of the British Empire and retired to the backbenches – probably with a certain amount of relief.

Two more Conservative women had entered the House in by-elections, and one of these, Edith Pitt, would later hold ministerial rank. The 1955 general election saw the number of Conservative women MPs increase to ten. One of the new ones was Evelyn Emmet, whom we have already come across through her activities in the party hierarchy and in the London County Council. She had, as we have seen, tried for a number of years to get into Parliament and was now a 56-year-old widow with four children. Although a dedicated worker with a great deal of influence in the party, she was not a particularly good speaker and rarely intervened in parliamentary debates. Joan Vickers, another activist in the party's women's organizations, also entered Parliament at this time. Eden was now prime minister, and he decided to keep Hornsby-Smith in her position at the Ministry of Health. A few months later he also promoted Edith Pitt to the position of Parliamentary Secretary at the Ministry of Pensions and National Insurance. It was a rapid promotion, but one that was deserved because of her previous experience in the field. The disastrous Suez intervention which led to the resignation of Anthony Nutting, the Foreign Minister, in 1956 also caused the addition of another Conservative woman MP. A 38-year-old businesswoman, Mervyn Pike, was chosen to replace him. Even more remarkable was the fact that she was adopted for one of the agricultural constituencies, which traditionally have not been very friendly to women candidates. In fact, her adoption did provoke some hostility in the constituency, for a group of Conservatives broke off from the local association and campaigned against her, insisting that a woman should not be the candidate. In any case she won the election, although with a much decreased majority. Some commentators felt this decline was because of her sex, but it is far more likely that it was simply part of the public's response to Suez and had nothing to do with her personally. In 1957 the number of Conservative women in Parliament reached 12 with the return of another woman in a by-election.

With Anthony Eden's resignation in 1957, Harold Macmillan became prime minister. He appointed Hornsby-Smith to become one of the under-secretaries at the Home Office, where, among other things, she was charged with examining the refugee problem. Edith Pitt continued her job at the Ministry of Pensions and National Insurance. In 1958 Mervyn Pike became a Parliamentary Private Secretary at the Home Office. The 1959 general election, on the other hand, saw fewer Conservative women candidates than had the 1955 election. Two major figures retired: Lady Davidson, who had been in Parliament since 1937 and who, though, rarely speaking in the House, had been an influential figure behind the scenes both in the women's organization and the 1922 Committee, and Florence Horsbrugh who now accepted a life peerage and moved up to the House of Lords. The most important Conservative woman to enter Parliament at this election was undoubtedly Margaret Thatcher. There were now twelve Conservative women in the House and three of these held ministerial positions. True, they were the same three women with Mervyn Pike now Assistant Postmaster-General, Edith Pitt as Parliamentary Secretary to the Ministry of Health and Pat Hornsby-Smith in the same position at the Ministry of Pensions and National Insurance. The last of these, however, soon tired of her political career, seeing, in spite of her own obvious talents, little room for advancement. She voluntarily resigned her post and became director of a large company. Macmillan was determined to find a woman to replace her and so, after only two years in the House, Margaret Thatcher achieved her first ministerial position.

In 1962 the situation changed again as Edith Pitt became one of Macmillan's victims in his infamous reshuffle (popularly known as the 'night of the long knives') in July 1962. However, a few months later the number of women ministers was returned to three for Lady Tweedsmuir, after sixteen years in the House, was finally given office and became under-secretary of state at the Scottish Office. She had also recently been elected to the executive of the 1922 Committee, the backbenchers' organization, which showed the respect with which she was now held in Parliament. In 1963, meanwhile, Mervyn Pike was moved to the post of under-secretary of state at the Home Office. In the two general elections of 1964 and 1966 the swing to the left caused a number of Conservative women to lose their seats including Lady Tweedsmuir and Hornsby-Smith. Furthermore, Harold Wilson, the new Labour prime minister, was sympathetic to the claims of women and determined to appoint them to office. In 1964 out of eighteen Labour women MPs, seven were given positions. Undoubtedly the most important appointment was that of Barbara Castle, the old Bevanite radical who had worked closely with Harold Wilson since the days of the Attlee government. Castle became Minister of Overseas Development (the first woman to hold a non-domestic appointment) and was given cabinet rank. In January 1966 she was given the even more important position of Minister of Transport, which was once again outside the traditional departments for women. All of this obviously put pressure on the Conservatives to show that they too could give women important offices. Douglas-Home appointed both Thatcher and Pike to the shadow cabinet for the positions which they had held when the party had been in office. When Edward Heath took over as party leader he showed even more sympathy. In 1966, for example, Pike was made opposition spokesman on the social services. From 1970 to 1974 there were fourteen Conservative women in the House of Commons. Margaret Thatcher was undoubtedly the most important, being Minister of Education and a member of the cabinet (only the second Conservative woman to hold this rank). Heath too broke with tradition and placed women in positions outside the usual spheres. Peggy Fenner served as Parliamentary Secretary to the Ministry of Agriculture, Fisheries and Food from 1972–4, and Betty Harvie Anderson was appointed to be the first woman Speaker of the House of Commons. Women in the House of Lords also made considerable progress at this time. Lady Tweedsmuir served as Minister of State for the Scottish Office for the first two years of the Heath government and then moved on to the Foreign Office for the last two years – the first time a woman had been appointed there. Baroness Young became the first woman whip in 1972 and then became Parliamentary Under Secretary of State to the Department of the Environment from 1973–4. The two 1974 elections, however, went against the Conservatives and as a result the number of Conservative women MPs declined to only seven.

In spite of these undoubted achievements, there is no doubt that leading women in the Conservative Party were feeling resentful about their treatment by party leaders. Barbara Brooke wrote to the party chairman in 1963 to express the feelings of the parliamentary subcommittee. As she explained:

> In the course of a general discussion at the end of the business on the agenda, it emerged how strongly a number of people were feeling about the way in which over and over again the women's point of view seems to be neglected, disregarded or never even sought. Burning indignation was expressed about the way in which no woman was invited to be present at Harold Macmillan's gathering of Ministers and Party officials at Chequers last spring.[21]

The women leaders were also upset because no woman had been asked to support Sir Alec Douglas-Home when he was chosen to become the new party leader. Irene Ward complained that women had not been sufficiently consulted about the party manifesto for the election of 1964 and believed that, as a result, party propaganda was not attractive enough to professional and younger women.[22] They felt they were being ignored when decisions about jobs were being made and that they did not have a real role in formulation of policy, in spite of the fact that leading male figures in the party talked about how important women were to the party. Many women felt that this was simply 'lip service' and that the party leadership really could not care less about women.

Women MPs complained that office was not given to them on the basis of merit but on that of percentage.[23] This was particularly discouraging since it was so difficult for women to enter the House anyway, and most of them had to be fairly exceptional and more talented than their male rivals just to get elected in the first place. Women also objected to the fact that they seemed to be considered only for certain 'feminine' ministries like health and education.[24] Of course, they were not always fair in their criticism. By 1962, for example, it was generally accepted that two or three MPs should be appointed to supplement the United Kingdom's delegation to the United Nations General Assembly and that one of these should be a woman. In 1962 the government asked several women to go but all of them were unable to accept the invitation. No woman was sent, therefore, and there were numerous complaints about this.[25] The same problem recurred in 1963 with the same result. It was clear, however, that, given the scarcity of Conservative women MPs and the numerous obligations they had assumed, that such events were certain to happen.

In other cases, women MPs complained that they were not kept informed of business before Parliament. Ian MacLeod observed that: 'There seems to be a feeling among many Conservative women Members of Parliament that they could be kept more fully informed of the Government's intentions on legislation especially affecting women and this came out very strongly over Lord Balniel's Bill on the Employment of Women when these Members felt many of the difficulties which beset that Bill could have been avoided if their advice had been taken earlier.'[26] Thus, by the mid-1960s many women in the Conservative Party were feeling increasingly dissatisfied with their allotted role in the party. Evelyn Emmet, now an MP, summed up the feelings of many:

As far as women Members are concerned, there is still a lot of custom and prejudice to overcome in the House. The tendency to overlook the women when there is interesting work to be done or jobs to be filled, is still very evident. It isn't that the men are deliberately obstructionist but they just do not remember we are there at such times! Women approach the task in a spirit of service and are perhaps not ambitious enough and dislike having continually to push. Most men who come into the House, come with definite ambitions. No doubt there are many disappointed Prime Ministers. They are reluctant to see a woman fill any place which might be theirs. In this matter we are falling behind other countries, who recognize more generously the contribution women could make in responsible positions. Where are our women Ambassadors, High Commissioners, Governors, Cabinet Ministers? If for the good of the country this is to be altered, and it should be, it must come through the force of Public Opinion and especially through the Women's Societies and Organizations. We Members in the House must live at peace and in harmony with our men colleagues and this could not be if we were for ever complaining.[27]

Emmet wanted more outside pressure to be put on the government and party leadership to appoint women to responsible positions. Her point was simple: that women already in Parliament could not be expected to be constantly lobbying for positions with no outside support. They did have to live in some harmony with their fellow MPs and, therefore, could not be seen as always hunting for posts.

Of course, the most extraordinary event of this period was the advent of a woman, Margaret Thatcher, as leader of the Conservative Party. There was a great deal of luck involved in this. Thatcher was born Margaret Roberts in 1925 in Grantham, Lincolnshire. Her father owned a shop over which the family lived, and her first memories were of struggling to keep the business going during the great depression. She was a bright child and did well at school – so well that she eventually landed a place in chemistry at Somerville College Oxford. She also threw herself into politics at Oxford, becoming president of the Oxford University Conservative Association. In this she was certainly going against the grain of the times for the fashion was in favour of the Beveridge Report and Attlee's consensus. After leaving Oxford, she very briefly joined the women's section of the party, but did not find it at all to her taste. At 24 she became a candidate for Parliament in the Labour safe seat of Dartford in the 1950 general election – the youngest woman to contest that election. Of course, she lost but she persevered. In the 1951 general election she contested and lost Dartford again. Meanwhile, she had decided that chemistry was not the field for her and decided instead to study law, passing her bar exams in 1953. At around the same time, in December 1951, she married Denis Thatcher, a wealthy businessman and committed Conservative, who would give her the support – both materially and emotionally – that she would need to pursue her political career. Within two years she had become the mother of twins, Mark and Carol – a fact which basically ensured that she would not be chosen by any Conservative constituency association in the immediate future. As we have already seen, the mid-1950s was a time of popular domesticity, on the surface at least, and there was little chance that the mother of two babies would be chosen as a Conservative candidate. This did not deter her, and barely a year after the twins' birth she was back trying to convince constituency associations to adopt her as their candidate – although she found no one willing to take her until after her children had started school.

Thatcher, as we have already seen, entered Parliament in 1959 for the safe seat of Finchley. She was very quickly noticed by Harold Macmillan who was in search of a token woman after Hornsby-Smith resigned her position at the Ministry of Pensions and National Insurance. As a young mother, she attracted some hostility from the civil servants who felt that she would neglect her work for her family. The permanent secretary at the ministry, Sir Eric Bowyer, apparently disapproved of her new position as his condescending tone seems to imply:

He asked whether as a young mother she would work hard enough. Twenty years on, he also pulled out of the past a recollection that had surely by then become a misleading cliché. 'She would turn up looking as if she had spent the whole morning with the coiffeur and the whole afternoon with the couturier.' However, in the end the civil service had 'got at least as much work from her as anyone else and probably a bit more'.[28]

The condescension he felt towards Thatcher is quite obvious in this statement and goes a long way towards explaining her own hostility towards the Civil Service. As we have already seen, many women felt that the Civil Service was by nature anti-feminine, and, it must be admitted, that there is a great deal of evidence to support their point of view. Whitehall's desire to preserve the status quo meant that they were usually more hostile than politicians to any change in women's legal status. On every issue considered by the parliamentary sub-committee of the WNAC, whether it be joint guardianship of children or the end of marriageability, the Whitehall mandarins always objected that it would cause more problems to change the law. In every case, when the law was eventually changed, the fabric of British society remained fundamentally intact in spite of the bureaucrats' predictions. Thatcher undoubtedly had a difficult time in her new position, and perhaps its greatest handicap was that it gave her little exposure or publicity.

Thatcher's career only really began to take off after Ian MacLeod, a major party leader, picked her out to be one of his assistants as shadow Chancellor of the Exchequer in 1965. When the Conservatives returned to power in 1970, Heath appointed Thatcher to be Minister of Education with a seat in the cabinet – yet another case of women's ministerial positions reflecting their supposed preoccupation with domestic affairs. She was, however, only the second Conservative woman to sit in the cabinet, and the first to do so through an entire Parliament. Nothing could be a greater contrast to Horsbrugh's pathetic tenure of office than Thatcher's. It was during her time in Heath's cabinet that her formidable intelligence was noticed, and that the party leadership began to see in her a major figure. Lord Home, earlier Sir Alec Douglas-Home told his wife: 'You know, she's got the brains of all of us put together, and so we'd better look out.'[29] Heath, however, never actually liked her, although their backgrounds were similar. John Campbell, in his biography of Heath, commented perceptively on Heath's feelings about Thatcher:

It is by no means the case that he [Heath] dislikes all women; but she – with her perfect complexion, well-cut clothes and precious accent – was exactly the type of Tory woman he most abhorred and least knew how to handle. He likes mannish women who place little overt value on their femininity, who talk like men and do not expect to be complemented on their appearance: Mrs Thatcher may have been as tough and businesslike as any man, but throughout her career she also used her femininity ruthlessly to disarm her male colleagues. With Heath this was counterproductive; it only irritated him.[30]

It was perhaps for this reason that Heath later did not take her challenge to his leadership seriously. There is no doubt that she did not like him either. She was generally viewed as being on the right of the party, at least with regard to economic questions, along with Enoch Powell, Keith Joseph, Geoffrey Howe and others. In private she talked about the need for market forces, but in public she was a loyal member of the cabinet and followed the party line. Although she plainly disagreed with Heath on occasions, once the decision had been taken, she generally stifled her disagreement. Thatcher clearly did not get along well with Heath, although she had always behaved in a loyal fashion. Although Heath promoted her, after the party left power, to the shadow Environment office, he sat her far from him at shadow cabinet meetings. Throughout his final year as leader Heath, much to his later sorrow, placed her in positions where she would get maximum exposure and where her debating skills could be shown off to their best advantage.

After the Conservative losses in the two elections of 1974, there was talk of replacing Heath as party leader, but a survey of the Areas by the WNAC showed that there was little support for this idea in the party organization in the country.[31] Perhaps for this reason, few of the leading figures in the party were willing to stand against him. His most likely opponent was Sir Keith Joseph who, like Thatcher, had become fascinated by monetarism, and was, therefore, strongly opposed to many of Heath's economic policies. By this time Thatcher had decided that Heath should go and all evidence points to the fact that she strongly supported Joseph's candidacy.[32] Joseph, however, shipwrecked his own campaign by giving a speech on 19 October in which, at the very end of an otherwise innocuous speech, he talked about the need for birth control among the lower class. This point, and some of the rather sinister sounding phrases used to argue it like 'our human stock' and 'these classes of people' caused an outcry in the press.[33] Very few people seriously thought Joseph was in favour of eugenics, and this controversy might have been quickly forgotten, but Joseph went to pieces over the press campaign. He kept trying to justify himself, and, therefore, kept the issue alive for weeks. In the end, Joseph withdrew from the campaign. At first sight there seemed to be no other reasonable alternative to Heath left in the party, but one did exist. On being informed of his refusal to stand against Heath, Margaret Thatcher immediately responded: 'If you are not, I shall.'[34] It was Margaret Thatcher's great good luck that no other major figure came forward to stand against Heath. The way was open for her to take advantage of the party's dissatisfaction with Heath's leadership.

However, the reaction to her candidacy did not always do justice to the Tory Party. In September 1974 Thatcher had given an interview to an obscure journal called *Pro-Retirement Choice* in which she had recommended that elderly people should stock up on tinned food when the price was low. After she announced her candidacy as Tory Party leader this fairly harmless comment was blown out of all proportion by the press, and Thatcher was accused of telling people to hoard food. Thatcher, at least, certainly believed this was an attempted smear campaign by the Heathites. In any case, it unquestionably did Thatcher no harm: most people either thought the debate absurd or thought that what she said had been quite reasonable. It may actually have helped her campaign since it allowed her to portray herself as the innocent lower-class victim of sinister forces in the party. As she said in her memoirs:

> Someone had clearly used this obscure interview in order to portray me as mean, selfish and above all 'bourgeois'. In its way it was cleverly done. It allowed the desired caricature to be brought out to the full. It played to the snobbery of the Conservative Party, because the unspoken implication was that this was all that could be expected of a grocer's daughter.[35]

Thatcher, then, turned the whole issue into a class question. She insisted that it showed the contempt felt by many aristocratic Conservative politicians for people from a humbler background. This is a classic example of how she took what might, on the surface, be weaknesses – her class origins and her sex – and turned them into advantages. She was, of course, outside the Tory Party elite, but she made this into a virtue.

Her campaign was certainly better run than Ted Heath's. The latter suffered from the severe handicap of believing he could not lose – and particularly that he could not lose to a relatively inexperienced woman. Heath's personality also worked against him: he had never been very friendly with the backbenchers, and his natural stiffness made his sudden effort to take an interest in them an unpleasant experience for all involved. Kenneth Baker reminisced of his call to meet with Heath that 'it was rather like being summoned to the Head-master's study'.[36] Thatcher capitalized on this discontent by meeting with groups of banckbenchers and listening sympathetically to their problems. To make matters worse, Heath helped bring about his own downfall by making her part of the Treasury team in late 1974. She was supposed to have played second fiddle to the Shadow Chancellor, Robert Carr, but she very quickly stole the show with her attack on Denis Healey's budget. In one of her more offensive attacks on the Chancellor she actually got the Tory backbenches cheering and made herself something of a hero. The effect on the party was like lightning, for nothing could contrast more with Heath's academic speaking style. Thatcher seemed to have the fighting spirit that the Tory Party so desperately wanted. As a later critic, Francis Pym, said: 'amidst the shambles and doubts of that time, here was one person who could articulate a point of view with conviction'.[37] Her performance convinced many people that she had the necessary forensic talents to hit hard at Harold Wilson.

The drawback, of course, was that she was a woman, and everyone knew that certain elements in the Conservative Party were strongly anti-feminist. *The Times*, at least, hypothesized that they would find it difficult to accept a woman leader. The press in general did not take Thatcher's candidacy seriously until after she had won the first round of voting. *The Economist* was condescending enough to comment: 'If Mr Edward Heath is capable, under whatever election procedure is devised... of being beaten by Mrs Margaret Thatcher, then he is well out of a job... Mrs Thatcher is precisely the sort of candidate... who ought to be able to stand and lose, harmlessly.'[38] Thatcher certainly did not think she could win at first and did not organize a serious campaign. However, when it became clear that Edward Du Cann, chairman of the 1922 Committee, would not stand, Airey Neave, a talented backbencher whose career had been thwarted by Heath, threw his support to her and directed her leadership bid. He galvanized it and soon after he joined the bandwagon it became clear that Thatcher's prospects were improving. Pressure was then put on several right-wing male backbenchers to also stand against Heath. The hope of many of those on the left of the party who were hostile to

Heath, was that this new candidate would take votes from Thatcher and, therefore, break her momentum, while forcing the vote to a second round. In this second round, a new frontbench candidate could appear – probably Willie Whitelaw – and win the party leadership.[39] If this was the plan it also backfired. A few days later, under much pressure, Hugh Fraser, brother of Lord Lovat and, at that time, husband of Lady Antonia Fraser, announced his candidacy for the post of party leader. He admitted that politically his ideas were very similar to those of Thatcher but felt that, being a man, he would be more acceptable to the party.[40] Fraser's candidacy, however, was never popular and actually caused more support to develop for Thatcher. There was no doubt that a certain, perhaps grudging, admiration was developing for her in the party. Even Harold Wilson could not help commenting: 'I have no doubt at all that Margaret was elected because of her courage. I agree with Lord Shinwell's view that she stood because she was the only man in the Conservative party.'[41]

Heath's popularity was undoubtedly high in the party. Constituency chairmen clearly wanted him to continue as leader, while poll after poll showed that he was far more popular with Tory voters than was Thatcher.[42] The constituency associations wanted Heath to continue as leader – perhaps, *The Times* hypothesized, because of their own anti-feminist tendencies.[43] The Young Conservatives and the women's sections also declared their support for Heath. On the other hand, none of these people had a vote and the MPs could hide behind a secret ballot. On 4 February 1975 the first round of voting took place for Conservative Party leader, and the result showed exactly how far Thatcher had come: 130 votes for her, 119 for Heath and 16 for Fraser. Thatcher did not, however, have the needed majority to win on the first ballot and so a second ballot was necessary. The result was an absolute sensation, since most people had expected Heath to win. It was clear, though, that the MPs had voted not so much for Thatcher as against Heath, and the outcome did not in any way guarantee that she would become party leader. Many people had voted for her in the hope that a more acceptable candidate – from their point of view – would then come forward in the second round.

This fact was quickly illustrated because, with Heath out of the running, major party leaders suddenly materialized as candidates: Willie Whitelaw, Jim Prior, Geoffrey Howe and John Peyton. Whitelaw forthwith became the favourite, at least as far as the press was concerned. *The Times* clearly felt that anti-feminine feeling – not so much in Westminster, they admitted, but in the constituency associations – would cause many MPs to hesitate about voting for Thatcher. Women Conservatives were particularly believed to be hostile to a woman leader, although it was admitted that their influence on MPs' decisions was limited.[44] The large number of candidates certainly worked to Thatcher's advantage as it threatened to split the votes of the centre and left-wing members. There was no doubt that Thatcher was gaining momentum, and by 11 February, it was clear that Thatcher was picking up support both in Westminster and in the constituencies. There was undoubtedly a certain amount of contempt felt for their last minute appearance: many people were heard to say openly that the four male candidates had left the dirty work to Thatcher and were now trying to capitalize on her deserved victory. Barbara Castle of the Labour Party shared this point of view:

> The newspapers are all full of the Tory leadership farce. So many brave warriors have now crept out of hiding to rush to climb on the second ballot bandwagon! Margaret looks the epitome of cool courage compared with them.[45]

Many others felt like Castle – to such an extent that a canvass of opinion in the Conservative constituency associations on 10 February showed support leaving Whitelaw and going to Thatcher. The chairman of the National Union told the 1922 Committee executive that support in the constituencies was believed to be as high as two to one in favour of Thatcher.[46] This probably sealed the situation, for on 11 February, when voting took place, Thatcher easily won and became the first woman leader of a British political party. The tradition-bound Tory Party had, once again, broken with tradition and chosen as leader a totally unexpected person. John Ranelagh in his book *Thatcher's People*, summed up what happened quite well: 'The Parliamentary Party, surprised by what it had done on the first ballot, was carried away by the thrill of the new.'[47] It was no longer possible to argue that MPs were simply voting against Heath. If this had been the case her support would have faded on the second ballot. Instead, it actually increased, and she won more votes than the other candidates combined. By the second round it was clear that the backbenchers were voting in favour of Thatcher and, as such, in favour of a new political style and philosophy.

This period saw an important, although hardly earth-shaking increase in women's involvement in politics. Obviously it was Thatcher's elevation to the party leadership that attracted most attention, but it is arguable that the growth of women membership in local government was, at least, equally as important. Local government has traditionally been one of the recruiting areas for MPs, and an augmentation in the number of women in local government should eventually lead to an increase in women MPs. A major constitutional reform by a Conservative government also opened the doors to women in the House of Lords. It soon became clear that this move had been a success for, by 1975, women made up a substantially higher proportion of the House of Lords than they did the House of Commons. Women's role in politics was obviously growing, although at a slow rate, and Thatcher's rise was the most spectacular expression of this ascent. It was, however, an isolated triumph and did not mean that the way had opened overnight for women in the Conservative Party. They still remained a tiny minority and generally far from positions of real influence.

9 A Woman Leader and Beyond, 1975–97

When news came out that Thatcher had been elected leader of the Conservative Party, the Labour leadership, for the most part, was delighted. They were convinced that she would be a serious disadvantage to the party, and cabinet members were heard to cry: 'We're home and dry!'[1] Certainly, Margaret Thatcher found herself in an extremely difficult position as leader of a divided party that had just been through a bruising leadership battle and as a woman in a man's world. She was highly suspicious of most members of the shadow cabinet she had inherited from Heath, and there is little doubt that they were equally dubious about her. Thatcher's major asset was probably her own popularity, and in particular that of her aggressive speaking manner with the backbenchers – but politics is a notoriously changeable business. Her major preoccupation was to solidify her position in the party and establish a power base. To do this, Thatcher combined in a remarkable fashion sweet femininity and hectoring aggression. Barbara Castle, although sitting on the opposite side, could not resist being enthusiastic:

> Margaret's election has stirred up her own side wonderfully – all her backbenchers perform like knights jousting at a tourney for a lady's favours, showing off their paces by making an unholy row at every opportunity over everything the Government does... She sat with bowed head and detached primness while the row went on: hair immaculately groomed, smart dress crowned by a string of pearls. At last she rose to an enormous cheer from her own side to deliver an adequate but hardly memorable intervention with studied charm.[2]

Of course, some of this may simply be the product of Barbara Castle's overactive imagination. Castle did, however, seize on one essential point: Thatcher knew how to turn her gender to her political advantage. There is little doubt that some MPs were emotionally affected by the sight of Thatcher dwarfed by the male party leaders, looking in comparison small and frail. This image caused some of them at least to develop an emotional loyalty to her.[3] Kenneth Baker, later a member of her cabinet, observed that: 'In both Party Conferences and television appearances she used her clothes, style and manner to convey the strength and vitality of her character, employing with devastating effect the fact that she was a woman.'[4] The cabinet secretary, Robert Armstrong, told of a cabinet meeting in which her earrings obviously hurt her. He explained that: 'As the meeting went on, she removed one of them...and as she did so she gave me a sidelong look of total amused complicity. It was a completely male-female moment.'[5] There is no doubt that she could have – when she wanted to – a certain sex appeal. It is repeatedly attested to in the memoirs of those who worked closely with her.

Thatcher clearly used her sex to her advantage in taming the back-benchers and the shadow cabinet. The male MPs simply did not know how to deal with her, not only because she was a woman but because she was a shopkeeper's daughter. Most of them had had no experience of women from her class, being used to upper- and middle-class women. Many of them had gone to public school and Oxford or Cambridge where, at that time, women were segregated into their own colleges. Certainly, very few of them had ever had to take orders from a woman before, and they really were unsure of how to react. Kenneth Harris, in his biography of Thatcher has commented percept-ively: 'They were not used to being in a subordinate relationship with a self-made woman used to saying what she thought without being asked, who liked to begin a discussion by putting forward her own views, would interrupt the subsequent speaker as soon as he said something with which she did not agree, and appeared to have the conviction, which she did not trouble to conceal, that the opinion she held was almost certain to be right.'[6] There was a certain ingrained chivalry in many of them that made it very difficult for them to argue back to a woman. Equally clearly, she exploited this chivalry to assert dominance over them. It had always been the tradition of the 1922 Committee to remain seated when the party leader entered the room. In Thatcher's case, however, a natural politeness caused them, as a body, to stand. Thatcher shamelessly exploited this according to one person present: 'She made a procession to her seat, as though she expected them to remain up standing; and when she got there turned as though to say, "Please be seated".'[7]

In 1979 Margaret Thatcher scaled yet another height by becoming the first woman prime minister in British history. During the campaign her gender was certainly not ignored by the particularly sexist British media. *The Daily Telegraph*, for example, described one of her campaign speeches by giving more information about her clothes than about her policy: 'Mrs Thatcher, in one of her favourite navy gabardine suits with a navy scarf at the neck, talked about the need to create wealth.'[8] This is typical of descriptions of Thatcher, for the press consistently paid as much, if not more, attention to her dress than to what she had to say. Clearly no voter was going to be allowed to forget the gender of Thatcher. Cecil Parkinson, at least, argued that the Labour Party based its campaign on the electorate's supposed fear of a woman prime minister. He insisted that:

> In spite of all this there were many people who felt that Britain was not ready for a woman Prime Minister, and that having her as our leader would prove a disadvantage to us and provide our opponents with a substantial electoral bonus. Certainly many people in the Labour Party took this view which was why Labour chose to fight a presidential-style election campaign contrasting the reassuring, experienced, down-to-earth Uncle Jim Callaghan with the inexperienced, radical and challenging Margaret Thatcher.[9]

Parkinson was trying to portray the Labour Party as the reactionary one where women were concerned. In this he undoubtedly struck a chord, for, as we have seen, the Labour Party had long been perceived by the general public as male-dominated and more hostile to ambitious women than the Conservative Party. The response of the Labour leaders to her election shows that they did not take a woman leader seriously – although it is, admittedly, highly doubtful that, if the positions had been reversed, the Conservatives would have reacted any differently to a woman leader of the Labour Party.

Thatcher never played down the fact that she was a woman and frequently insisted in public on the stereotypically womanly tasks she did: buying Denis's bacon, preparing breakfast for the family, doing housework on weekends. She constantly presented the image of herself as housewife to the general public. Her favourite metaphor was that of the housewife planning her budget, and she loved to contrast that with the government's own formation of its budget – much to the latter's disadvantage. Her implication was obvious: having been a housewife she would know better how to manage the nation's money than all the well-educated mandarins of Whitehall or the male politicians. It was certainly an attempt to show how practical and ordinary she was, and, as such, it did not work with the voters. Poll after poll showed that people did not consider her 'down to earth' at all.[10] Still, at least one journalist saw her preoccupation with inflation as being due not to the fact of being a monetarist, but to her feminine role. As a writer in *The Times* commented: 'Women tend to feel strongly about inflation not only because shopping makes price increases real to them but because inflation threatens the security of the family and changes relationships within it.'[11] In an interview with *The Observer*, Thatcher stressed her involvement in domestic chores: 'At weekends I cook and do some housework because there is no one else to do it.' Castle, at least, was incredulous, commenting in her diary: 'Sorry but I don't believe it.'[12]

Her love of clothes is legendary. Once she even showed her favourite clothes and talked about them on the BBC, going so far as to announce that she had bought her underwear at Marks and Spencer. Nor is the question ignored in her memoirs where she writes:

> From the time of my arrival in Downing Street, Crawfie [Cynthia Crawford, Thatcher's personal assistant] helped me choose my wardrobe. Together we would discuss style, colour and cloth. Everything had to do duty on many occasions so tailored suits seemed right. (They also have the advantage of gently passing by the waist.) The most exciting outfits were perhaps those suits I had made – in black or dark blue – for the Lord Mayor's Banquet. On foreign visits, it was, of course, particularly important to be appropriately dressed. We always paid attention to the colours of the national flag when deciding on what I should wear.[13]

Her preoccupation was not without a basis: we have already seen that the press focused on her clothing from the beginning and gave detailed accounts of it. When Parliament began to be televised in November 1989, Thatcher began to receive letters from viewers commenting on her clothes and noting if she had worn the same outfit two times in a row. Nigel Lawson perceptively commented on the logic behind Thatcher's obsession with her appearance:

> Some of the time saved through her economy of sleep was devoted to what was frequently her first appointment of the day: the visit of her hairdresser. She was convinced that her authority – in a world in which a woman's appearance is always a subject of comment, a man's only occasionally – would be diminished if she were not impeccably turned out at all times. She was probably right – and certainly this was one aspect of her with which the great mass of women voters could readily identify, however much it may have been derided in NW1.[14]

Another part of Thatcher's femininity was her tears.[15] She certainly made no effort to hide her parental concern when her son Mark disappeared in 1982 during a motor rally in the Sahara. During the six days in which there was no news of him, her anxiety was evident, and she wept often – even sometimes in public. Other occasions also called forth tears like an IRA attack, for example. Sometimes the tears seemed too theatrical as when she reminisced about her father on television. She also showed her femininity in her interest in Downing Street and its furnishings. She describes in loving detail in her memoirs how she redecorated the residence and brought in fine art work.

Femininity then was part of Thatcher's image and undoubtedly a carefully cultivated part, but it was not the only or even the predominate element. François Mitterrand perhaps summed up Thatcher best in his comment that she had 'eyes like Stalin and the voice of Marilyn Monroe'.[16] His point is clear: that she combined femininity with extreme ruthlessness. The general public, however, seem to have retained the toughness more than the gentle femininity. Opinion polls taken in 1985 showed that most people in Britain viewed her as tough, decisive and shrewd but as someone who lacked the ability to listen to reason, to care for others or to be sympathetic to their needs.[17] At the same time there is an undoubted – although frequently grudging – admiration for Thatcher. Her nicknames show this ambivalence: the Iron Lady or Attila the Hen. In her defence it must be stated that women from lower-class backgrounds cannot become prime minister unless they are tough and aggressive – and more tough and more aggressive than the men around her. Aggressivity and dominance are traditionally male characteristics, and there is undeniably an element of sexism in criticizing Thatcher for possessing 'male' traits. What is acceptable in a male is much less acceptable in a woman. Perhaps the most remarkable achievement of Thatcher was to reverse gender stereotyping to some extent. It was the Labour leader Neil Kinnock who came across as warm and caring while Thatcher was viewed as combative and abrasive. Yet she managed to combine this with a preoccupation with dress and hair that does not fit into her image at all.

On the other hand, it would be wrong to confuse Thatcher's femininity with feminism. Given her philosophy, it is not surprising to discover that she was often severely criticized by feminists for not doing much for women during her years as party leader and prime minister. When Kenneth Baker, for example, suggested mentioning in the Conservative manifesto for the 1987 election that nearly 50 per cent of university and polytechnic students were women, Thatcher dismissed the idea as 'irrelevant'.[18] Only one other woman sat in the cabinet, Janet Young as Leader of the Lords, but she was never powerful, and it was not long before she was asked to resign to make room for Willie Whitelaw. Thatcher herself placed a great emphasis on home and family in many of her speeches. When she gave the first Dame Margery Corbett Ashby lecture in 1982, she underplayed the feminist aspect of things and stressed maternal duty:

> But I remain totally convinced that when children are young, however busy we may be with the practical duties inside or outside the home, the most important thing of all is to devote enough time and care to their needs and problems. There are some things for which only a parent will do. I will never forget the comment of a headmaster of a school I visited when Secretary of State for Education. He said that as many problem children came from rich as from poor homes. Some were from homes where the children have everything they wish for except perhaps enough of their parents' attention. Material goods can never be a substitute for loving care.[19]

This speech has been greatly criticized for being anti-feminist and even insulting to the memory of Margery Corbett Ashby. Beatrix Campbell, for example, has asserted that Thatcher's '"tribute" to her [Ashby] did not celebrate the suffrage struggle but the protagonists' domesticity'.[20] This is not an entirely fair assessment. While on the surface this excerpt sounds traditionalist, notice that Thatcher does not say that mothers should stay at home with their children all the time. She simply says that parents (note that she never specifies the mother) need to devote time to their children. This quote is very revealing about Thatcher's concept of the family and of her own role in it. She certainly was not a housewife, except for a short period of time after the twins' birth, but she constantly stresses that she always arranged time to be with her children. There is no doubt that she believed this and that she viewed herself as combining, as well as possible, a demanding political career with that of a parent. Nor, in this speech, does she fail to mention the achievements of Ashby and the legal, professional and political disabilities from which women suffered that Ashby helped remove. At the end she even acknowledges her debt to Ashby, although perhaps in less generous terms that she should, saying simply: 'I am very much aware of how much I owe to Dame Margery.'

On the other hand, there is no doubt that she did make some deliberately provocative comments like: 'The battle for women's rights has been largely won. The days when they were demanded and discussed in strident tones should be gone forever.' This quote is a clue to Thatcher's form of feminism, for there is no doubt that Thatcher was a feminist of sorts, or she would not have arrived at 10 Downing Street. A passage from her memoirs is even more revealing about her feminism:

> My experience is that a number of the men I have dealt with in politics demonstrate precisely those characteristics which they attribute to women – vanity and an inability to make tough decisions. There are also certain kinds of men who simply cannot abide working for a woman. They are quite prepared to make every allowance for 'the weaker sex': but if a woman asks no special privileges and expects to be judged solely by what she is and does, this is found gravely and unforgivably disorienting.[21]

Thatcher felt that past legislation had removed the basic obstacles to women's professional and political success and that it was now up to them, through their own dynamism and ambition, to force their way to the top, as she had done. Thatcher argued that many contemporary feminist demands were essentially asking for special treatment for women and thus reinforcing male stereotypes about the weakness of the female sex. Her theory was that any exceptional assistance given to women encouraged men to continue to see themselves as superior and to look down on women. She wanted women to succeed without any special programmes to help them, and clearly felt that this was her case. Of course, Thatcher was helped. Central Office made a determined effort to get her a seat in the 1950s because they felt she was exactly the kind of woman that the party needed to attract: a young, highly educated, and articulate, professional. She was also assisted by the fact that she married a wealthy and supportive man and, therefore, could afford child care and household help.

Certainly there has been a general tendency for Tory women MPs to play down their interest in feminism, at least in recent times. Edwina Currie, who was a junior minister in Thatcher's government, said of the Equal Opportunities Commission:

> I despair of that ragbag of a body which finds it so easy to waste time and public money fiddling around with stuff like this. It merely encourages women to think that equality grows out of a law book, which it does not ... It comes from women taking the opportunities open to them. It comes when women face the demands of a

responsible job, and, like the men, ensure that they have made the arrangements accordingly.[22]

Angela Rumbold's response after being appointed to the Home Office with responsibility for, among other things, women's issues is typical. During an interview with *The Observer*, when asked about her new role as 'Minister for Women' – as the press decided to call her – she commented: 'Your profession has dumped that name on me. My major responsibility is Prisons.'[23] This does not mean they are not feminists. It is simply part of their free market ideas and individualist political philosophy that, once the legal disqualifications have been removed – for no one denies that in the past women suffered from disabilities that kept them out of public life – women should be allowed to achieve on their own. Their contention is that providing women with extra help undervalues their accomplishments and plays into the hands of sexist males.

On the other hand, the Conservatives did introduce legislation to expand the definition of equal pay from equal pay for equal work to equal pay for work of equal value, although it must be said that they did so rather grudgingly after they were forced to do so by the European Community. The sexist comments at the time by some of the Tory extremists became infamous. It has not infrequently been suggested that Thatcher's government made the legislation extremely complex so that it would be unworkable.[24] It must also be stated that Thatcher's government did establish a ministerial group in 1986 to consider the effect of legislation on women. It was handicapped from the beginning, however, by the fact that, since there were few women ministers, few women could belong to the group. Certainly there is little evidence that Thatcher took much interest in it or attended any of its meetings. It is perhaps significant that it was not until the 1992 election – two years after the departure of Thatcher – that this group became a cabinet committee and increased its power from that of mere persuasion. It must be also said in Thatcher's favour that it was her government, in 1988, that ordered the Civil Service to scrutinize all legislation and policies to make sure that they did not hurt women. This order, however, did not apply to earlier legislation and so its impact was perhaps not felt immediately. The party also issued a number of publications at this time, like 'Opening Doors for Women' and *A Britain without Barriers*, to emphasize what they had done for women.

Of course, in 1990 Thatcher fell from power, a victim of her own dominating personality. She was replaced by a man, John Major. The loss of Thatcher caused the party to relinquish a large part of its feminine image. Furthermore, Major made the initial mistake of not including any woman in his first cabinet, and this provoked an outcry from women MPs and party supporters. He soon rectified this by placing in his next cabinet Gillian Shephard at the Department of Employment and Virginia Bottomley at the Ministry of Health. Both of these women had supported him in the leadership contest and were well-qualified for their positions. It must be noted too that when John Major appointed Gillian Shephard to be Employment Secretary he gave her responsibility for women's issues, a task for which she showed considerable enthusiasm. In 1994 Shephard was moved to the Ministry of Education where she immediately improved relations with union leaders. This was not terribly difficult since her predecessor, John Patten, had been forced to pay damages to Birmingham's Director of Education for describing him as 'a nutter' and 'a madman'.[25] He also appointed a number of other women to important public posts. After the 1992 election the party chairman, Norman Fowler announced that he wanted the party to have at least one hundred women candidates for the next general election.[26] Major did not, however, feel able to take action on the method of selecting parliamentary candidates. The constituency associations have always been extremely touchy about any incursions on their power, and Major – perhaps understandably given the rows over Europe and economic policy which were tearing the party apart – probably felt that he could not add another controversy to fuel party conflict. He did, however, make one particularly eye-catching appointment in 1996 when he named Jacqui Lait to be the first woman in the Conservative whips office in the House of Commons. She became the seventh woman in the government – which given the number of women MPs was a remarkably high percentage. The whips' office was one of the last purely masculine domains left at Westminster, and it was said that even Thatcher would only go there when she was invited.[27] Major also supported in 1991, for example, Opportunity 2000, a programme designed to help women climb the professional and corporate ladder. These successes, though, must be balanced by the departure of Emma Nicholson. Nicholson comes from a family with a centuries-old history of being MPs. She had long been active in Conservative Party politics, and had made a determined attempt while at Central Office to increase the number of women MPs. Eventually, she herself became an MP. However, Nicholson decided to leave the party in 1996. She joined the Liberal Democrats because she was so angry over her treatment by the party leaders. She felt that no matter what she did, the very fact of being a woman meant that she was unlikely to receive any major promotion. Once again, there was a complaint that women were not judged on merit but rather that they were given jobs on the basis of percentage.

In both local and national government at this time, women made significant progress. It was estimated in 1994 that women made up approximately one-quarter of local councillors.[28] In London, which has a long tradition of female involvement in local government, one-third of its local councillors were women. In the 1986 metropolitan borough elections, for example, women made up about 22 per cent of all candidates. The Conservatives had the largest number of women candidates: 27 per cent.[29] In general, it has been found that Conservatives field the largest number of women in local government elections, although one study has shown that Conservative women are less likely to win than those in other parties. Furthermore, Labour Party women candidates are significantly more likely to win.[30]

Furthermore, this period was, in many ways, a breakthrough one for women in Parliament. Paradoxically the number of women in Parliament actually declined in the 1979 election – in spite of the election of a woman prime minister – and it remained low in 1983. The 1987 one, however, saw 41 women arrive in Westminster – nearly double the previous amount. In the 1992 election this figure reached 60, which was obviously a significant improvement, although women still made up under 10 per cent of the House of Commons.[31] At the same time, there were repeated complaints by women MPs from all parties about the conduct of men in Parliament. Most of the complaints were about a group of Tory men – although Labour was not exempt from criticism. Since they made their remarks in a relatively low voice which was usually not picked up by the microphones, their comments are rarely to be found in *Hansard*'s record of Parliamentary debates. For all this, they were real enough and frequently designed to hurt. The situation has improved a great deal now – not least because of much publicity given to the question and because of the televising of parliamentary debates. Personally offensive remarks persist, however, and focus very commonly on appearance. The Labour MP, Clare Short, was amazed the first time she made a point of order during a division, for which you are required to sit down and put on a top hat. Apparently the male MPs associated women in top hats with cabarets and the Folies Bergères and went crazy when she did it – much to her embarrassment.[32] In particular, debates on subjects of specific interest to women, like abortion or parental leave, provoke a hostile response among these extremist Tories. They are frequently very insulting to women speaking on such a subject – particularly if they are from the Labour Party. Numerous complaints have also been made about the lack of facilities for women in Westminster and notably the lack of women's toilets, changing rooms and tea rooms. Many women feel there are too many bars which reinforce a masculine atmosphere.

In relation to the voters, the famous gender gap virtually disappeared in the elections of 1979, 1983 and 1987, only to reappear in 1992. In 1979, 45 per cent of men and 48 per cent of women were estimated to have voted Conservative, which is within the margin of error for such a poll. In 1983 the results were similar: 45 per cent of both men and women appeared to have voted Conservative. In 1987 the figure was also identical – 44 per cent for both men and women.[33] In 1992, however, the gender gap re-emerged, but not in a clear male/female divide. As had already been observed in the 1960s, the split was between younger and older women, and Conservative support seems to have been primarily concentrated among women over the age of 35. Younger women seem to have, if anything, voted to the left of men of their age.[34] However, recent research has shown that the gender gap is far more complex than previously thought. On the question of women's rights, for example, Conservative women voters, in general, are well to the left of their male counterparts. One survey that asked the question of whether women's rights had not gone too far, found that, while male Conservatives tended to agree with this statement, women did not. On some questions like abortion it was even found that the average Conservative woman supported women's rights more strongly than did the average male Liberal Democrat.[35] In general it was found that on almost every major issue, women were slightly to the left of men in the Conservative Party. This clearly conflicts with the often-presented image of the Conservative woman as a wild-eyed reactionary.

Undoubtedly the gender gap was responsible to a large extent for the surprise victory of the Conservatives. The reappearance of the gender gap certainly helped galvanize the Labour Party to make an effort to shed its masculine image. Labour had already conducted a study after the 1987 defeat which showed that women saw the Labour Party as the most masculine of all parties. Labour was also shocked to discover that most people thought the Conservatives had more women MPs than they did, which was clearly not the case.[36] Perhaps the presence of a woman leader with a strong personality was enough to give a feminine cast to the entire party. In any case, Labour made a concentrated effort to increase the number of women MPs. They even went so far as to impose all-women shortlists on some constituencies – a practice which, apparently to Blair's relief, was stopped in January 1996 after an industrial tribunal ruled that they violated the Sex Discrimination Act. To a large extent, it appears that Labour's masculine image is due to its heavy trade union membership. Under Neil Kinnock the party began distancing itself from the unions – a policy which was continued under John Smith and Tony Blair. Blair, in particular, has paid attention to developing the number of individual members in the party, and this, in and of itself, has increased women's membership. In 1992 women made up 40 per cent of the Labour Party's individual members, but under Tony Blair 45 per cent of new members have been women.[37] By 1997 it was obvious that Labour was losing its masculine image.

During this period the Conservative Party continued to be dominated by women at the grassroots level, although there was a noticeable falling off in numbers. It was estimated that in 1992 about one-half of the members of the Conservative Party were women. Since most earlier records are not always reliable, it is hard to establish exactly what change may have occurred. It seems likely, though, that fewer women are joining the Conservative Party and, in particular, fewer young women. We have already seen in the previous chapter that this phenomenon had been diagnosed in the 1960s and had caused quite a lot of alarm in the party hierarchy. It is safe to say that it persisted and even accelerated during the period under consideration here. Central Office continued to make efforts to attract younger, professional women into the party. Essentially, by this period two sorts of women's groups existed within the party, and they each had quite different kinds of meetings. One type of meeting was designed for the traditional Conservative woman and included all the popular old favourites: teas, luncheons, garden parties, etc. This part was controlled, to a large extent, by increasingly elderly housewives and was increasingly rejected by younger, more ambitious Conservative women. Edwina Currie's cry: 'I'm not a woman, I'm a Conservative' expressed the views of many women, who did not want to find themselves outside the mainstream of the party.[38] The other kind was created, as we have seen, with busy, career women in mind, who did not have time for the older, more leisurely type of social meeting. These two types of women were obviously very different, and, unfortunately for the Conservatives, both were less and less interested in Conservative politics during this period. Certainly the increasingly large number of working women, especially in the middle class, played a role here, for they simply no longer had the time to devote to volunteer work anymore. There is evidence, however, that the problem goes even deeper and involves both the Conservative and the Labour Parties. A 1993 poll, for example, found that 82 per cent of women between the ages of 18 and 24 were uninterested in political activities – a finding which should be of significance for all politicians.[39] One thing that certainly had not changed since the 1920s was that women were far more numerous at the bottom of the pyramid than in the higher positions. While a large number of officers at constituency rank or lower were women, considerably fewer held office at the regional level. The closer one got to the top, the lower the proportion of women. Women, for example, made up 20 per cent of the National Union and only 6 per cent of the parliamentary party.[40]

Certainly, the party attempted to modernize its image with women and, in particular, tried to raise the number of women MPs. Emma Nicholson worked in the 1980s to increase the amount of women on candidate lists and to organize conferences to attract successful women into party politics. Lady Seccombe, party vice-president in charge of women during the early 1990s, also tried to multiply the number of women candidates. It seems clear, then, that Central Office has made a continuous effort to increase the number of Conservative women MPs. The case of Virginia Bottomley tells us something about their efforts. She was undoubtedly one of the most important of the new women to enter Parliament at this time. In some ways, her background was a bit odd for a Tory MP, for she had been a social worker, magistrate and chairman of the Juvenile Court. Already deeply interested in politics, she was the wife of an MP but had not really thought of a political career for herself:

> We had a family joke that many women had got into politics on the death of their husband, taking over their seats. Peter [her husband] and myself always had this view that, if in the unfortunate circumstance the Clapham omnibus ran him over, the obvious step would be for me to try and take over his constituency. But I don't think I ever thought it was possible for me to go in for Parliament off my own bat, myself.[41]

In fact, she did not put herself forward, but Sir Anthony Royle, at that time vice-chairman of the party, contacted her husband and told him:

'I'd like your permission to approach Virginia.'[42] This incident illustrates perfectly well the traditionalism within the party, and its leaders' desire to present a more modern image. The first step taken by Royle was not to talk to Virginia Bottomley but to sound out her husband. At the same time it does show that the party is on the look-out for good women candidates and willing to take the initiative by approaching someone suitable. She entered Parliament in a by-election in 1984 and quickly climbed to the top. It did not take her long to reach ministerial rank at the Department of the Environment. At this time her husband was also in the government as Minister for Transport, so they became one of the rare ministerial couples in the House's history. As we have already seen, she later became Minister of Health under John Major. Bottomley's time as Health Secretary, however, was not happy as she oversaw a period of major change and gross underfunding in the Health Service. Bottomley was most criticized for the closure of London's hospitals. In the case of St Bartholomew's, for example, a hospital that had been founded in 1123, she announced its closure in the written answer to a parliamentary question.[43] The extensiveness of the London hospital closures was fiercely attacked, particularly after the death of a patient for whom doctors could not find a hospital bed.[44] The final result was that the government was forced to modify its policy, and Bottomley was moved from Health. She became Heritage Secretary in a cabinet reshuffle of that year.

In spite of this, complaints continued to be voiced at this time that selection committees remained generally opposed to women MPs. Teresa Gorman, a right-wing feminist, wrote an article in *The Daily Mail* which recounted some of the more hair-raising examples of sexism that prospective women candidates had encountered during meetings with constituency associations. During one interview she observed that the chairman was staring at her:

> He finally put the question that made me realise I would not be chosen to fight an election for the Conservatives in his town. 'We liked your speech,' he said. 'But tell me, why did you wear high heels?' For a moment I was speechless. I'd expected him to ask my views on the economy, Northern Ireland, the police. 'I mean to say,' he went on, 'you couldn't go canvassing around the streets in those, could you?'[45]

She cited innumerable instances of sexist remarks to candidates, most of them concerning their appearance. One woman was told that she was too fat, another that she was too small, a third that they did not like her hairstyle. One woman was even told that she was too glamorous. Teresa Gorman was one of the lucky ones for she managed to get a safe seat in 1987. In some ways it was a fluke – at the last minute the sitting MP had to resign over a scandal, and the committee had only a few days to find a new candidate. They chose Gorman, and nineteen days before the vote, she became a candidate for one of the safest seats in Britain.

For all of this, there were clear signs of resistance to change at the base of the party. One investigation of local Tory associations found that segregation of the sexes was still the rule in many areas:

> Benton Conservative Club, like almost every other Conservative Club in the country, is a bastion of male privilege. It started out as a men-only club, somewhere to shelter from domestic duties and, as in hundreds of other clubs, Conservative or otherwise, the conversation in the men's bar relies still heavily on nudges and winks about telling the wife or not telling the wife. The gulf between the sexes has only been bridged to the extent of admitting women as associate members, who pay half the £20 annual subscription. They know that they are only allowed in by kind male permission, restricted to certain areas of the building.[46]

The popular image of the party then tended towards the reactionary. The Carlton Club, that bastion of the Conservative Party, continued to refuse to admit women. The only exception they made was for Thatcher since the party leader had always belonged to the club – but even this they did rather grudgingly. Apparently, it would have been a greater sacrilege not to have had the party leader a member than to allow a woman to enter. In particular, however, the women's sections have been criticized for their anti-feminist position. It has been accepted wisdom that women members of the party are more right-wing than the average Conservative female voter, but this is also true of men. According to the 'law of curvilinear disparity', the rank-and-file of the Conservative Party tend to be to the right of both the electorate and their leaders, and the exact same phenomenon is repeated in the Labour Party, although this time on the left.[47] This sounds logical, since people who have strong political ideas are more likely to become party militants. There is nothing particularly extraordinary or unusual, then, about the fact that Conservative women party activists tend to be on the right of the political spectrum. It must be admitted, however, that recent research on British politics has called into question the 'law of curvilinear disparity'. A 1995 study found little difference between the views of party members and voters in either Labour or the Conservatives, with the important exception of education.[48] It is safe to say that the reactionary nature of Conservative Party members has been exaggerated.

A 1994 study of Conservative Party members characterized the typical one as retired, coming from a middle-class background, owner of his or her house and possessing few educational degrees.[49] Since most of the party's members are retired, they are also elderly with about one-half of the membership over the age of 66. In contrast only about 5 per cent are under the age of 35. This, of course, has serious implications for the party's future and shows that all the efforts made since the 1960s to attract younger members have failed for the most part. In the Whiteley, Seyd and Richardson study it was estimated that the party should lose about 40 per cent of its membership by the early twenty-first century. The advanced age of Conservative Party militants certainly had a role in the decline in the party structure which was so evident in the 1997 election. Of course, the Labour Party also has problems attracting younger members, but not to anywhere near the extent of the Conservatives.

It is time now to consider the 1997 general election in more detail. Obviously, it devastated the Conservative Party, and Conservative women shared in this decimation. One of the most evident characteristics about this election was that the gender gap disappeared again. According to a Labour Party report leaked to the *Independent on Sunday*, about 45 per cent of women supported Labour which means that men and women voted in equal numbers for Blair's party. The same report estimated that 1.8 million people who had voted for the Conservatives in 1992 supported Labour in 1997 and that about one million Conservatives decided simply to stay at home.[50] Labour also succeeded in getting 101 women MPs elected – approximately one-third of their members. In all, 119 women were elected which makes the 1997 election a watershed for women's representation in Parliament: for the first time in history, women MPs totalled over 20 per cent of all members. The contrast with the Conservative Party could not be greater, for only seven women held their seats, and five new ones were elected. Of the latter group, three are considered to be pro-European and to the left of the party while the other two are resolutely opposed to the single currency. The major woman casualty was probably Edwina Currie, who ended her long parliamentary career then. Anne Widdecombe was one of the few to survive, although some Conservatives may have come to regret this because of the campaign she led against Michael Howard's bid to be party leader.[51] The arrival of all these Labour women certainly made an impression in Parliament and the nation.[52] One Conservative MP commented: 'I can't get over the visual impact of all those women on the Labour benches... It brings home the stark contrast with ours.'[53]

As this book goes to press, it is too early to tell if the momentum will be kept up and whether it will spread to the Conservative Party. Complaints were still being heard in May 1997 that Conservative selection committees – even those with a large proportion of female members – still did not like to nominate women candidates.[54] Of course there have been positive signs as well. Researchers for the British Candidate Study were told by many Conservative constituency associations that they make every effort to include women on their shortlist. One person said: 'I went down to 14 deliberately because the 14th happened to be a woman,' and another insisted: 'I was trying desperately to find a woman but from the CVs they didn't come out.'[55] This points to another problem: that women simply do not apply to be candidates in the same numbers as men – and this is especially true in the Conservative Party now. The selection committees are not the only ones to blame, since even with the best intentions they simply do not find enough women. We have already seen how Virginia Bottomley, whose husband was an MP and who was herself actively involved in politics, had never considered becoming an MP until she was approached by Central Office. While sexism undoubtedly remains a problem in some selection committees, it is also true that the best women candidates simply never consider politics as a career. The long hours and the often long distances between home, Westminster and the constituency are obviously a handicap for women with small children. The demands of work and family put enormous pressures on any woman, but when the career is as exacting as that of being a Member of Parliament, it must seem unbearable to most. Perhaps one of the first steps towards getting more women into the House is to make its working hours more normal and have sessions in the morning. It must also be said that many women delay going into politics until their children have grown, which makes them past the upper age limit considered by most constituencies. Most selection committees prefer someone under forty who can stay their MP for twenty-five or thirty years. It is often extremely difficult for anyone over that age to become a candidate for a winnable seat. Perhaps the sight of all those women MPs on television will have a good effect and accustom everyone – both men and women – to the idea. Women clearly still have a long way to go, but the numbers elected in 1997 are encouraging. Perhaps the Conservative Party will also be able to bring about such an increase in its number of women MPs.

10 Conclusion

In our analysis of the relationship between women and the Conservative Party from the time of Disraeli to the present, certain themes have clearly emerged. First, women's involvement in the Conservative Party has always emphasized conviviality and social events, and their respectability has been a major factor in their success. Conservative Party functions have simply been more feminine than their equivalents in the Labour Party and therefore have attracted more women. Second, from the political point of view, there has rarely been a large difference between Labour and the Conservatives with regard to women's issues. They both have, at least until recently, stressed woman in her role of wife and mother, and the dominant philosophy in both parties has been that woman's place is in the home – at least until a chronic shortage of workers forced them to re-evaluate this stand. Finally, a certain tension is apparent in the Conservative Party between femininity and feminism and between feminism and conservatism. There has been a long tradition of family first and a glorification of the housewife – although this has never kept Conservative women from high achievements in the workplace. Let us now consider these themes in more detail.

The social role of women in the Conservative Party has always been immensely important. The aristocratic basis of the party in the nineteenth century meant that most politicians were directly or indirectly related to each other. Particularly great families like the Cecils were linked to a large number of other families through marriage ties, and this, of course, tended to give a certain authority to women. The case of Georgina, Lady Salisbury is classic: with her husband, three sons, two nephews and numerous more distant relatives all involved in politics, she could hardly help being interested in it. Once she made up her mind on an issue too, she certainly could easily make her opinion be known to people of immense influence – who just happened to be in her home. The political hostess was probably the most obvious manifestation of this phenomenon. Until the 1922 Committee and other backbench organizations were formed, the Conservatives had no consultative mechanism between the leaders and the rank and file members in Parliament. This desperately needed communication took place at social events, and the political hostesses played an important part in the political process by organizing parties and, most importantly, by establishing the guest list. Rising MPs from outside the aristocracy often found that a female patron was an excellent way of getting a foothold on the ladder towards success.

The Primrose League transformed women's involvement in the Conservative Party into that of a mass movement, but here, once again, we see the importance of the social dimension. The Primrose League was a political organization, of course, but it fulfilled a major recreational function too. This was the key to its success: it gave leisured women something to do that made them feel worthwhile. It also educated them about politics, so that they could out-argue men, which, in and of itself, was something of a revolution. Although the mass engagement of women in politics was novel, the Conservatives justified this as an extension of women's domestic role. Indeed, philanthropic work for women was widely accepted by this time, and the Primrose League could be viewed as a simple transference of the philanthropic spirit to a new realm. Thus, politics became socially acceptable for women. The Primrose League also catered to the need of non-working women to do something in their spare time and provided them with a respectable source of entertainment. In the twentieth century the Conservative Party's organization for women repeated the success of the Primrose League – at least until the 1960s – and duplicated its traditions. It has thus been primarily viewed as a social group by its women members at the base of the organization, but it is one that does vital political work. These women simply found the Conservatives more feminine and more congenial than the trade union dominated Labour Party. Women became the foundation of the Conservative Party as a mass organization and, after 1918, of its electoral support. The so-called gender gap – the fact that more women than men vote Conservative – caused that party to return to power in 1951 and kept it there for much of the later period.

Now let us turn to the second theme: that of the similarity of Labour and Conservative policy towards women. It has long been a staple idea that feminism belongs to the left, but this book takes the position that this is not the case. Both left and right have been dominated by men and by their ideas. Until recently, the philosophy of both parties was the same: a woman's place is in the home, and both parties justified political changes because they helped women as wives and mothers. This is as true of the welfarism of the postwar Labour Party as of Conservatism. Furthermore, even when the parties have supported a more clearly feminist issue – as in the case of equal pay, for example – they have done so because they knew most people were in favour of it. Politicians generally wait until social attitudes have changed before introducing major reforms. Basically, the attitudes of both parties have been shaped by political advantage. This is most clearly seen in the debate over suffrage, when politicians discussed not whether it was right for women to vote, but whether it would help their party. The basic issue in all parties was that of universal manhood suffrage – the 'woman question' was simply a corollary to this.

This brings us to our third theme: that of feminism versus femininity. Conservative women have generally exhibited a preoccupation with home and family and have insisted that they always put family first. This characteristic appears in women as busy and powerful as Nancy Astor or Margaret Thatcher. Thatcher went so far as to portray herself as something of a housewife, insisting that she made breakfast, shopped for food and tidied the house like anyone else. Of course, no one believed her (unless she did), but it was all part of her image. Clothes, of course, are another subject of fascination. Thatcher had closets full of them and loved to talk about them. This, of course, is by no means peculiar to Conservatives, as Labour women like Barbara Castle have also shown an interest in fashion. However, Conservative women have, not infrequently, refused the title of feminist, and, in some cases, there has even been evidence of a certain hostility to feminism. The most obvious case is with regard to women candidates for constituencies. Source after source from the 1920s to the 1990s states that local women are more hostile than men to women candidates for Parliament. Throughout the years, Central Office has repeatedly made efforts to increase the number of women MPs and met with very little success. Of course, this is not entirely the fault of constituency associations, for in many cases women simply did not stand. Since very few women present themselves at the first stage as potential candidates, even fewer make it into Parliament. Furthermore, the fact that someone rejects the title feminist does not mean that they are not one. Feminism means different things to different people. Thatcher may have denied being one, but, at the same time, she would not have reached 10 Downing Street if she had not had a rather advanced notion of women's role.

For those who are successful or quite simply for those who are inclined towards feminism, a tension may develop between their feminism and their conservatism. We see this most clearly in the cases of Conservative suffrage leaders like Lady Selborne or Lady Frances Balfour. Here the dilemma is: which comes first, conservatism or suffragism? Suffragism pushed them towards the Labour Party which had a more progressive position on the question, but their politics on other questions was undoubtedly Conservative. This phenomenon was also repeated in the 1960s (and certainly more recently than that) when many women found themselves torn between their feminism and their conservatism. This accounts for the maverick behaviour of certain women, like Nancy Astor, Thelma Cazalet-Keir or Irene Ward, who were frequently at odds with their party. However, it would still be wrong to see feminism as the sole possession of the left. The Labour Party – and in particular one of its major components the trade unions – has often been anti-feminist in outlook, notably over questions relating to employment. The exact same tension has existed on the left as well, for women there too have anguished over whether they were first a feminist or first a socialist, since very often the two have not agreed. There is nothing peculiar to conservatism about this dilemma. In fact, in recent times Conservative women have developed their own idea of feminism: one that refuses special assistance specifically for women on the grounds that it encourages men to continue to think of them as in some way inferior. While it may not be agreeable to all feminists, there is a certain element of truth in it.

Recent history has seen the decline of that once mighty force, the Conservative women's organization. To a large extent this has come about because women's role in society is changing. Since the war, more and more women have entered the workforce, and they therefore have less time for volunteer activities. Furthermore, much of what the party offered women was entertainment and companionship – a way of livening up otherwise boring days at home. As more and more women go to work, this is less and less necessary. The result of this social change has been that the Conservative women's organization has appeared to be more and more out of touch with its times and that ambitious women have been abandoning it in droves. In recent times, Thatcher, Edwina Currie and, in fact, most other prominent women in the party have had little to do the women's sections. To many people their members seem almost caricatural. This fact has been clearly shown by the declining numbers and the ageing membership of the women's sections since the 1960s. Although the party made various attempts to arrest this trend, they have never made much headway against it. At the same time the gender gap has disappeared – although it did reappear briefly in the 1992 election – and Labour has managed to develop a feminine image for itself, especially after the 1997 election. Labour has been making continual efforts since the war to attract women, and it has made a concerted effort to promote women to visible positions. This is certainly one of the reasons for the decline of the gender gap since women seem to perceive Labour as a less and less masculine organization. To some extent, this tendency was arrested in the 1970s and 1980s, first, by Edward Heath's dynamic espousal of women's causes and then by the election of a woman as party leader. Since 1992, however, Labour has become perceptively more feminine than the Conservatives. On the surface, the future relationship between women and the Conservative Party does not look as if it will be as intimate as in the past. Things, however, can still change.

The history of women and the Conservative Party, then, has been long and varied. It contains many remarkable figures and many very ordinary ones. More than anything else, it has reflected women's position in society. It would be wrong to judge people in the past by our standards today – an error which feminist writers make not infrequently. While progress towards sexual equality may seem slow to some, it has been steady and consistent since the nineteenth century. The problem is that the definition of progress has changed constantly as each generation takes for granted the hard-won achievements of the previous one. At the time of the Primrose League, the very fact of belonging to a political organization was often excitement and liberation enough, but for us it inspires simply a yawn. Not everyone can be a Pankhurst, loudly and militantly demanding rights. Nor can everyone be like John Stuart Mill, who was far in advance of his time on the question of women's rights. It would be a shame to discard Conservative women from the history of feminism simply because they were too polite and because they were too much a prisoner of their own times. They belong to the history of feminism as much as do women on the left or those on the militant fringe. In some ways, they are a far more accurate measure of the changing role of women simply because of their social conservatism. They have contributed in their own way to the liberation of women, and in many cases their contribution has been of the highest importance. In the past, conservatism and feminism have not necessarily been opposed terms. What they may be in the future is still to discover.

Notes

INTRODUCTION

1   Olive Banks, *Faces of Feminism* (Oxford, 1981).
2   Martin Pugh has been instrumental in detailing the relationship between the right and feminism, notably in *The Tories and the People* (Oxford, 1985).
3   Christabel Pankhurst was an approved candidate of the Lloyd George Liberal-Conservative coalition in 1918. Even stranger, perhaps, Mrs Emmeline Pankhurst was a Conservative candidate at the time of her death. It would not be difficult to qualify each woman – at least in her later life – as Conservative.
4   Secret report on policy for women by Douglas?, 24.9.69, CRD 3/38/4, Conservative Party Papers, Bodleian Library, Oxford (henceforth cited as CPP).

1 WOMEN IN THE POLITICAL BACKGROUND

1   Quoted in Brian Harrison, *Separate Spheres: The Opposition to Women's Suffrage in Britain* (London, 1978), 81.
2   For more on Mary Anne Disraeli see Elizabeth Lee, *Wives of the Prime Ministers* (London, 1918).
3   The Primrose League will be discussed in more detail in Chapter 2.
4   For Lady Salisbury's correspondence with Disraeli see the Disraeli Papers, 93/2, Bodleian Library, Oxford (henceforth cited as BLO).
5   On being asked by another woman if the Primrose League was not vulgar, Lady Salisbury replied: 'Vulgar? Of course it is. That is why we've got on so well.' In Mrs George Cornwallis-West (ed.), *The Reminiscences of Lady Randolph Churchill* (Bath, 1908, repub., 1973), 100.
6   For more on this see Patrick Joyce, 'Popular Toryism in Lancashire 1860–1890' (DPhil, Oxford, 1975).
7   Randolph Churchill, *Lord Derby, 'King of Lancashire'* (London, 1959), 65–6.
8   J. C. C. Davidson to Miss Law, 6.12.1916 in Robert Rhodes James, *Memoirs of a Conservative: J. C. C. Davidson's Memoirs and Papers 1910–37* (London, 1969), 46.
9   For more on Mary Derby see Esther Shkolnik, *Leading Ladies: A Study of Eight Late Victorian and Edwardian Political Wives* (London, 1987).
10 Quoted in Winifred, Lady Burghclere, *A Great Man's Friendship: Letters of the Duke of Wellington to Mary Marchioness of Salisbury 1850–1852* (London, 1927), 36.
11 Richard Shannon, *The Age of Disraeli* (London, 1992), 169.

12   Salisbury to Lady Salisbury, 15.2.1874 in Lady Gwendolyn Cecil, *Life of Robert Marquess of Salisbury, Vol. 2* (London, 1921), 46–7.
13   Disraeli to Salisbury, 16.2.1874 in Cecil, Vol. 2, 48.
14   Mary Salisbury to Disraeli, 16.1.1865, Disraeli Papers, 113/4, BLO.
15   See Mary Salisbury to Disraeli, 29.6.1876 and 7.9.1876 in Disraeli Papers, 113/4, BLO.
16   A. J. P. Taylor called Derby 'the most isolationist foreign secretary that Great Britain has ever known' in *The Struggle for Mastery in Europe, 1848–1918* (London, 1954), 233.
17   For more on this see Robert Blake, *Disraeli* (London, 1967), 623 ff. and Shkolnik, 222–3.
18   See Blake, 634–5.
19   Mary Derby to Disraeli, 6.10.1878 in Disraeli Papers, 113/4.
20   See, for example, Gladstone to Lady Derby, 17.5.1882 on Derby's refusal to take office, in H. C. G. Matthew (ed.), *The Gladstone Diaries, Vol. X* (Oxford, 1990), 263–4.
21   Memorandum by Queen Victoria, 20.2.1874 in G. E. Buckle (ed.), *The Letters of Queen Victoria, Vol. 2, 1870–1898* (London, 1926), 822.
22   Quoted in Blake, 546.
23   Disraeli to Victoria, 17.4.1874, in Buckle, Vol. 2, 333–4.
24   Blake, 546.
25   Victoria to Disraeli, 11.7.1874 in Buckle, Vol. 2, 341–2.
26   Victoria to Disraeli, 26.1.1875 in Buckle, Vol. 2, 373.
27   Disraeli to Victoria, 26.1.1875 in Buckle, Vol. 2, 373–4. Disraeli eventually gave way to Victoria on this issue, in spite of the fact that he knew it would cause unfavourable criticism. He did, however, have his price and immediately afterwards asked Victoria to agree to his friend, Sydney Turner, for a future appointment.
28   Victoria to the Earl of Beaconsfield (Disraeli), 28.9.1876 in Buckle, Vol. 2, 480.
29   Quoted in Stanley Weintraub, *Victoria* (London, 1987), 414.
30   I have followed here Richard Shannon, *The Age of Salisbury* (London, 1996), 91.
31   Victoria to Salisbury, 31.10.1884 in Buckle, Vol. 3, 563.
32   For more on this see H. C. G. Matthew, *Gladstone, 1875–1898* (Oxford, 1995), 149.
33   Victoria to Salisbury, 3.12.1885 in Buckle, Vol. 3, 706–7.
34   Although as Matthew has noted in *Gladstone, 1875–1898*, 260, the reverse was not true. The Conservative opposition did not write to her on such questions. This clearly shows that while they differed in form from the Liberals, they did not differ in content.
35   We shall hear more about her activities in Chapter 2.
36   H. Montgomery Hyde, *The Londonderrys* (London, 1979), 94–5.
37   Martin Pugh, *The Tories and the People* (Oxford, 1985), 57.
38   Blake, *The Unknown Prime Minister* (London, 1955), 88
39   Hyde, 151–2.
40   Ibid., 159.
41   There is no doubt though that Lord Londonderry's obvious limits were also responsible for his lack of advancement. The correspondence

between Davidson and Lady Londonderry contained in the Davidson Papers, 188, House of Lords Record Office, London gives a good idea of the tense relationship between the party chairman and the Londonderrys. A letter written by Lady Londonderry on 11.12.29, is quite interesting. Although, in the opinion of this author, Davidson's letter was perfectly polite, Lady Londonderry thought otherwise: 'I have received your letter of this morning, and it is exactly the kind of letter I expected from you. If you do not realise yourself how rude the whole thing is, it only confirms in my mind how hopeless the management of our Central Office is. If you treat me in this very off hand fashion, I hardly like to contemplate what occurs elsewhere.' She goes on to insist that: 'Considering that it is I who organised the ball which produced all the money for the Anti-Socialist campaign in the north, and it is to my husband that you owe everything in these quarters, the only time there has been a failure was at the last election, when the Central Office ran the campaign and they lost nearly every seat. I do not accuse the Central Office naturally of any intentional discourtesy, but of gross ignorance in the management of affairs of this sort.' Lady Londonderry apparently thought that Davidson and Central Office were not showing her enough deference.

42   Marquess of Londonderry, *Ourselves and Germany* (London, 1938).
43   Marchioness of Londonderry, *Retrospect* (London, 1938), 127–8. It was Lady Londonderry who removed her hostess's name and replaced it by a blank.

2 THE PRIMROSE LEAGUE

1   Quoted in Michael Bentley, *Politics without Democracy* (London, 1984), 267.
2   For more on Churchill see R. F. Foster's biography, *Lord Randolph Churchill* (London, 1981).
3   See Janet Robb, *The Primrose League, 1883–1906* (New York, 1942), 33. Strangely enough, Lady Salisbury had come to the same conclusion as Churchill: 'We must have caucuses' she wrote in 1880. Quoted in Shannon, *The Age of Disraeli*, 330.
4   See Lady Dorothy Nevill, *The Reminiscences of Lady Dorothy Nevill* (London, 1906).
5   Martin Pugh, *The Tories and the People* (Oxford, 1985), 12–13. Throughout this account of the Primrose League, I have depended heavily on Pugh.
6   Mrs George Cornwallis-West (ed.), *The Reminiscences of Lady Randolph Churchill* (Bath, 1908, repub. 1973), 98. Note that membership was open to Roman Catholics and Protestant Dissenters, which in and of itself was revolutionary, particularly for a Conservative organization. The Church of England, after all, was often said to be the Tory Party at prayer. The recruitment of non-Anglicans would be one of the League's greatest successes.
7   See page 8.

8   Quoted in Martin Pugh, *The Making of Modern British Politics 1867–1939* (Oxford, 1982, 2nd ed. 1992), 55.
9   Pugh, *The Tories and the People*, 144.
10 Richard Shannon, *The Age of Salisbury* (London: 1995), 114. Martin Pugh in *The Making of British Politics*, 55, says that the League claimed that nine-tenths of its membership was working class.
11 Pugh, *The Tories and the People*, 123.
12 Minutes for 15.12.1883, in MSS.PL.1, Primrose League Papers, BLO (henceforth cited as PLP).
13 Jennie Churchill, preface to 'The Primrose League: How Ladies Can Help It' (London, 1885).
14 Cornwallis-West, 124.
15 Ibid., 125
16 Cited in Martin Pugh, *The Tories and the People*, 48.
17 Robb, 49.
18 Pugh, *The Tories and the People*, 49
19 Ibid., 50.
20 Cornwallis-West, 98. See also the meeting of 2 March 1885 when the Ladies Grand Council was officially constituted in MSS.PL.10/1, PLP.
21 Meeting of 6.6.1885 in MSS.PL.10/1, PLP.
22 *The Morning Post*, 22.2.1886.
23 Report on the annual meeting of the LGC in *The Morning Post*, 14.5.1892.
24 'Report of the Executive Committee of the LGC', May 1887 in MSS.PL/11, PLP.
25 *The Morning Post*, 22.2.1886.
26 Cornwallis-West, 128–9.
27 Quoted in Pugh, *The Tories and the People*, 53.
28 'Report of the Executive Committee of the LGC', May 1887 in MSS.PL/11, PLP.
29 *Primrose League Gazette*, 19.11.1897.
30 Report on a meeting of the LGC in *The Morning Post*, 26.5.1887.
31 *Primrose League Gazette*, 19.11.1887.
32 Lady Montagu, 'Why Should Women Care for Politics?', paper read at the annual meeting of the LGC, 1.5.1888, MSS.PL/11, PLP.
33 One need only think of Margaret Thatcher, when she was Minister of Education ending an important meeting with civil servants in order to buy bacon for Denis. Of course, Thatcher had no love for civil servants. In any case, it was certainly an original and even rather tactful way of ending a discussion.
34 Report on a meeting of the LGC in *The Morning Post*, 26.5.1887.
35 Lady Montagu, op. cit.
36 Minutes of the Ladies Grand Council, 9.3.1897, MSS.PL/13, PLP.
37 See, for example, *Primrose League Gazette*, 19.11.1887.
38 *Primrose League Gazette*, 25.2.1893. By 'what they held most beloved' the speaker is referring to the union of Great Britain and Ireland, because the home rule crisis was going on at this time.
39 Jean Gaffin, 'Women and Cooperation' in Lucy Middleton (ed.), *Women in the Labour Movement* (London, 1977), 114.

40 Ibid., 117.
41 Pugh, *The Tories and the People*, 68.
42 Ibid., 69.
43 Sheila Ferguson, 'Labour Women and the Social Services' in Middleton, op. cit., 40.
44 Ibid., 69.
45 Cornwallis-West, 127.
46 *The Morning Post*, 25.5.1887.
47 Pugh, *The Tories and the People*, 68.
48 Ibid., 69.
49 Quoted in Beatrix Campbell, *Iron Ladies: Why do Women Vote Tory?* (London, 1987), 15.

3 THE CONSERVATIVE PARTY AND THE CAMPAIGN FOR WOMEN'S SUFFRAGE

1   Quoted in Pugh, *The Tories and the People*, 57.
2   Quoted in David Morgan, *Suffragists and Liberals: The Politics of Woman Suffrage in Britain* (Oxford, 1975), 69.
3   Ibid., 63.
4   As late as 1924, the Duchess of Atholl, then a Member of Parliament, moved rejection of an equal franchise bill on the grounds that it would extend the vote to 'people who live in caravans' and to 'those who travel the roads as hawkers ... [and to] tinkers', *Parliamentary Debates*, 5th series, 29.2.1924, col. 866.
5   For more on this see, for example, Martin Pugh, *Women and the Women's Movement in Britain* (London, 1992) and *Electoral Reform in Peace and War* (London, 1978).
6   Morgan, 16.
7   Les Garner, *Stepping Stones to Women's Liberty* (London, 1984), 11.
8   *The Conservative and Unionist Women's Franchise Review*, November 1910.
9   *Primrose League Gazette*, 15.12.1886.
10 Mrs Henry Fawcett, 'The Constitutional Policy and Its Developments', in *The Men's League Handbook on Women's Suffrage* (London, 1914), 45.
11 Ibid., 50.
12 Lord Selborne to Bonar Law, April 1911, box 18/7, Bonar Law Papers, House of Lords Record Office (henceforth cited as HLRO).
13 *Primrose League Gazette*, 1.9.1910.
14 Eleanor Cecil to Maud, Countess of Selborne, 6.2.1914, MS.Eng. Lett.d.424, Countess of Selborne Papers, BLO.
15 Brian Harrison, *Separate Spheres: The Opposition to Women's Suffrage in Britain* (London, 1978), 84.
16 I have followed Edwardian use for the terms suffragist (constitutional feminist) and suffragette (militant feminist).
17 Eleanor Cecil to Maud Selborne, 3.11.1909, MS.Eng.Lett.d.424, Countess of Selborne Papers, BLO.

18   Robert Cecil to Maud Selborne, 29.6.1911, MS.Eng.Lett.d.427, Count-
     ess of Selborne Papers, BLO.
19   Christabel Pankhurst to Arthur Balfour, 6.10.1907, Add. 49793, Balfour
     Papers, British Library (henceforth cited as BL).
20   Morgan, 34.
21   Christabel Pankhurst to Arthur Balfour, 28.10.1907, Add. 49793,
     Balfour Papers, BL.
22   Morgan, 47.
23   Arthur Balfour to Christabel Pankhurst, 23.10.1907, Add. 49793,
     Balfour Papers, BL.
24   Arthur Balfour to Mrs Templeton, 29.10.1909, Add. 49793, Balfour
     Papers, BL. He sent this as a circular to various suffrage associations.
25   Balfour to Pankhurst, op. cit.
26   Pugh, *The Tories and the People*, 60–1.
27   These results are all taken from Pugh, *The Tories and the People*, 61.
     Pugh took his figures from Harrison, *Separate Spheres: The Opposition
     to Women's Suffrage in Britain* and recalculated them so as to exclude
     Liberal Unionists. If they are included, the results show a significantly
     higher number of votes against women's suffrage.
28   Entry for 19 January 1913 in John Ramsden (ed.), *Real Old Tory
     Politics: The Political Diaries of Sir Robert Sandars, Lord Bayford,
     1910–1935* (London, 1984), 59.
29   Austen Chamberlain to Mary Chamberlain, 26.3.1909, in Austen Cham-
     berlain, *Politics from Inside: An Epistolary Chronicle 1906–1914* (Lon-
     don, 1937), 169.
30   Stanley Baldwin, 29.3.1928, col. 1480, *Parliamentary Debates*, 5th series,
     Vol. 215.
31   Quoted in Harrison, 204.
32   I have closely followed here the reasoning used by Martin Pugh in his
     books, *Electoral Reform in War and Peace* and *Women and the Women's
     Movement in Britain 1914–1959*.
33   Pugh, *Women and the Women's Movement in Britain 1914–1959*, 39.
34   *Parliamentary Debates*, 5th series, 29.2.1924, col. 866.
35   John Ramsden, *The Age of Balfour and Baldwin* (London, 1975),
     120.
36   Note the use of the word 'virtual'. It has been calculated that 94.9 per cent
     of English males were given the vote by this act. The main hindrance to
     complete male suffrage was the need to meet a residency requirement.
     See Kenneth O. Morgan, *Consensus and Disunity: The Lloyd George
     Coalition Government, 1918–1922* (Oxford, 1979), 152.
37   Harrison, 205.
38   Report in *The Times*, 10.1.1918.

4 THE PARTY MOBILIZES FOR WOMEN

1   Not infrequently the word 'Amalgamated' is dropped from its name,
     and its initials then become WUTRA.

2   In Oxfordshire for example, 24 habitations were taken over by the party. John Ramsden, 'The Organization of the Conservative and Unionist Party in Britain, 1910–1930' (Oxford, DPhil, 1974), 172.

3   Pugh, *The Tories and the People*, 178.

4   For more on the party structure see Anthony Seldon and Stuart Ball, *Conservative Century* (Oxford, 1994).

5   National Union minutes, transcript of Special London Conference, 30.11.1917, quoted in John Ramsden, *The Age of Balfour and Baldwin* (London, 1975), 119.

6   Pugh, *Women and the Women's Movement in Britain*, 63.

7   Arthur Fawcett, *Conservative Agent* (Yorkshire, 1967), 23.

8   *Conservative Agents' Journal*, November 1927, 302. Of course, many men also preferred keeping women in a separate organization so as to preserve the all-male atmosphere of many conservative clubs. For more on this see David Jarvis, 'The Conservative Party and the Politics of Gender', in Martin Francis and Ina Zweiniger- Bargielowska (eds.), *The Conservatives and British Society 1880–1990* (Cardiff, 1996).

9   *Conservative Agents' Journal*, June 1924, 138–9.

10 The use of the term 'women organizers' did not appear immediately. At first they were generally called 'women agents', but 'agent' implied that they, like their male counterparts, had passed the examination to become certified Conservative Party agents. This was clearly not the case at first and so the term 'organizer' had to be used instead.

11 *Conservative Agents' Journal*, October 1922, 19–20.

12 Fawcett, 25.

13 *Conservative Agents' Journal*, November 1927, 303.

14 Central Women's Advisory Committee, 18th Annual Conference Handbook, 10 May 1939, CCO 170/3/1, CPP.

15 Beatrix Campbell, *Iron Ladies: Why do Women Vote Tory?* (London, 1987), 51.

16 Pugh, *Women and the Women's Movement in Britain*, 126.

17 Robert Rhodes James, *Memoirs of a Conservative: J. C. C. Davidson's Memoirs and Papers 1910–1937* (London, 1969), 266.

18 Memorandum by Davidson, n.d., some time in early 1930, DAV/190, Davidson Papers, HLRO.

19 His conflict with Lady Londonderry, which we saw in Chapter 1, was typical of Davidson. He wanted a modern professional party and had little time for the old aristocracy.

20 Davidson to Sir Charles Nall-Cain, 8.12.1929, DAV/188, Davidson Papers, HLRO.

21 Memorandum by Davidson, op. cit.

22 Pugh, *Women and the Women's Movement in Britain*, 125.

23 Quoted in J. Lovenduski, P. Norris and C. Burness, 'The Party and Women', in Seldon and Ball, *Conservative Century*, 623–4.

24 Pugh, *The Tories and the People*, 179–81.

25 See, for example, the minutes of the formation of the Southwestern Area Committee on 13 May 1920 in ARE/11/11/1, Women's Advisory Committee, CPP.

26   Minutes of the Women's Parliamentary Council, Western Area, 4.11.1926, ARE/11/11/1, op. cit.
27   Eva Hubback to Lady Astor, 14.5.1923, 1416/1/1/260, Astor Papers, Reading University Library (henceforth cited as RUL).
28   For more on this see Pugh, *Women and the Women's Movement in Britain*, 61.
29   For more on this see D. Jarvis, 'Mrs Maggs and Betty, the Conservative Appeal to Women Voters in the 1920s', in *Twentieth Century British History* (No. 5, 1994).
30   This election consecrated the split in the Liberal Party for Lloyd George and his Liberal supporters decided to continue the coalition with the Conservatives. It was called the 'coupon' election by Asquith because official coalition candidates received a letter of support from Lloyd George and Bonar Law. This same election in Ireland led to an overwhelming victory by Sinn Féin in what is now the Republic of Ireland and the formation of a separate Irish Parliament.
31   Quoted in Pamela Brookes, *Women at Westminster* (London, 1967), 9.
32   See Chapter 1 for information on the great aristocratic families and their interconnections. Elizabeth Vallance, *Women in the House* (London, 1979), 27.
33   Stuart Ball, *Baldwin and the Conservative Party* (London, 1988), 21.
34   Until then ladies had only been allowed to watch the debates from behind a grille so that the men could not see them. It was believed that the sight of women would distract the MPs from their work.
35   *The Times*, 2.12.1919.
36   *The Times*, 16.5.1930.
37   This question is discussed in more detail in Chapter 7.
38   Quoted in R. T. McKenzie, *British Political Parties* (London, 1955), 277.
39   Sue McCowan, *Widening Horizons: Women and the Conservative Party* (London, 1975), 7. This is a Conservative Political Centre publication.
40   Quoted in Brian Harrison, *Prudent Revolutionaries* (Oxford, 1987), 79.
41   Nancy Astor, draft address to the annual meeting? Plymouth, 22.7.1921, 1416/1/1/621, Astor Papers, RUL.
42   Nancy Astor to Mrs Bucknill, 25.2.1925, 1416/1/1/261, Astor Papers, RUL.
43   See, for example, entries for 21.11.1925 and 15.03.1929 in Stuart Ball (ed.), *Parliament and Politics in the Age of Baldwin and MacDonald: The Headlam Diaries, 1923–1935* (London, 1992), 73 and 167.
44   Harrison, *Prudent Revolutionaries*, 90.
45   Lady Astor, 'No More War' in 'The Vote: The Organ of the Women's Freedom League', 27.7.1923, 1416:1:1:260, Astor Papers, RUL.
46   Katherine, Duchess of Atholl, *Working Partnership* (London, 1958), 126.
47   Ibid.
48   Yet another case of 'male equivalence'.
49   S. J. Hetherington, *Katherine Atholl, 1874–1960: Against the Tide* (Aberdeen, 1989), 110–11.
50   Ibid., 116.
51   Atholl, 176–7.

52 Ibid., 223.
53 A complete list of the women's legislation enacted during this period can be found in Pugh, *Women and the Women's Movement in Britain*, 108–9. This is followed by a detailed discussion of the laws.
54 For a more detailed discussion of this see Pugh, *Women and the Women's Movement in Britain*, 113–19.
55 Appendix II of 'Minutes of Equal Franchise Committee of Cabinet', 21.2.1927, HO 45/13020, part 1, Public Record Office, Kew (henceforth cited as PRO). All references on this subject in this paragraph come from this document.
56 It is interesting to note that no woman either belonged to the committee or was invited to attend its deliberations.
57 Memorandum by Home Office, some time in 1926, HO 45/13020, part 1, PRO.
58 Joynson-Hicks to Davidson, 11.5.1927, HO 45/13020, part 1, PRO.
59 The 'one person, one vote' principle would only become law under the Attlee government. Until then a person could exercise a maximum of two votes in their residence and in either their university or in the constituency of their business.
60 *The Times*, 14.3.1928.

5 FROM DOMESTICITY TO WAR, 1928–45

1 Quoted in Harrison, *Prudent Revolutionaries*, 305.
2 See page 50.
3 *The Times*, 9.3.1928.
4 For more on this see Pugh, *Women and the Women's Movement in Britain*, 209–10.
5 Minutes of the meeting of the Women's Advisory Council (Western Area), 2.7.1929 in ARE 11/11/2, CPP.
6 Ibid.
7 *Conservative Agents' Journal*, January 1936, 9.
8 Minutes of the annual general meeting of the National Society of Women Organizers (NSWO), 28.5.1937 in CCO 170/2/1/1, CPP.
9 Minutes of NSWO, 10.9.37 in CCO 170/2/1/1, op. cit.
10 Minutes of NSWO, 7.10.37 in CCO 170/2/1/1, op. cit.
11 History of qualified women agents, n.a., n.d. in CCO 500/9/20, CPP.
12 Pamela Brookes, *Women at Westminster* (London, 1967), 60.
13 Numerous analyses of this phenomenon have been made. See, for example, Jorgen Rasmussen, 'Women's Role in Contemporary British Politics', in *Parliamentary Affairs* (Vol. 36, No. 3, Summer 1983).
14 Entry for 3 November 1936, Robert Rhodes James (ed.), *Chips: The Diaries of Sir Henry Channon* (London, 1967), 75.
15 This preoccupation with the dress of women members is evident from the day Lady Astor first entered the House and continues to the present. Both the press and other MPs notice and comment upon women's clothes far more than they do for men. Lady Iveagh, for example,

did not appear in Parliament very often, but when she did the word spread quickly, and MPs came just to see her stylish clothes. As we shall see, the same attention was paid to Margaret Thatcher's dress. This is undeniably a sign that women still have some progress to make.

16 Diana Cooper, *Autobiography* (Salisbury, 1979), 392.
17 Evelyn Emmet to an unknown person, 21.11.1935, MS. Eng. hist. c. 1055, Baroness Emmet Papers, BLO.
18 Evelyn Emmet, 'A Day in the Life of a Woman County Councillor', 1930? in MS. Eng. hist. 1059, Baroness Emmet Papers, BLO.
19 Annual report of Women's Advisory Committee, June 1934 to May 1935, Lancashire, Cheshire and Westmorland Provincial Area in ARE 3/11/3, CPP.
20 Annual report of the Women's Advisory Committee, NW Provincial Area, June 1935–May 1936 in ARE 3/11/1, CPP.
21 Annual report of Women's Advisory Committee, June 1934 to May 1935, Lancashire, Cheshire and Westmorland Provincial Area in ARE 3/11/3, CPP.
22 Annual Report of the Women's Advisory Committee, NW Provincial Area, June 1935–May 1936, op. cit.
23 Women's Advisory Committee, Annual Report, June 1936–May 1937, NW Provincial Area in ARE 3/11/1, op. cit.
24 Women's Advisory Committee, Annual Report, June 1937–May 1938, NW Provincial Area, op. cit. Unless otherwise noted, other quotes in this paragraph come from this source.
25 Many of the girls in the Hindley Club worked in Wigan, whose sufferings during the Depression were immortalized at this period by George Orwell. See *The Road to Wigan Pier*.
26 Women's Advisory Committee, Annual Meeting, NW Provincial Area, June 1938–May 1939, ARE 3/11/1 op. cit. Other quotations in this paragraph are taken from this report.
27 Minutes of Women's Advisory Committee, Western Area, 29.1.1932, in ARE 11/11/2, CPP.
28 Minutes of Women's Advisory Committee, Western Area, 8.11.1932 in ARE 11/11/2, op. cit.
29 Annual Report, North-western Area, June 1941 in ARE 3/11/1, op. cit.
30 Somerset and Bristol County Committee Minutes, 7.11.1940, ARE 11/11/4, CPP.
31 For more on this, see the opening chapters of John Ramsden, *The Age of Churchill and Eden* (London, 1995).
32 Note on approximate position of qualified women organizers, March 1945?, in CCO 170/2/1/3, CPP.
33 Quoted in CWAC minutes, 12.3.1947, CCO 170/1/1/3, CPP.
34 CWAC Minutes, 13.1.1944 in CCO 170/1/1/2, CPP.
35 Pugh, *Women and the Women's Movement in Britain*, 275.
36 Memorandum by the National Council of Women to the Select Committee on Equal Compensation, December 1942, *Parliamentary Papers, 1942–43, Vol. 3*, appendix J, 189.
37 Quoted in Pugh, *Women and the Women's Movement in Britain*, 278.

38   *Social Insurance and Allied Services* (Beveridge Report), Cmd 6404 (London, 1942), 134.
39   CWAC minutes, 7.2.1945 in CCO 170/1/1/2, op. cit.
40   WNAC minutes, 11.4.1945 in CCO 170/1/3/1, CPP.
41   CWAC minutes, 8.7.1942, CCO 170/1/1/2, CPP.
42   CWAC minutes, 13.4.1943, CCO 170/1/1/2, op. cit.
43   Pugh, *Women and the Women's Movement in Britain*, 281.

6 THE CONSERVATIVE PARTY AND WOMEN VOTERS, 1945–75

1   Mr Watson to Brigadier Clarke, 15.2.1950, CCO 180/1/5, CPP.
2   Brigadier D. W. Clarke to the G.D., 2.2.1950, CCO 180/1/5, op. cit.
3   PORD, memorandum on the floating vote, 6.12.1949, CCO 180/1/3, CPP.
4   PORD report 'The Characteristics of the Floating Voter', November 1949, CCO 180/1/3, op. cit.
5   Pippa Norris and Joni Lovenduski, 'Gender and Party Politics in Britain', in Lovenduski and Norris, *Gender and Party Politics* (London, 1993), 38–9.
6   Secret report on policy for women, by Douglas?, 24.9.1969, CRD 3/38/4, CPP.
7   During this period the CWAC changed its name to the Women's National Advisory Committee (WNAC). For clarity's sake, I have used WNAC throughout in the body of the text and kept CWAC for the references.
8   CWAC sub-committee on Party Literature for women, minutes, 14.2.1946, CCO 170/1/4/1, CPP.
9   In their analysis of women's educational deficiencies they were unfortunately correct. See pages 126–8.
10   CWAC sub-committee on party literature for women, minutes, 13.12.1945, CCO 170/1/4/1, op. cit.
11   CWAC minutes, 26.6.1946, CCO 170/1/1/2, CPP.
12   Article published in the Conservative publication *Onward* in 1954. Reprinted in *The Guardian*, 21.3.1990.
13   Which was at least partly linked to the need to maintain a large army and the continuation of conscription.
14   Public Opinion Survey No. 27, April 1951, CCO 180/2/3, CPP.
15   Confidential report on women's rights, Conservative targets, n.a., 11.4.1973, CRD 3/38/2, CPP.
16   Pugh, *Women and the Women's Movement in Britain*, 288.
17   WNAC minutes, 11.1.1962, CCO 170/1/1/6, CPP.
18   Ministry of Labour, 'The Future Employment of Women, Manpower Studies No. 1 The Pattern of the Future', n.d.
19   Confidential report on women's rights, Conservative targets, op. cit.
20   WNAC's working party on women and employment, July 1964, CCO 4/9/467, CPP.
21   Ministry of Labour, 'The Future Employment of Women', op. cit.

22 No author, Draft for meeting with Party Chairman, 18.4.1969, CCO 500/9/21, CPP.

23 WNAC, parliamentary sub-committee, points for discussion with the party chairman, November 1968, CCO 20/36/5, CPP.

24 'Women in Party Politics', n.a., probably by Evelyn Emmet and written in 1958, MS. Eng hist. c. 1055, Baroness Emmet Papers, BLO.

25 WNAC's working party on women and employment, op. cit..

26 Pugh, *Women and the Women's Movement in Britain*, 288.

27 Public Opinion Survey No. 36, May 1952, CCO 180/2/4, CPP.

28 Addendum to WNAC minutes, 10.1.1957, CCO 170/1/1/5, CPP.

29 CWAC minutes, 12.3.1947, CCO 170/1/1/3, CPP.

30 Meeting of the General Purposes Committee, 14.5.1947, ARE 9/11/5, CPP.

31 Outside Organizations sub-committee of WNAC, minutes, n.d., probably mid-1950s, CCO 170/1/3/2, CPP.

32 Miss Walton to Mr Chapman-Walker, 17.6.1947, CCO 4/2/60, CPP. The emphasis is hers.

33 A claim which most women viewed rather cynically. Lady Davidson, for example, said on 11.11.1946 on the *Woman's Hour* programme: 'This assumption enters into the realm of speculation and appears to mean that men wouldn't enter into equal competition with women as teachers. Is this due to fear, sex prejudice, or is it merely the hypothesis of the Royal Commission? Normally open competition for posts stimulates entry rather than discourages it.'

34 Marjorie Maxse to Miss Spencer, 6.11.1946, CCO 4/2/60, CPP.

35 Report by Evelyn Emmet, CWAC minutes, 6.5.1948, CCO 170/1/1/3, op. cit.

36 Outside Organizations sub-committee of WNAC, minutes, 24.2.1955, CCO 170/1/3/2 op. cit.

37 WNAC, 29th Conference, 21.5.1957, conference handbook, CCO 170/3/10, CPP.

38 *The Observer*, 31.3.1968.

39 Working Party of Area Women Chairmen and Area Deputy Central Office Agents, 26.1.1960, CCO 500/9/7, CPP.

40 Mrs Walsh's report on the 1964 general election, n.d., CCO 60/4/25, CPP.

41 Robert McKenzie and Allan Silver, *Angels in Marble: Working Class Conservatives in Urban England* (London, 1968), 86.

42 The work of the Cripps Committee will be discussed in more detail in the next chapter.

43 Opinion Research Centre, A survey on women's interests and problems carried out for Conservative Central Office, 28–31 March 1968, CRD 3/38/4, CPP.

44 Ibid.

45 Douglas?, Policy for Women (secret), 24.9.1969, CRD 3/38/4, op. cit.

46 Beryl Cooper and Geoffrey Howe, 'Opportunity for Women', CPC, 1969, CRD 3/38/4, op. cit.

47 This will be discussed in more detail in the next two chapters.

7 WOMEN IN THE CONSERVATIVE PARTY ORGANIZATION, 1945–75

1 No author, 'Draft: Notes on women's organisation', 8.5.1967, CCO 20/36/2, CPP.
2 CWAC minutes, 16.3.1950, CCO 170/1/1/4, CPP.
3 South-East Area's Women's Advisory Committee, minutes, 29.6.1948, ARE 9/11/5, CPP.
4 WNAC, minutes, 2.9.1954, CCO 4/6/409, op. cit.
5 Emmet to unknown correspondent, some time in 1963, op. cit.
6 Working Party Report, 4.7.1957, CCO 500/9/2, op. cit.
7 WNAC, 'Report on the Chelmer Committee', some time in 1973, CCO 4/10/316, CPP.
8 Quoted in Rupert Morris, *Tories: From Village Hall to Westminster: A Political Sketch* (London, 1991), 52.
9 No author, 'Routine duties of woman vice-chairman', 26.6.1968, CCO 20/4/3, CPP.
10 No author, 'Draft notes on women's organization', 8.5.1967, CCO 20/36/2, CPP.
11 CWAC minutes, appendix A, 8.12.1949, CCO 170/1/1/4, CPP. Other quotes in this paragraph are taken from this source.
12 CWAC minutes, 14.6.1951, CCO 170/1/1/4, CPP.
13 Marjorie Maxse to Mrs Geoffrey Wilson, 12.3.1948, CCO 3/1/12, CPP.
14 Chapman Walker to Marjorie Maxse, 15.12.1947, CCO 3/1/12, op. cit.
15 Lord Woolton to Dorothy Crisp, some time in February 1948, CCO 3/1/12, op. cit.
16 Miss Sturges-Jones to Miss Fletcher, 14.12.1948, CCO 3/1/12, op. cit.
17 CWAC minutes, 8.9.1949, CCO 170/1/1/4, CPP. Unless otherwise stated, all other information in this paragraph comes from this source.
18 South-East Area Women's Advisory Committee minutes, 24.10.1946, ARE 9/11/3, CPP.
19 CWAC minutes, 8.1.1948, CCO 170/1/1/3, CPP.
20 CWAC minutes, 16.3.1948, CCO 170/1/1/3, op. cit.
21 Quoted in J. D. Hoffman, *The Conservative Party in Opposition, 1945–1951* (London, 1964), 180.
22 For more on *A True Balance* and on other aspects of postwar Conservatism and women see Ina Zweiniger-Bargielowska's excellent article 'Explaining the Gender Gap: The Conservative Party and the Women's Vote, 1945–1964', in M. Francis and I. Zweiniger-Bargielowska (eds.), *The Conservatives and British Society 1880–1990* (Cardiff, 1996).
23 Lovenduski, Norris and Burness, 'The Party and Women', in Seldon and Ball, *Conservative Century*, 624.
24 See the two files on that conference in CCO 4/7/440 and 441, CPP.
25 1964 Women's Conference handbook.
26 Outside Organizations sub-committee of WNAC, minutes, 23.2.1960, CCO 170/1/3/2, CPP.
27 Gerald O'Brien to Chairman, Conservative and Unionist Central Office, R. J. Webster, 23.6.1967, CCO 20/36/3, CPP.

28   Meeting of Women Chairmen and Honorary Secretaries of Area Women's Advisory Committees, 7.12.1961, CCO 120/4/23, CPP.

29   'Women in the Party Organization: Progress Report, November 1961', CCO 500/9/7, CPP.

30   Meetings of secretaries of Area Women's Advisory Committees, 25.9.1963, CCO 500/9/9, CPP.

31   WNAC, Opinion Poll, October 1960, CCO 500/9/7, CPP.

32   Report on leadership conferences for women, 1957–1958, January 1959, CCO 500/9/2, CPP.

33   'Women in the Party Organization: Progress Report, November 1961', op. cit.

34   No author, 'The family in the community', May 1968, CCO 20/36/4, CPP.

35   Joan Varley was a prominent figure in Conservative women's politics. She was secretary of the WNAC's parliamentary sub-committee, secretary of the Cripps Committee and in the early 1970s became Director of Central Administration and Chief Woman Executive at Central Office. She is in some way involved in almost every initiative with regard to women during Heath's period as leader and even later.

36   Notes of a meeting held between Mrs Morrison, Mrs G. Pawson, JP, Chairman of the Yorkshire Area Women's Advisory Committee, Miss Joan Varley and Miss B. Lowe, 6.7.1972, CCO 60/4/10, CPP.

37   Joan Varley to Women's Departments in all areas, 14.2. 1969, CCO 500/9/20, CPP.

38   Sara Morrison to Geoffrey Howe and other ministers, 30.6.1971, CCO 500/9/20, CPP.

39   R.W. to Douglas Hurd, 29.2.1972, CCO 500/9/20, op. cit.

40   Women's Rights, Conservative Targets, 11.4.1973, confidential, CRD 3/38/2, CPP.

41   WNAC minutes, 14.2.1952, CCO 170/1/1/4, CPP.

42   Parliamentary Sub-committee, Ad-hoc drafting Committee meeting, 29.10.1946, CCO 500/9/1, CPP.

43   Memorandum on parliamentary sub-committee, n.d., CCO 500/9/19, CPP.

44   Memorandum from the chairman of the WNAC, February 1952, CCO 170/1/5/1, CPP.

45   Parliamentary sub-committee, minutes, 8.12.1954, CCO 170/1/5/1, op. cit.

46   WNAC, minutes, 8.12.1955, CCO 4/6/409, CPP.

47   Jury Service recommendations, n.d., CCO 4/9/464, CPP.

48   Parliamentary sub-committee, minutes, 7.2.1962, CCO 170/1/5/1, op. cit.

49   CRD report on National Insurance benefits for married women, January 1955, CCO 4/6/409, op. cit.

50   Report of the Women's Policy Group, n.d., CCO 60/4/7, CPP.

51   Parliamentary sub-committee minutes, 12.11.1958, CCO 170/1/5/1, op. cit.

52   Parliamentary sub-committee minutes, 11.3.1959, CCO 170/1/5/1, op. cit.

53   Parliamentary sub-committee minutes, 31.5.1962, CCO 170/1/5/1, op. cit.

54   Emmet to unknown correspondent, some time in 1963, MS. Eng. hist. c. 1057, Emmet Papers, BLO.

55 Parliamentary sub-committee minutes, 17.7.1952, CCO 170/1/5/1, op. cit.
56 'Women's rights, Conservative targets', 11.4.1973, op. cit.
57 Cripps Committee on Women's Rights, 'About this Report', February 1969, CRD 3/38/2, op. cit.
58 Memorandum by Emmet, 5.4.1960, MS. Eng. hist. c. 1062, Emmet Papers, BLO.
59 For more on the achievements of the Heath government in relation to women see 'Women's Lib is not new', February 1972, CCO 20/4/6.

8 CONSERVATIVE WOMEN IN PARLIAMENT, 1945–75

1   See Joni Lovenduski and Pippa Norris, *Gender and Party Politics* (London, 1993), 45.
2   Addendum to WNAC minutes, 10.1.1957, CCO 170/1/1/5, CPP.
3   WNAC Local Government Working Party report, January 1955, CCO 4/6/408, CPP.
4   Ibid.
5   WNAC Area reports, 12.9.1968, CCO 4/10/313, CPP.
6   Sue McCowan, 'Widening Horizons: Women and the Conservative Party' (London, 1975), 18. This is a Conservative Party publication.
7   CWAC minutes, 9.12.1948, CCO 170/1/1/3, op. cit.
8   CWAC minutes, 14.11.1946, CCO 170/1/1/2, CPP.
9   *The Sunday Times*, 26 April 1964.
10 It must be noted, however, that the same complaint has been voiced by women in the Labour Party. See Jorgen Rasmussen, 'Female Political Career Patterns and Leadership Disabilities in Britain: The Crucial Role of Gatekeepers in Regulating Entry to the Political Elite', in *Polity* (Vol. 13, No. 4, Summer, 1981).
11 Elizabeth Hodder, *Hats Off! to Conservative Women* (London, 1990), 24. This is a Conservative Party publication.
12 Parliamentary sub-committee of WNAC, minutes, 13.2.1952, CCO 170/1/5/1, CPP.
13 Parliamentary sub-committee, WNAC, minutes, 20.3.1952, CCO 170/1/5/1, op. cit.
14 Memorandum from the chairman of WNAC, February 1952, CCO 170/1/5/1, op. cit.
15 See, for example, Beverley Stobaugh, *Women and Parliament 1918–1970* (New York, 1978), Jill Hills, 'Candidates, the Impact of Gender' in *Parliamentary Affairs* (Vol. 34, No. 2, Spring 1981) and, more recently, Joni Lovenduski, 'Sex, Gender and British Politics' in *Parliamentary Affairs* (Vol. 49, No. 1, January 1996). Numerous other studies have found the same thing.
16 Lady Howe, 'Wives of Tory MPs and Candidates', November 1971, CCO 60/4/10, CPP.
17 Pugh makes the same point in *Women and the Women's Movement in Britain*, 306.

18 Evelyn Emmet, Address to an unknown constituency committee, 1945, MS. Eng. Hist. 1059, Lady Emmet Papers, Bodleian Library, Oxford.
19 Lovenduski, Norris and Burness, 'The Party and Women', in Seldon and Ball, *Conservative Century*, 626.
20 Pamela Brookes, *Women at Westminster* (London, 1967), 182.
21 Barbara Brooke to Party Chairman, 21.11.1963, CCO 4/9/469, CPP.
22 Irene Ward to Miss Brant, 6.11.1964, CCO 500/9/6, CPP.
23 'Women in Party Politics', n.a., probably by Evelyn Emmet and written in 1958, MS. Eng. Hist. c. 1055, Baroness Emmet Papers, BLO.
24 Parliamentary sub-committee minutes, 7.11.1956, CCO 170/1/5/1, op. cit.
25 Rab Butler to Viscount Blakenham, 3.12.1963, CCO 60/4/5, CPP.
26 Ian MacLeod to Miss Brant, 24.6.1963, CCO 500/9/6, op. cit.
27 Article or address by Evelyn Emmet, 1961, MS. Eng. Hist. c. 1056, Baroness Emmet Papers, BLO.
28 Hugo Young, *One of Us* (London, 1989), 47.
29 Quoted in Hugo Young, 27.
30 John Campbell, *Edward Heath* (London, 1993), 385.
31 Area Reports, WNAC minutes, 8.11.1974, CCO 4/10/316, CPP.
32 Margaret Thatcher, *The Path to Power* (London, 1995), 261.
33 For more on this episode see John Ramsden, *The Winds of Change: Macmillan to Heath* (London, 1996), 441.
34 Ramsden, 442.
35 Thatcher, 268.
36 Kenneth Baker, *Turbulent Years* (London, 1993), 44.
37 Francis Pym, *Politics of Consent* (London, 1985), 5.
38 *The Economist*, 30.11.1974.
39 *The Times*, 16.1.1975.
40 *The Times*, 21.1.1975.
41 Quoted in Patricia Murray, *Margaret Thatcher* (London, 1980), 95.
42 Ramsden, 447.
43 *The Times*, 4.2.1975.
44 *The Times*, 7.2.1975.
45 Entry for 5.2.1975, Barbara Castle, *The Castle Diaries, 1974–76* (London, 1980), 304.
46 *The Times*, 11.2.1975.
47 John Ranelagh, *Thatcher's People* (London, 1991), 149.

9 A WOMAN LEADER AND BEYOND, 1975–97

1 Quoted in Melanie Phillips, *The Divided House: Women at Westminster* (London, 1980), 15.
2 Entry for 4.3.1975, *The Castle Diaries, 1974–76*, 330.
3 Ramsden, *The Winds of Change*, 454.
4 Kenneth Baker, *The Turbulent Years: My Life in Politics* (London, 1993), 270.

5   Young, 310.
6   Kenneth Harris, *Margaret Thatcher* (London, 1988), 60.
7   Quoted in Harris, 97.
8   *The Daily Telegraph*, 1.5.1979.
9   Cecil Parkinson, *Right at the Centre* (London, 1992), 143.
10   Young, 312. It is interesting to note that the creation of the image of the Chancellor preparing his budget in parallel to the housewife preparing hers was frequently used in Conservative Party propaganda aimed at women during the 1950s.
11   Patricia Hodgson, 'A Woman at the Helm', in *The Times*, 30.3.1979.
12   *The Observer*, 12.10.1975. Entry for 13.10.1975, *The Castle Diaries, 1974–1976*, 518.
13   Margaret Thatcher, *The Downing Street Years* (London, 1992), 575.
14   Nigel Lawson, *The View from No. 11* (London, 1992), 127.
15   She was certainly not the only woman MP to use this ploy. Witness Barbara Castle's tears when her trade union reform plan, *In Place of Strife*, was rejected.
16   *The Times*, 7.5.1993. The exact words of Mitterrand's comment have never been clear, although the point is obvious. This is the version of his personal assistant, Jacques Attali. Another version is that he said she had the eyes of Caligula and the mouth of Marilyn Monroe. This makes more sense, since Thatcher definitely does not have Monroe's voice – but perhaps Mitterrand's ignorance of the English language led him to colour the sounds he heard.
17   Juliet and Wayne Thompson, *Margaret Thatcher: Prime Minister Indomitable* (Oxford, 1994), 10.
18   Kenneth Baker, 266.
19   Reprinted in Juliet and Wayne Thompson.
20   Campbell, 235.
21   Margaret Thatcher, *The Downing Street Years* (London, 1992), 129.
22   Quoted in Beatrix Campbell, 212.
23   *The Observer*, 29.7.1990.
24   For more on this, see J. Lovenduski and V. Randall, *Contemporary Feminist Politics* (Oxford, 1993).
25   Peter Catterall and Virginia Preston, *Contemporary Britain: An Annual Review 1995* (Aldershot, 1996), 301.
26   Lovenduski and Norris, *Gender and Party Politics* (London, 1994), 56.
27   *The Times*, 24.7.1996.
28   Lovenduski and Norris, *Gender and Party Politics*, 44.
29   Donley Studlar and Susan Welch, 'The Party System and the Representation of Women in English Metropolitan Boroughs', in *Electoral Studies* (Vol. 1, No. 1, 1992).
30   Colin Rallings and Michael Thrasher 'Women in Local Politics', *Association of County Councils Gazette* (No. 83, 1991).
31   Pippa Norris, 'Women Politicians: Transforming Westminster?', in *Parliamentary Affairs* (Vol 49, No. 1, January 1996).
32   Lesley Abdela, *Women with X Appeal* (London, 1989), 24.

33   Figures are taken from Joni Lovenduski and Pippa Norris, *Gender and Party Politics* (London, 1993), 39.
34   Joni Lovenduski and Vicky Randall, *Contemporary Feminist Politics* (Oxford, 1993), 161 and Pippa Norris, 'Mobilising the Women's Vote: The Gender-Generation Gap in Voting Behaviour', in *Parliamentary Affairs* (Vol. 49, No. 2, April 1996).
35   Ibid.
36   Clare Short, 'Women and the Labour Party', in *Parliamentary Affairs* (Vol. 49, No. 1, January 1996).
37   Lovenduski, 'Sex, Gender and British Politics', in *Parliamentary Affairs* (Vol. 49, No. 1, January 1996).
38   Quoted in Beatrix Campbell, 275.
39   A. J. Davies, *We the Nation: the Conservative Party and the Pursuit of Power* (London, 1995), 161.
40   Lovenduski and Norris, 40.
41   Quoted in Abdela, 85.
42   Ibid.
43   *The Times*, 6.4.1995.
44   *The Times*, 10.3.1995.
45   Teresa Gorman, 'Why the Tories are Really Failing Women', *The Daily Mail*, 5.11.1985.
46   Morris, 96.
47   See J. D. May, 'Opinion Structure of Political Parties: The Law of Curvilinear Disparity', in *Political Studies* (1973).
48   Patrick Seyd and Paul Whiteley, 'Labour and Conservative Party Members: Change over Time', in *Parliamentary Affairs* (Vol. 48, No. 3, July 1995).
49   Paul Whiteley, Patrick Seyd and Jeremy Richardson, *True Blue: The Politics of Conservative Party Membership* (Oxford, 1994), 42.
50   *Independent on Sunday*, 25.5.1997.
51   *Independent on Sunday*, 18.5.1997.
52   The usually sexist British press dubbed them 'Blair's babes', and numerous weekly magazines featured them on the covers in a remarkably condescending fashion.
53   *New Statesman*, 16.5.1997.
54   Ibid.
55   Quoted in Lovenduski, Norris, and Burness, 'The Party and Women', 630.

Select Bibliography

MANUSCRIPT COLLECTIONS

I. Bodleian Library, Oxford

Conservative Party Papers:
  ARE Area Office Papers
  CCO 3 Special Subjects
  CCO 20 Chairman's Office
  CCO 60 Vice-Chairman's Office – Women
  CCO 120 General Director's Office
  CCO 170 Women's Organization Office
  CCO 180 Public Opinion Research Department
  CCO 500 Chief Organization Officer: Director of Organization
  Conservative Research Department Papers
  Director of Organization and Constituency Organization Papers
  Executive Committee Minutes
Benjamin Disraeli Papers
Lady Emmet Papers
Primrose League Papers
Selborne Papers
Lord Woolton Papers

II. British Library, London

Arthur Balfour Papers

III. House of Lords Record Office, London

J. C. C. Davidson Papers
Bonar Law Papers

IV. Public Record Office, Kew

Cabinet Papers
Home Office Papers

V. Reading University Library

Astor Papers

NEWSPAPERS, PERIODICALS AND REPORTS

Conservative Agents' Journal
Conservative and Unionist Women's Franchise Review
The Daily Telegraph
The Economist
The Guardian
The Independent on Sunday
The Morning Post
The New Statesman
The Observer
The Primrose League Gazette
The Spectator
The Sunday Times
The Times

PUBLISHED PRIMARY SOURCES

I. Official and Semi-official Documents

Ministry of Labour, *Manpower Studies*
Parliamentary Debates, House of Commons
Parliamentary Papers
Social Insurance and Allied Services (Beveridge Report) Cmd. 6404 (London, 1942)

II. Letters and Private Papers

Boyce, D. G. *The Crisis of British Unionism: Political Papers of the Second Earl of Selborne* (London, 1987)

Buckle, G. E. (ed.) *Letters of Queen Victoria* (3 vols., London, 1930)

Burghclere, Lady. *A Great Man's Friendship: Letters of the Duke of Wellington to Mary, Marchioness of Salisbury 1850–1852* (London, 1927)

—— *A Great Lady's Friendships: Letters to Mary, Marchioness of Salisbury, Countess of Derby 1862–1890* (London, 1933)

Chamberlain, Austen. *Politics from Inside: An Epistolary Chronicle 1906–1914* (London, 1936)

Guedalla, P. *The Queen and Mr Gladstone* (London, 1933)

James, Robert Rhodes (ed.) *Memoirs of a Conservative: J.C.C. Davidson's Memoirs and Papers, 1910–37* (London, 1969)

Minney, R. J. *The Private Papers of Hore-Belisha* (London, 1960)

Nevill, R. (ed.) *The Life and Letters of Lady Dorothy Nevill* (London, 1919)

Petrie, Sir Charles. *The Life and Letters of Austen Chamberlain* (2 vols., London, 1939–40)

Zetland, Marquis (ed.) *The Letters of Disraeli to Lady Chesterfield and Lady Bradford* (2 vols., New York, 1924)

III. Published Diaries and Speeches

Ball, Stuart (ed.) *Parliament and Politics in the Age of Baldwin and MacDonald: The Headlam Diary 1923–1935* (London, 1992)
Barnes, John and David Nicholson (eds.) *The Leo Amery Diaries* (2 vols., London, 1980, 1988)
Cartwright, Julia (ed.) *The Journals of Lady Knightley of Fowsley* (London, 1915)
Castle, Barbara. *The Castle Diaries* (London, 1980)
Colville, J. R. *The Fringes of Power: 10 Downing Street Diaries, 1939–45* (London, 1985)
Dilks, David (ed.) *The Diaries of Sir Alexander Cadogan, 1938–45* (London, 1971)
James, Robert Rhodes. *'Chips': The Diaries of Sir Henry Channon* (London, 1967)
Matthew, H. C. G. (ed.) *The Gladstone Diaries* (14 vols., Oxford, 1980–95)
Middlemas, Keith (ed.) *Thomas Jones: Whitehall Diary, 1916–30* (2 vols., London, 1969)
Nicolson, Nigel (ed.) *Harold Nicolson: Diaries and Letters, 1939–45* (London, 1967)
Ramsden, John (ed.) *Real Old Tory Politics: The Political Diaries of Sir Robert Sanders, Lord Bayford, 1910–35* (London, 1984)
Thatcher, Margaret. *Let Our Children Grow Tall: Selected Speeches* (London, 1977)
—— *The Revival of Britain* (London, 1989)
Vincent, J. R. (ed.) *The Crawford Papers: The Journals of David Lindsay, 27th Earl of Crawford and 10th Earl of Balcaries, 1871–1940, during the Years 1892–1940* (London, 1984)
—— (ed.) *The Later Derby Diaries: Home Rule, Liberal Unionism and Aristocratic Life in Late Victorian England* (London, 1981)
Williamson, Philip. *The Modernisation of Conservative Politics: The Diaries and Letters of William Bridgeman, 1904–1935* (London, 1988)

IV. Memoirs

Astor, Nancy. *My Two Countries* (New York, 1923)
Atholl, Duchess of. *Working Partnership* (London, 1958)
Baker, Kenneth. *The Turbulent Years: My Life in Politics* (London, 1993)
Balfour, Lady Frances. *Ne Obliviscaris: Dinna Forget* (London, 1930)
Cooper, Lady Diana. *Autobiography* (Salisbury, 1979)
Cooper, Alfred Duff (Viscount Norwich). *Old Men Forget* (London, 1953)
Cornwallis-West, Mrs George (ed.) *The Reminiscences of Lady Randolph Churchill* (London, 1908)
Howe, Geoffrey. *Conflict of Loyalty* (London, 1994)
Lawson, Nigel. *The View from No. 11* (London, 1992)

Londonderry, Marchioness of. *Retrospect* (London, 1938)
Macmillan, Harold. *Past Masters: Politics and Politicians, 1906–39* (London, 1975)
—— *Winds of Change, 1919–39* (London, 1966)
Nevill, R. (ed.) *Leaves from the Notebooks of Lady Dorothy Nevill* (London, 1907)
—— (ed.) *My Own Times by Dorothy Nevill* (London, 1912)
—— *The Reminiscences of Lady Dorothy Nevill* (London, 1906)
—— (ed.) *Under Five Reigns: by Lady Dorothy Nevill* (London, 1910)
Parkinson, Cecil. *Right at the Centre* (London, 1992)
Tebbit, Norman. *Unfinished Business* (London, 1991)
Thatcher, Margaret. *The Downing Street Years* (London, 1992)
—— *The Path to Power* (London, 1995)
Woolton, Lord. *Memoirs* (London, 1959)

SECONDARY SOURCES

I. Biographies

Arnold, Bruce. *Margaret Thatcher: A Study in Power* (London, 1984)
Aster, Sidney. *Anthony Eden* (London, 1976)
Balfour, Lady F. *Lord Balfour of Burleigh* (London, 1924)
Blake, Robert. *Disraeli* (London, 1967)
—— *The Unknown Prime Minister: The Life and Times of Andrew Bonar Law, 1858–1923* (London, 1955)
Campbell, J. *Edward Heath* (London, 1993)
—— *F. E. Smith: First Earl of Birkenhead* (London, 1983)
Carlton, David. *Anthony Eden* (London, 1981)
Cecil, Lady Gwendolen. *The Life of Robert Marquis of Salisbury* (4 vols., London, 1921 & 1931)
Charmley, John. *Churchill: The End of Glory* (London, 1993)
—— *Duff Cooper: The Authorised Biography* (London, 1986)
Churchill, Randolph. *Lord Derby: 'King' of Lancashire* (London, 1959)
Cosgrave, Patrick. *Thatcher: The First Term* (London, 1985)
Egremont, Max. *Balfour* (London, 1980)
Foster, R. F. *Lord Randolph Churchill: A Political Life* (London, 1981)
Gilbert, Martin. *Winston S. Churchill* (8 vols., London, 1980–8).
Grigg, John. *Nancy Astor: Portrait of a Pioneer* (London, 1980)
Harris, Kenneth. *Thatcher* (London, 1988)
Harrison, Brian. *Prudent Revolutionaries* (Oxford, 1987)
Hetherington, S. J. *Katherine Atholl, 1874–1960, Against the Tide* (Aberdeen, 1989)
Horne, Alistair. *Harold Macmillan* (2 vols., London, 1988 and 1990)
Hyde, H. M. *The Londonderrys: A Family Portrait* (London, 1979)
James, Robert Rhodes. *Anthony Eden* (London, 1986)
Junor, Penny. *Margaret Thatcher: Wife, Mother, Politician* (London, 1983)
Langhorne, Elizabeth. *Nancy Astor and her Friends* (London, 1974)

Lee, Elizabeth. *Wives of the Prime Ministers, 1844–1906* (London, 1918)
Lewis, Russell. *Margaret Thatcher* (London, 1975)
Masters, Anthony. *Nancy Astor: A Life* (London, 1981)
Matthew, H. C. G. *Gladstone, 1875–1898* (Oxford, 1995)
Middlemas, Keith and John Roberts. *Baldwin: A Biography* (London, 1969)
Mitchell, David. *Queen Christabel* (London, 1977)
Murray, Patricia. *Margaret Thatcher* (London, 1980)
Pankhurst, Richard. *Sylvia Pankhurst, Artist and Crusader* (London, 1979)
Romero, Patricia. E. *Sylvia Pankhurst: Portrait of a Rebel* (New Haven, 1987)
Rose, Kenneth. *The Later Cecils* (London, 1975)
Roth, Andrew. *Heath and the Heathmen* (London, 1972)
Rothwell, Victor. *Anthony Eden: A Political Biography 1931–1957* (Manchester, 1992)
Shkolnik, Esther. *Leading Ladies: A Study of Eight Late Victorian and Edwardian Political Wives* (New York, 1987)
Taylor, Rex. *Lord Salisbury* (London, 1975)
Thompson, Juliet and Wayne C. Thompson (eds.) *Margaret Thatcher: Prime Minister Indomitable* (Oxford, 1994)
Vincent, J. R.. *Disraeli* (Oxford, 1990)
Weintraub, Stanley. *Victoria* (London, 1987)
Young, Hugo. *One of Us* (London, 1989)
Ziegler, Philip. *Diana Cooper* (London, 1981)

II. General Works

Abdela, Leslie. *Women with X Appeal* (London, 1989)
Alberti, Johanna. *Beyond Suffrage* (New York, 1989)
Atholl, Duchess of. *Women and Politics* (London, 1931)
Baker, Kenneth (ed.) *The Faber Book of Conservatism* (London, 1993)
Ball, Stuart. *Baldwin and the Conservative Party* (London, 1988)
Banks, Olive. *Faces of Feminism* (Oxford, 1981)
Beard, M. *English Landed Society in the Twentieth Century* (London, 1989)
Behrens, Robert. *The Conservative Party from Heath to Thatcher* (London, 1980)
—— *The Conservative Party in Opposition 1974–77* (Coventry, 1977)
Bentley, Michael. *Politics without Democracy: Great Britain 1815–1914* (London, 1984)
Berrington, Hugh. *Backbench Opinion in the House of Commons 1945–1955* (Oxford, 1973)
Blake, Robert. *A Century of Achievement: An Illustrated Record of the National Union of Conservative and Unionist Associations 1867–1967* (London, 1967)
—— *The Conservative Party from Peel to Thatcher* (London, 2nd edn., 1985)
—— and John Patten (eds.) *The Conservative Opportunity* (London, 1976)
Blewett, Neal. *The Peers, the Parties and the People: The General Elections of 1910* (London, 1972)
Block, Geoffrey. *A Source Book of Conservatism* (London, 1964)
Bourne, M. *Patronage and Society in Nineteenth-Century England* (London, 1986)

Brookes, Pamela. *Women at Westminster* (London, 1967)
Brown, Rosemary. *Going Places: Women in the Conservative Party* (London, Conservative Political Centre, 1980)
Bruce-Gardyne, Jock. *Mrs Thatcher's First Administration* (London, 1984)
Butler, Lord. *The Art of the Possible* (London, 1971)
—— *The Conservatives: A History of Their Origins to 1965* (London, 1977)
Button, Sheila. *Women's Committee: A History of Gender and Local Government Policy Formulation* (University of Bristol, 1984)
Campbell, Beatrix. *Iron Ladies: Why Do Women Vote Tory?* (London, 1987)
Cannadine, David. *The Decline and Fall of the British Aristocracy* (New Haven, 1990)
Charmley, John. *A History of Conservative Politics 1900–1996* (London, 1996)
Christie, O. F. *The Transition to Democracy, 1867–1914* (London, 1934)
Cockburn, C. *Women, Trade Unions and Political Parties* (London, 1987)
Coleman, Bruce. *Conservatism and the Conservative Party in Nineteenth Century Britain* (London, 1988)
Conservative and Unionist Central Office. *Handbook for Women Organizers and Workers* (London, 1928)
Conservative Party. *A True Balance: in Home, in Employment, as Citizens* [Women] (London, 1949)
Cooper, Beryl and Geoffrey Howe. *Opportunity for Women* (London, 1969)
Cosgrave, Patrick. *Thatcher: The First Term* (London, 1985)
Crisp, Dorothy. *The Rebirth of Conservatism* (London, 1931)
Currell, Melville. *Political Woman* (London, 1974)
Davis, A. J. *We the Nation: the Conservative Party and the Pursuit of Power* (London, 1995)
Dutton, David. *'His Majesty's Loyal Opposition': The Unionist Party in Opposition, 1905–1915* (Liverpool, 1992)
Evans, Brendan and Andrew Taylor. *From Salisbury to Major: Continuity and Change in Conservative Politics* (Manchester, 1996)
Fawcett, A. *Conservative Agent* (London, 1967)
Feuchtwanger, E. J. *Disraeli, Democracy and the Tory Party* (London, 1968)
Fforde, Matthew. *Conservatism and Collectivism 1886–1914* (Edinburgh, 1990)
Francis, Martin and Ina Zweiniger-Bargielowska (eds.) *The Conservatives and British Society, 1880–1990* (Cardiff, 1996)
Fulford, Roger. *Votes for Women: The Story of a Struggle* (London, 1957)
Gamble, Andrew. *The Conservative Nation* (London, 1974)
Garner, Les. *Stepping Stones to Women's Liberty* (London, 1984)
Garrison, Terry. *Mrs Thatcher's Casebook* (Cambridgeshire, 1984)
Gash, Norman. *The Radical Element in the History of the Conservative Party* (London, 1989)
Githens, Marianne, Pippa Norris and Joni Lovenduski. *Different Roles, Different Voices* (New York, 1994)
Green, E. H. H. *The Crisis of Conservatism: The Politics, Economics, and Ideology of the Conservative Party 1880–1914* (London, 1995)
Hall, Stuart and Martin Jacques (eds.) *The Politics of Thatcherism* (London, 1983)
Hanham, J. *Elections and Party Management, Politics in the Time of Disraeli and Gladstone* (London, 1969)

Harrison, Brian Howard. *Separate Spheres: The Opposition to Women's Suffrage in Britain* (London, 1978)
Heath, A., R. Jowell, J. Curtice, G. Evans, J. Field and S. Witherspoon. *Understanding Political Change: The British Voter 1964–1987* (Oxford, 1991)
Hodder, Elizabeth. *Hats Off to Conservative Women* (London, 1990)
Hoffman, J. D. *The Conservative Party in Opposition 1945–51* (London, 1964)
Hollis, Patricia. *Ladies Elect: Women in English Local Government, 1865–1914* (Oxford, 1987)
—— *Women in Public: The Women's Movement 1850–1900* (London, 1979)
Holton, Sandra Stanley. *Feminism and Democracy: Women's Suffrage and Reform Politics in Britain 1900–1918* (Cambridge, 1986)
Hume, Leslie Parker. *The National Union of Women's Suffrage Societies, 1897–1914* (New York, 1982)
Hunt, E. H. *British Labour History 1815–1914* (London, 1981)
Jalland, Patricia. *Women, Marriage and Politics 1860–1914* (London, 1986)
Jenkins, Peter. *Mrs Thatcher's Revolution* (London, 1987)
Kavanagh, Dennis. *Margaret Thatcher: A Study in Prime Ministerial Style* (Glasgow, 1986)
—— *Thatcherism and British Politics* (Oxford, 1987)
—— and Anthony Seldon (eds.) *The Thatcher Effect: A Decade of Change* (Oxford, 1989)
Kent, Susan Kingsley. *Making Peace: the Reconstruction of Gender in Interwar Britain* (Princeton, 1993)
—— *Sex and Suffrage in Britain, 1860–1914* (Princeton, 1987)
Layton-Henry, Zig (ed.) *Conservative Party Politics* (London, 1980)
Lewis, Jane (ed.) *Before the Vote Was Won: Arguments for and against Women's Suffrage* (New York, 1987)
Lindsay, T. F. and M. Harrington. *The Conservative Party 1918–1979* (2nd edn., London, 1979)
Lovenduski, Joni. *The Politics of the Second Electorate: Women and Public Participation* (London, 1981)
—— and Vicky Randall. *Contemporary Feminist Politics* (Oxford, 1993)
—— and Pippa Norris. *Gender and Party Politics* (London, 1993)
—— (eds.) *Women in Politics* (Oxford, 1996)
Ludlam, Steve and Martin Smith. *Contemporary British Conservatism* (London, 1996)
Lytton, Earl of, et. al. *The Men's League Handbook on Women's Suffrage* (London, 1914)
Marsh, P. *The Discipline of Popular Government: Lord Salisbury's Domestic Statecraft, 1881–1902* (London, 1978)
Mayer, Frank. *The Opposition Years: Winston S. Churchill and the Conservative Party 1945–1951* (New York, 1992)
McCowan, Sue. *Widening Horizons: Women and the Conservative Party* (London, 1975)
McDowell, R. B. *British Conservatism 1832–1914* (London, 1959)
McKenzie, R. T. *British Political Parties* (London, 1955)
—— and Allan Silver. *Angels in Marble: Working Class Conservatives in Urban England* (London, 1968)
Mitchell, Dennis. *Cross and Tory Democracy* (New York, 1991)

Morgan, David. *Suffragists and Liberals: The Politics of Woman Suffrage in Britain* (Oxford, 1975)

Morgan, Kenneth O. *Consensus and Disunity: The Lloyd George Coalition Government, 1918–1922* (Oxford, 1979)

—— *The People's Peace: British History 1945–1990* (Oxford, 1990)

Morris, Rupert. *Tories: From Village Hall to Westminster* (London, 1991)

National Union of Conservative and Unionist Associations. *Final Report of the Conservative Party Organization* (London, 1949)

Norris, Pippa. *Political Recruitment: Gender, Race and Class* (Cambridge, 1995)

—— *Political Representation: Gender, Class and Race in the British Parliament* (Cambridge, 1994)

—— *Politics and Sexual Equality* (Brighton, 1987)

—— *Women and Politics: Different Voices, Different Lives* (London, 1994)

Norton, Philip and Arthur Aughey. *Conservatives and Conservatism* (London, 1981)

Pankhurst, Sylvia. *The Suffragette Movement* (London, 1977)

Phelps, Barry. *Power and the Party: A History of the Carlton Club 1832–1982* (London, 1983)

Phillips, Melanie. *The Divided House: Women at Westminster* (London, 1980)

Pinto-Duschinsky, M. *The Political Thought of Lord Salisbury 1854–1868* (London, 1967)

Pugh, Martin. *Electoral Reform in War and Peace, 1906–18* (London, 1978)

—— *The Making of Modern British Politics 1867–1939* (Oxford, 1982, 2nd edn. 1993)

—— *The Tories and the People 1880–1935* (Oxford, 1985)

—— *Women and the Women's Movement in Britain 1914–1959* (Basingstoke, 1992)

—— *Women's Suffrage in Britain, 1867–1928* (London, 1980)

Purvis, Jane. *Women's History, Britain 1850–1945* (London, 1995)

Radice, Lisanne, Elizabeth Vallance and Virginia Willis. *Member of Parliament* (London, 1987, 1990)

Ramelson, Marian. *The Petticoat Rebellion: A Century of Struggle for Women's Rights* (London, 1967)

Ramsden, John. *The Age of Balfour and Baldwin* (London, 1975)

—— *The Age of Churchill and Eden, 1940–1957* (London, 1995)

—— *The Making of Conservative Policy since 1929: The Conservative Research Department* (London 1980).

—— *The Winds of Change: Macmillan to Heath, 1957–1975* (London, 1996)

Rendall, Jane (ed.) *Equal or Different: Women's Politics 1800–1914* (Oxford, 1987)

Robb, Janet Henderson. *The Primrose League* (New York, 1942)

Rogers, Barbara. *52%: Getting Women's Power into Politics* (London, 1983)

Ross, John. *Thatcher and Friends: The Anatomy of the Tory Party* (London, 1983)

Rover, Constance. *Women's Suffrage and Party Politics in Britain 1866–1914* (London, 1967)

Seldon, Anthony. *Churchill's Indian Summer: The Conservative Government, 1951–55* (London, 1981)

―― and Stuart Ball (eds) *Conservative Century* (Oxford, 1994)

Seyd, Pat and Paul Whitely. *Labour's Grassroots: The Politics of Labour Party Membership* (London, 1992)

Shannon, Richard. *The Age of Disraeli: The Rise of Tory Democracy* (London, 1992)

―― *The Age of Salisbury, 1881-1902: Unionism and Empire* (London, 1996)

Shiman, Lilian Lewis. *Women and Leadership in Nineteenth Century England* (London, 1992)

Smith, Paul. *Disraelian Conservatism and Social Reform* (London, 1967)

Southgate, Donald. *The Conservative Leadership, 1832-1932* (London, 1974)

Stacey, Margaret and Marion Price. *Women, Power and Politics* (London, 1981)

Stewart, Robert. *The Foundation of the Conservative Party 1830-1867* (London, 1978)

Stobaugh, Beverly Parker. *Women and Parliament, 1918-1970* (Hicksville, NY, 1978)

Strachey, Ray. *The Cause: A Short History of the Women's Movements in Great Britain* (London, 1928, repub. 1978)

Taylor, A. J. P. *The Struggle for Mastery in Europe* (London, 1954)

Thompson, F. M. L. *English Landed Society in the Nineteenth Century* (London, 1963)

Vallance, Elizabeth. *Women in the House* (London, 1979)

Watkins, Alan. *A Conservative Coup: The Fall of Margaret Thatcher* (London, 1991)

Weeks, Jeffrey. *Sex, Politics and Society* (London, 1981)

Whiteley, Paul, Patrick Seyd and Jeremy Richardson. *True Blues: The Politics of Conservative Party Membership* (Oxford, 1994)

Young, Hugo and Anne Sloman. *The Thatcher Phenomenon* (London, 1986)

Young, James. *Women and Popular Struggles* (Edinburgh, 1985)

Young, Ken. *Local Politics and the Rise of Party: The London Municipal Society and the Conservative Intervention in Local Elections 1894-1963* (Leicester, 1975)

III. Articles and Theses

Close, D. 'The Collapse of Resistance to Democracy: Conservatives, Adult Suffrage and Second Chamber Reform, 1911-1928', *Historical Journal* (Vol. 20, 1977)

Cooper, A. F. 'The Transformation of Agricultural Policy, 1912-1936: A Study in Conservative Politics' (DPhil, Oxford, 1979)

Fforde, Matthew. 'The Conservative Party and Real Property in England' (DPhil dissertation, Oxford, 1984)

Harrison, B. 'Women in a Man's House: The Women MPs 1919-45', *Historical Journal* (Vol. 29, 1986)

Hills, Jill. 'Candidates, the Impact of Gender', *Parliamentary Affairs* (Vol. 34 No. 2, Spring 1981)

Hogg, S. 'Landed Society and the Conservative Party in the late Nineteenth and Early Twentieth Centuries' (B.Litt dissertation, Oxford, 1972)

Jarvis, D. 'Mrs Maggs and Betty, The Conservative Appeal to Women Voters in the 1920s', *Twentieth Century British History* (No. 5, 1994)

Joyce, Patrick. 'Popular Toryism in Lancashire, 1860–90' (Oxford, D.Phil, 1975)

Lawrence, J. 'Class and Gender in the Making of Urban Toryism 1880–1914', *English Historical Review* (Vol. 108, 1993)

Lovenduski, Joni. 'Sex, Gender and British Politics' in *Parliamentary Affairs* (Vol 49, No. 1, January 1996)

McRae, Susan. 'Women at the Top: The Case of British National Politics', *Parliamentary Affairs* (Vol. 43, July 1990)

Norris, Pippa. 'Mobilising the Women's Vote: the Gender-Generation Gap in Voting Behaviour', *Parliamentary Affairs* (Vol. 49, No. 2, April 1996)

—— 'Women Politicians: Transforming Westminster?' *Parliamentary Affairs* (Vol 49, No. 1, January 1996)

Quinault, R. E. 'Warwickshire Landowners and Parliamentary Politics, 1841–1923' (Oxford, D Phil, 1975)

Rallings, Colin and Michael Thrasher, 'Women in Local Politics' in *Association of County Councils Gazette* (No. 83, 1991)

Ramsden, John. 'The Organisation of the Conservative and Unionist Party in Britain 1910–1930' (Oxford, DPhil, 1974)

Rasmussen, Jorgen. 'The Electoral Costs of Being a Woman in the 1979 British General Election' *Comparative Politics* (Vol. 15, July 1983)

—— 'Female Political Career Patterns and Leadership Disabilities in Britain', *Polity* (Vol. 13, Summer 1981)

—— 'The Role of Women in British Parliamentary Elections', *Journal of Politics* (Vol. 39, Nov. 1977)

—— 'Women Candidates in British By-elections', *Political Studies* (Vol. 29, June 1981)

—— 'Women's Role in Contemporary British Politics', *Parliamentary Affairs* (Vol. 36, Summer 1983)

Short, Clare. 'Women and the Labour Party', *Parliamentary Affairs* (Vol. 49, No. 1, January 1996)

Sreberny-Mohammedi, Annabelle and Karen Rowe. 'Women MPs and the Media: Representing the Body Politic', *Parliamentary Affairs* (Vol. 49, No. 1, January 1996)

Studlar, Donley and Susan Welch. 'The Party System and the Representation of Women in English Metropolitan Boroughs', *Electoral Studies* (Vol. 11, March 1992)

Vallance, Elizabeth. 'Two Cheers for Equality: Women Candidates in the 1987 General Elections', *Parliamentary Affairs* (Vol. 41, Jan. 1988)

—— 'Women Candidates in the 1983 General Election', *Parliamentary Affairs* (Vol. 37, Summer 1984)

—— 'Women in the House of Commons', *Political Studies* (Vol. 29, September 1981)

Welch, Susan. 'Sex Differences in Political Activity in Britain', *Women and Politics* (Vol. 1, No. 2, Summer 1980)

—— and Donley Studlar. 'British Public Opinion toward Women in Politics: A Comparative Perspective', *Western Political Quarterly* (Vol. 39, March, 1986)

Index

Index